ADVENTURE IN DIPLOMACY

Adventure in Diplomacy

Our French Dilemma

Kenneth Pendar

Simon Publications, Inc.
2003

Published by Simon Publications, P. O. Box 910455 San Diego, CA 92191-0455

THIS FIRST BOOK OF MINE I WISH TO DEDICATE TO MY FRENCH FRIENDS AND THEIR COMPATRIOTS IN NORTH AFRICA AND FRANCE, STAUNCH ALLIES OF MY COUNTRY, WHO DURING THE BLACKEST HOURS OF HISTORY SILENTLY GUARDED THEIR COUNTRY'S UNITY AND SERVED HER TRUE INTERESTS IN RESISTING BY COUNTLESS MEANS OUR COMMON ENEMY.

PREFACE

I HAVE written this book for three reasons: first, because as a very American American I love France deeply. I have had more chances than most Americans to know her in happier days and, during her years of agony, to see her colonial policies, personalities, and watch her rebirth. Secondly, I have tried to make this book a page of American diplomatic history—a sort of laboratory specimen of a period during which our diplomacy was, I believe, unsuccessful; because I think it is always instructive for a country to observe such moments under a microscope. My third reason is that it seems to me we must know more about our actual practical diplomacy if we are to have a foreign policy that works. After surveying the scene and the interplay of interests, I point out certain instances which I feel could have been handled with greater chances for success.

I have written this book as a private citizen during a period when I had resigned from any official connection with the United States Government. If in places I seem too critical, I can only assure my readers that my motivating spirit has been a constructive one.

The failures of personality I shall have to mention are brought out only because they illuminate some important problem or policy. Similarly the criticism of Foreign Office operations are not founded on any anti-British feeling on my part. I am one of the people who believe that close ties between Britain and America are not only advisable but a necessity for both countries. I do feel, however, that the Foreign Office policies and practices during the period I record were far from being in the best long range interests of Great Britain—just as many of our own diplomatic manoeuvers worked against over-all American interests.

Foreign affairs of the type discussed in this book are never an easy subject, especially when they concern democracies.

I am told that during a dinner with Marshal Stalin at Teheran, Mr. Churchill rose to his feet and made the following toast: "I should like to propose a toast to the President of the United States who has steered the Ship of State through the stormy waters of partisan politics amidst the violent freedoms of democracy."

This violence, this complexity, we understand in our own country —and expect foreigners to understand also. Yet we are all too likely to think that foreign politics, especially French, are far too complicated for us. Democracies by their very nature are complicated. It must be this very complexity and the political indolence that comes over democracies in peace time that explains that strange popularity foreign dictators have had with the American and British people. It is only necessary to reread the American press during the early years of Mussolini and even Hitler to be struck by the praise these men received for the so-called "good" they were doing for their countries. In those days they had enthusiastic support from American public opinion,— the same hopeful support we later gave de Gaulle. It would pay us better to try to understand foreign politics and foreign democracy, as we expect them to understand us. Yes, democracy is complex; only fascism has the deceptive facade of simplicity.

There are many misgivings in this book about the future of French democracy unless she has better leadership. I have based them on facts, and with apprehension for the future of France—that key to continental Europe. For behind this detailed story of an episode in diplomacy lies a basic question, "Will Europe become,?" Paul Valéry asked in 1940, "a little peninsula of the Asiatic continent, or remain a precious part of the earth, the pearl of the globe, the brain of a vast body?" The answer is important to all of us. Our North African and French adventure is another clue to that answer.

References made to documents and articles are marked in the text by numbers referring to the Appendix at the back of the book.

Kenneth Pendar,
Washington, D.C., 1945.

~~~~~~

TABLE OF CONTENTS
~~~~~~

CHAPTER I

American Adventure

From June, 1941 until July, 1943, I was lucky enough to have an inside view of one of the most dramatic chapters in American diplomatic history—our dealings with Vichy, with de Gaulle and with the French generally in North Africa. That story was intertwined with another—the secret development of our pre-landing underground, with all its E. Phillips Oppenheim atmosphere of mystery and intrigue in the Arab world and the Vichy world, its contacts with the Nazi agents in Africa, and its glimpses of the network of spies and political intrigue. Neither story has ever been completely or even accurately told. Both are important, I think, to Americans. They are case histories in diplomacy, and as johnny-come-latelies in the international world, we know all too little about how diplomacy actually works.

We hear a great deal about the big issues, a great deal about the interplay of the top personalities. The smaller drama I happened to see played out in North Africa explained and illuminated something else: the manner in which broad international policies are actually implemented and worked out by diplomats on the scene. As a witness of this drama, I came to realize something I had never suspected as a private citizen: the way in which Presidential and Congressional policy can be distorted and even reversed as it filters down through the State Department and the hundreds of Embassies and Consulates, as it encounters the apparently inevitable differences of opinion between different government agencies, and as it is misunderstood or misinterpreted by public opinion at home. Good policies, I gradually realized, are not enough. We need to know as much of the actual mechanisms of diplomacy as we know of the structure of a corporation or of a government bureau in Washington. Otherwise our international policies will be unrecognizable by the time they have been handled by the long line of personalities between the Senate's Foreign Affairs Committee and the young Third Secretary in some far-off Legation in a dimly known land. Until we, as citizens, know the diplomatic world as we know the business, military and governmental world, until we choose and support our diplomats as carefully as we choose and support our generals and admirals, our diplomacy will continue to be defeated as it was in North Africa, and as it was in our final wartime dealings with France.

To say that we were defeated diplomatically in North Africa and in our French policies generally is, I realize, a strong statement. It is a statement, however, that is privately made by many leading American officials and by all of the numerous liberal Frenchmen with whom I have discussed this entire story. It seems almost incredible, in retrospect, that the most powerful country in the world, girded with military might and holding every card in the deck in the early stages of this diplomatic game, should have fumbled, misplayed and thrown away its political, moral and diplomatic strength as we did. It was a sad but instructive drama that I saw played out under the hot African sun.

Our original difficulty was perhaps unavoidable. That was the fact that we went to North Africa to do one job—a basically military one—and were forced into doing another, a diplomatic and political one. In the traditional American way, we wanted to keep hands off French politics, to let France, like other nations, work out its own political salvation in its own way. We succeeded brilliantly in the military job we originally set out to do, but we found ourselves in the meantime hopelessly and almost helplessly submerged in a witch's brew of international intrigue and internal French bickering. And while we hesitated and fumbled, we allowed de Gaullism—which most of our top leaders recognized at the time as an extremely dubious political movement—to become, to all outward appearance, a shining anti-Nazi crusade. We allowed de Gaulle himself to assume supreme and dictatorial power over the destiny of France.

While England pursued a line that was at least vigorous and considered in British interest, we were swayed by a dozen hesitancies and divided by a sharp difference of opinion in Washington as well as in North Africa itself. Our attention was concentrated on the military aspects of our job. Our whole American hands-off-foreign-interests tradition was strong. We simply did not realize in time that

we were allowing American prestige to fall to something minus zero
in both Africa and France, and long-term American interests to be frustrated and betrayed. If our traditional friendship with France is today
clouded and strained, it is because we awkwardly and grudgingly
allowed de Gaulle to come to power. If de Gaulle still represents lib-
eralism and patriotism to many British and American citizens, it is
because neither the British nor the American Government ever frankly
told their people the inside story of our dealings in North Africa and
in London with de Gaulle.

I first came in contact with this drama in the spring of 1941. The
Army and Navy were recruiting men to act as observers in North Africa
under the terms of the Weygand-Murphy economic agreements.
When a Navy friend of mine told me of the project, I left my job
at the Harvard Library to volunteer. It seemed—as it was—a chance
to do something for the anti-Nazi cause, for my own country and for
France, where I had worked from 1937 to 1940.

These Weygand-Murphy agreements were the first fruit of our
much criticized relations with Vichy in the early days of the war.
They were negotiated in North Africa between Robert Murphy, then
Counselor of our Embassy at Vichy, and General Weygand, the
strange and interesting figure whom Vichy delegated, as a sort of
pro-Consul, to oversee French interests in North and West Africa.
Under them, we promised to ship French North Africa substantial,
though not lavish, amounts of coal, cotton goods, petroleum products,
binder twine, tea, sugar and other much-needed necessities.[1] The
French promised in return to allow a reasonable number of American
observers to act as "control officers," scrutinizing the shipments closely
from the time they were unloaded until they reached the ultimate
French or Arab consumer. This was necessary, of course, in order to
make sure that the French lived up to the second part of their agreement: their promise that they would not export these or any similar
goods from North Africa.

The Weygand-Murphy agreements were immediately under heavy
fire from both the American and British press and from the British
Foreign Office. Our own press saw in them a sort of appeasement of

[1] These numbers appearing throughout the text refer to articles and documents
in the appendix at the back of this book.

Vichy, and a possibility of strengthening the Axis war machine through bootlegged American goods. The British were still in the darkest phase of the war and understandably afraid that their most potent weapon, the European blockade, might be weakened by any American exports to North Africa. They were increasingly mistrustful of the French, and refused to believe that the Vichyites in North Africa would abide by the terms of our agreement. Even after they were somewhat re-assured by our promises to keep a strict watch on every shipment, the British remained dubious about the whole venture. They even viewed our group of control officers with considerable distrust, and apparently considered their presence in North Africa a sort of economic infiltration into a British sphere of influence. From the start, our North African venture, therefore, was clouded in international misunderstanding and confusion.

President Roosevelt and Secretary of State Hull actually had very good and definite reasons for the Weygand-Murphy agreements but they were not reasons that could be stated publicly in the early months of 1941. No one explained them to me when I first volunteered, in Washington, but I later realized their validity in North Africa.

The first reason was a psychological one. At a time when the democratic world was uneasy about France, we wanted to show the French people as a whole that we kept an abiding friendship for them and that we believed, in spite of all appearances, that they remained our friends at heart. Our second reason was strategic. Our shipments to North Africa were an early part of what later came to be known as economic warfare. The Germans had promised the North Africans that Germany could supply all their needs. The Nazis were never able to carry out even a small part of this rash promise. Our goods, therefore, made a profound impression on the needy French and Arabs, and won us much friendship and prestige.

Our third reason was purely military. Well aware of the Axis menace to our own safety, the President and our top military leaders wanted to keep observers in strategic posts in North Africa, which was a sort of whispering gallery for every military rumor, near the Libyan battle-front and constantly in touch with the French homeland. If the Axis menace to us increased, North Africa was also our best line of battle against its aggressions. Through North Africa we could defend Dakar and West Africa, and beyond them South America. Through North Africa we could attack Axis Armies in the Near East and eventually liberate southern Europe. It was a key point in our whole system of defense. The British lifeline passed just north of it: Gibraltar was across the way, Malta and Suez to the east. Warring ships and submarines constantly circulated off its shores and Germany drew many materials of war from its rich fields and mines. It also contained a potential weapon of great importance: scores of thousands of French soldiers who had been disarmed under the armistice terms of 1940. If they kept their faith in the anti-Nazi cause, they could be rearmed to help in the final battles.

Our North Africa strategy, founded on our Vichy strategy, actually made our whole military problem enormously easier when war came. But in 1941 few people outside of what Washington calls the highest echelons seemed to realize this. Few outside the inner circle of diplomacy knew the violence with which American and British policies diverged, or the reasons for President Roosevelt's desire to keep close, if critical, relations with Vichy. This misunderstanding made our job in North Africa much more difficult. We had little backing from anyone at home during the early stages of our work. Even in the State Department itself, there was much difference of opinion about the whole North African adventure, and, almost up to the time of the 1942 landings, a feeling in the Department itself, as well as in other Washington agencies, that the whole thing was a mistake. The general public felt uneasy about our activities, and definitely uncomfortable about our Vichy policy as a whole.

The British policy with Vichy was, on the surface at least, a much easier one to justify. As we saw it develop in our daily dealings with the British representatives in Tangier and their secret agents in French North Africa, the general tendencies were quite different from our official ones, though close to what many Americans felt.

After France fell, in 1940, Britain viewed her late ally with suspicion which was widely shared over here. Even before the period of all-out collaboration that followed Laval's return to power, the British were cynical about Vichy's sincerity and unwilling to believe in any promises made by the French. Long-accumulated complaints dating from the Twenties and Thirties played their part in the mutual and growing dislike between the British and the French. Each country felt badly let down after the military debacle. Each had a long list of grievances against the other. France resented the long-term British refusal to back her in a "strong" policy against the Germans after World War I, and what seemed to her a half-hearted participation in the early stages of World War II. She complained that the British expeditionary force in 1940 was not only small but ill-equipped. England, on the other hand, was embittered by what she thought was too easy a capitulation to the Nazis, the French refusal of Churchill's offer of joint nationality with the British, and Vichy's alacrity in working out a *modus vivendi* with the Nazi conquerors. As Britain held the lines alone, this failure grew to the proportions of treachery in the British mind, and the British Government genuinely feared that Vichy would enter the war on the German side and hand over French colonies and the French fleet.

The French fleet became an almost morbid preoccupation with Anglo-American diplomacy during those unhappy years, and we felt the resulting repercussions later in North Africa. Both London and Washington discussed it so much with Vichy, and scolded Vichy so much about it, that you would have thought, as one correspondent remarked, that it was our own fleet which the French had somehow managed to steal from us. Our own Navy had not reached its present magnificent strength and Britain's naval power was stretched to the utmost; her very existence hung from a perilously thin supply line of ships. Though the French Government gave its word of honor that the fleet would not pass into German hands, neither Washington nor London felt easy about it. British unease culminated in an episode that left a bitter residue of anti-British feeling in North Africa, and confirmed the numerous Vichyites there in the cynicism and chauvinism we later found so trying. A British fleet took action against the French fleet at Mers-el-Kébir, a French naval station near Oran, Algeria, in July, 1940, and some 1200 French sailors were killed. Whether or not this rather impulsive action was justified, the results in both Algeria and Morocco were deplorable for the Allied cause. Many of the sailors' families lived in North Africa, and Mers-el-Kébir was publicly memorialized and remembered for years afterwards.

As the British pursued this all-out anti-Vichy policy, they made and strengthened connections with the French military underground. I was surprised to discover, in North Africa and London, something that was never clearly explained over here: the fact that this military underground had no original connection whatever with de Gaulle. It was formed by the French Army and started almost the day the armistice was signed. It had its own GHQ, its own organization, and its own channels of communication with the British. It was not until 1942, when the British decided to channel all their relations with France through de Gaulle, that he had any official contact with this original resistance movement.

In the midst of this vigorous anti-Vichy line of action, however, the British made at least one effort to work out some sort of compromise with Vichy. A basis for an understanding was actually drawn up between the two governments.[2] These negotiations were later used by Pétain in his own defense, and were instanced by Pierre Flandin to justify his having entered the Vichy Government. The idea was proposed by an emissary from Vichy, Professor Louis Rougier, and drawn up by him and Sir William Strang at the Foreign Office in October, 1940. The original text shows corrections in the Prime Minister's own hand. It was merely a negotiation and never became a treaty as it was not signed or implemented, partly, at least, because of opposition from the same General Weygand who signed the agreements with Robert Murphy. With a military man's approach, he argued that Britain had no chance of living up to its military terms unless and until the United States entered the war. But these negotiations remained a symbol of the fact that Britain still hoped to strengthen Vichy resistance to Germany. Her differences with our own Vichy policy may therefore, as one observer pointed out, have been more apparent than real. We ran into opposition from London only when, as in North Africa, we seemed about to break the European blockade, or when, later, we diverged from Foreign Office policy with de Gaulle.

This policy was the last line of British action in dealing with France. She felt around at once for a French leader who could produce a warmer climate of friendship between the two countries. At one point, as will be seen later, Prime Minister Churchill toyed with the idea of bolstering up the French pretender, the Comte de Paris. But the British finally fixed upon a sometimes enthusiastic, sometimes exasperated support of General de Gaulle. In the early days after the fall of France, he stood out as a courageous and dynamic figure, a refreshing sight to democratic eyes after the venality and timidity of Vichy. Like many other historical figures, his faults were not at first apparent. He was given all the facilities of the British Broadcasting Corporation, and soon became a symbol, to French patriots as well as to the democratic world, of the enduring spirit of France. By the time Prime Minister Churchill fully realized the anti-democratic, totalitarian tendencies of de Gaullism, the General had a deep hold on British as well as exiled French hearts.

While the British fought Pétain, tried to reach a *modus vivendi* with his government, and groomed his successor, we followed an entirely different policy. Our underlying idea, in Vichy as in North Africa, was to keep diplomatic relations with Vichy just as long as possible, so that we could observe what went on there, intercede whenever possible for the democratic cause, and keep American influence high in France, to counteract Nazi manoeuvering. Our policy was, I learned from our diplomats, a triple-barreled one. From a strictly military standpoint, we wanted to be able to move freely in Unoccupied France and in the colonies, using them as listening posts and also creating and strengthening our secret military contacts. From a political standpoint, we wanted, while the British used force and the threat of force, to use moral and economic arguments to keep Pétain from all-out collaboration. While the British scolded, we cajoled. Our North African economic agreements were the most dramatic of our attempts to keep Vichy from swinging wholly into the Nazi camp.

Finally, we had a third reason for our Vichy–North-African policies. This reason was more permanent and profound. We wanted to keep traditional American-French understanding and friendship alive. We wanted to show our friendship for *all* Frenchmen, whether they had been able to escape to the outer world or not, and whatever their brand of politics. Though we never condoned Vichy's policies and, in fact, openly and consistently criticized them, we did not condemn any Frenchman who sincerely thought they represented the best solution for France. We said, in effect: "We know that you are under tremendous pressure and are doing the best you can. We know France so well that we know only a tiny minority of Frenchmen could ever be pro-Nazi. In spite of outward appearances, we, your old friends, have faith in you. If you honestly think your Marshal Pétain is doing his best for

France, if you honestly think he is anti-Axis at heart, we are not going to interfere or condemn. While you are in prison like this, we shall stand by and keep in close contact with you. We shall strengthen you in any way we can." We believed in short, that all Frenchmen were potential allies, and treated them accordingly.

Though this Vichy policy of President Roosevelt's had looked extremely dubious from Cambridge, Massachusetts, I soon discovered its wisdom and far-sightedness when we reached North Africa. There is simply no question in the minds of people who were in North Africa during those trying years that Mr. Roosevelt's "appeasement" made our military job enormously easier and quicker. Rightly or wrongly, millions of men and women in France and especially in North Africa preserved an almost mystic faith in Marshal Pétain throughout those years. In North Africa, especially, the Pétainists formed an overwhelming majority. No attack on our part could have shaken that faith; the British attacks merely confirmed and strengthened it. They were not unpatriotic or pro-German, those Pétainists: in our two years in North Africa, we met almost no pro-Nazis. They were simply blindly, idolatrously sure that Pétain was wisely and skillfully preserving all that could be saved of France. No one could sway that belief; they had to discover its erroneousness for themselves. Our patience with them, our enduring friendship, did much to keep totalitarian poisons from seeping into many misguided French minds. We proved to them that they had strong, loyal friends on the democratic side.

Like almost all Americans, I was pro-de Gaulle and inclined to think all Vichyites must be traitors when I volunteered for the North African assignment. I was also deeply and gloriously ignorant of the job we were assigned to do. I did know France, had many friends among British and French political and military figures, and spoke French without too much of my original South Dakota accent. I had lived in many parts of England and Europe, and knew something of the Arabs from archaeological trips in the Near East. But North Africa was a closed book to me.

I soon discovered that my fellow control officers knew little more than I did. Though some of us felt, often, that the professional diplomats we encountered in North Africa were fumbling and bureaucratic, we were ourselves no shining example of what the representatives of a great power should be. Plucked from banks, stores, other business backgrounds, and picked largely for our knowledge of France, we were a heterogeneous, and sometimes confused group. Though we secretly saw ourselves as Scarlet Pimpernels, serving American interests in a strange and dangerous world, we had an obstinately naïve suburban touch. Our success in North Africa, which was considerable, was due partly to Robert Murphy, who stayed on there to carry out his agreements with General Weygand. He handled his oddly assorted assistants with consummate skill. It was partly due, too, to the fact that the cards were stacked in our favor. American prestige was very high in North Africa in 1941 (it has dwindled sharply since) and the Axis was heartily loathed by French and Arabs alike.

Still, our entrance into North Africa in the summer of 1941 was an inexperienced and unprepared one, and our whole performance there was ominously prophetic of the political and diplomatic fumbling we have apparently continued in Europe. Our awkwardness, as control officers, was not entirely our own fault. Though the Army and Navy selected us, we became part of the State Department's Foreign Service—non-career vice consuls—and were presumably to be trained by them. Actually, no one gave us any training or indoctrination at all. There was an almost reckless confidence about the way in which our Government projected us onto the international scene armed with nothing more than a knowledge of French and good intentions.

When I went down to Washington to get my instructions, in the spring of 1941, I expected to find someone in the State Department in charge of training our group of amateurs. I thought we would be given a course in North African history, politics and culture, and some instruction in diplomatic techniques and procedures. To my amazement, I found that no one in Washington seemed to know much more about North Africa than we did. What maps existed in government files were antiquated and inadequate. There was a "post report," also rather out-of-date, in the State Department files, describing Morocco and Algeria for the benefit of future consular officers, but it dwelt almost entirely on what seemed to be a singularly unhealthy climate and intolerable health conditions. Morocco was said to be damp and unwholesome (which it most certainly was not in my experience) and the natives were described as suffering from diseases ranging through malaria to bubonic plague. Other Washington governmental departments could report only that the communications system in North Africa was reputed to have broken down, and that the railroads were disrupted and gasoline not to be had. As far as the political situation went, we were told merely that it was black. The Germans were said to be infiltrating all Africa, disguised as tourists, via Spain and Spanish Morocco. They were reported to be planning a *coup* in North Africa, and best opinion was that we would find ourselves in Nazi hands soon after we arrived.

We did learn a little about our specific job. We found that we had both a disclosed and an undisclosed mission. Our more publicized job was to keep an eye on American shipments, check them at the port of entry, and follow them into every little Arab bazaar to their ultimate consumer. We were also to make sure that no similar goods were shipped out of North Africa. Our secret job was a more dramatic one. We were to be undercover American agents, acting as observers and organizers for the Army and Navy. We were to appraise the military and political situation, make friends with Arab chiefs and French officers, and set up contacts that might be useful to American defense. Later on, we were also—though we did not know this in 1941—to gather a great deal of highly secret military information in preparation for our landings.

Finally, we flew over, a dozen of us, to drop like so many Alices into the African wonderland. By midsummer of 1941, we were ready for two years of adventure, spying, political manoeuvering and international intrigue almost incredible to Yankee minds. After our years in banking, selling, and other sober American pursuits, we found the world of diplomacy, in the strange North African air, a shifty and shifting business, and seldom what it appeared from the outside. We had front line seats for two years at one of the most curious and important diplomatic dramas of our time.

CHAPTER II

Innocence Abroad

THE first glimpse of Casablanca was disappointing to my adventure-seeking eye. It could have been almost any seaside resort in California or Florida. The city was neat, white and shiny under the hot blue African sky. Our white Consulate, overlooking a little square set with geometrical palm trees, could have been a Federal building in Miami or Jacksonville. Even inside the impression persisted, because I found our consular staff in the same state of anxiety and confusion that I had left in Washington.

Our Casablanca Consul General, H. Earle Russell, a friendly and well-meaning career man, had not been told that I was coming and was obviously far from glad to see me, though he tried hard to be his agreeable and pleasant self. I was the sixth of this new series of non-career vice consuls who had been suddenly, and mysteriously, dropped in his lap by the far-off gods in Washington. It was obvious at once that Mr. Russell and his career vice consuls were upset. They seemed to share the feeling of almost the entire Allied world about the much misunderstood Weygand-Murphy agreements, and the State Department had made no effort to pave the way for our appearance. We found everyone in the Consulate in a state of dismay and agitation over our very existence. We were an unnecessary disturbance to their already confused but nevertheless traditional operations. They were afraid of what the Germans might do, and had already had a bad reaction from Vichy officials on the scene. They felt (with some justification) that a lot of amateurs were being sent in, to implement a policy they did not approve in the first place. From the very beginning, we encountered a fatal lack of unity and coördination in American policy abroad.

The whole Consulate was full of a strange atmosphere of nerves, panic and a sense of haste. The staff warned us not to be conspicuous. Mr. Russell warned us not to do anything other than learn to code and decode messages. We must not, he said, arouse German suspicions further or make trouble for the Vichy authorities in Morocco. Chances were we could stay only a few weeks anyway before the Germans forced our withdrawal. We must certainly stay within Casablanca. In fact, added Mr. Russell, we had better stay within a few blocks of the Consulate itself. If we tiptoed and whispered, if we assumed the very color of the plaster Consulate walls, the Germans might simply not notice that we were there.

This atmosphere of division and dissension surrounded our entire North African adventure during the next two years. Beginning with Mr. Russell and his staff in those early days, we lived in a constant state of suspicion, misunderstanding and distrust. No one loved us, and we were not always too confident of ourselves. We knew what we were doing, or thought we did, and were sure that Mr. Roosevelt and the Army and Navy were extremely anxious to have a job done, but we could never persuade other people of our validity. There was an almost universal feeling in the democratic world that we and our mission symbolized a truckling to the forces of totalitarianism, and were tarred with its brush. Our side in general wanted no dealing with Vichy or its works. They could see in the Weygand-Murphy agreements only a compromise with the forces of evil, and did not realize that they were a series of oblique moves on the military chess board.

This criticism, freely expressed in the Anglo-American press, actually helped us in the early days. It gave us sort of a "cover" with the Germans. Later, however, we discovered it had done so much toward misinforming and prejudicing public opinion that a true understanding of the later political issues became extremely difficult if not almost 'impossible. Large sections of the State Department, and, later, other wartime Washington agencies, remained unconvinced about the whole North African scheme until military action started.

In spite of this misunderstanding and distrust, we non-career men felt that the career men in Casablanca should play a more traditionally American role in launching us on our work that summer of 1941. We wanted a little more of the John Quincy Adams and John Jay spirit, a little less civil service caution. We didn't yet know North Africa, but we did know the French, and we knew that they admired enterprise and courage, and needed tough assurance to help them get over the deep-grained inferiority complex that grew like a cancer after their defeat. Later we learned that the Arabs admired these qualities even more. We also knew that German experts agreed that the way to treat a Nazi was to stand up to him. Above all, we knew that Americans had a unique weapon: we were the only country that still kept our extra-territorial rights in Morocco, and while it might be bad diplomacy to use those rights, it would be good diplomacy to let the French know we were fully aware of their existence.

Under a series of agreements made directly with the Sultan of Morocco, we could circulate freely in his realm and exercise certain definite and unique legal powers. Though the United States had formally recognized the French Protectorate, our relations were in theory exclusively with the sovereign state of Morocco. Except as an act of courtesy, we didn't even have to ask French permission to go anywhere we chose in Morocco. Finally, and aside from everything else, this diplomatic caution of our Consulate was a direct betrayal of our understanding with Great Britain, which had only agreed to the breaking of her blockade on condition that we watch the movement of every piece of American goods through the Moroccan bazaars and into the hands of the ultimate consumers. We could hardly do this from the United States Consulate, or even from inside the port of Casablanca.

Feeling utterly frustrated, I settled down in the Consulate and devoted myself to restudying the maps of Morocco and the data available about it on the spot. The maps were sketchy and tantalizing in their emptiness. Later, I was to see almost all those empty spaces for myself, and fall completely under their spell.

Morocco is one of the few authentically unspoiled countries remaining in the world. It is the most independent, vigorous section of North Africa. Tunisia, the easternmost part of North Africa, is more oriental than Algeria or Morocco, more influenced historically by empire-builders of all races. Even Algeria, with its rich coastal Mediterranean lands, has a long history as a colony of great powers. Its lands have been developed and exploited for many centuries, many of its natives corrupted and degraded. But Morocco, lying on the Atlantic, away from this stream of Mediterranean conquest, has remained comparatively untouched. Its climate, though hot, is swept by Atlantic winds on the coast and is very dry but not too enervating inland. A rather superior and enterprising type of Arab lives in its lowlands; and a proud, warrior race of Berbers, only lately subjugated (the last tribe in 1934), inhabits the high and wildly beautiful Atlas Mountains of the south and west. The French have done as good a colonizing job here as any white race has ever done anywhere. Arab cities have been preserved, while shining modern French cities have been built beside, rather than within, them. Arab and Berber culture and arts have been preserved, too, together with a shadowy but apparently fairly satisfactory simulacrum of their original political pattern.

The great expanse of fertile soil in Morocco, as well as this country's strategical location, makes it the most important of French North Africa. A vast mountain range, higher than the Alps, shelters it from the withering heat of the Sahara sands. In the foothills and plateaux are still to be found occasional magnificent trees, remnants of long since vanished forests. In the northern plains are extensive Roman ruins excavated under French auspices to prove to the Moroccans the priority of Latin civilization.

There are two distinct divisions in the physical character of Morocco —the fertile north and the more barren south. Within each of these divisions are two climates—one along the coast always temperate and agreeable, another inland, nearer the desert, with stinging summer heat and winters chilled by the nearby mountain snows and ice.

The capital of the north is the ancient town of Fez, built by the Arab conquerors, and today one of the most perfectly preserved medieval towns in the world. This white city lies in the fold of a green valley between the Riff mountains at the north and the Middle Atlas on the south. Its rich population and beautiful mosques, towers and white palaces, all topped with emerald green tile roofs, are concentrated into a small area between crenelated white walls. The mosques and universities make this city not only the spiritual and intellectual center of Morocco but of western Islam. Situated where a river rushes out of the earth, Fez is filled with a constant sound of rushing water, a music unique in Morocco.

To the west on the Atlantic coast is the French capital city of Rabat, built around one of the ancient sea-ports of the fierce Barbary pirates. In this delightful colonial town the French Protectorate Government is installed in a series of modern villas, white with green tiled roofs of Moroccan inspiration and architecturally most successful. Here, next door to the French Resident General lives most of the year his Shereefian Majesty, the Sultan of Morocco, in a snow-white palace that is a fantasy of odd-shaped windows, balconies and terraces set far back in a green field.

About fifty miles to the south on the coast is the commercial capital—Casablanca—built a generation ago on a plan drawn by Marshal Lyautey, the great French colonizer. It is the one great seaport north of Dakar on the Atlantic African coast, and because it is newly built is the cleanest city in North Africa, without the air of decay that hangs over most of the towns.

One hundred and fifty miles inland is Marrakech, the largest native city of North Africa. This orange-red city, built in a palm oasis at the foot of rocky snow-capped peaks rising with breath-taking majesty from the flat barren plain, lies like a "desert flower thrown over the wall of the Atlas." Scores of mosques rise above its extensive walls, but the greatest monument of all is the splendid rose-colored tower of the Koutoubiya Mosque, a masterpiece of the ancient glory of Islam. It dominates the town against the everchanging background of the mountains and serves as a symbol to the Arabs of the former grandeur of their civilization.

Into this city pour every day thousands of Berbers (Morocco, particularly the south, is predominantly Berber) from the mountains and the desert. They come on horseback, camelback, donkeyback, in auto buses, and on foot to trade and gossip in the market place. The fathers and ancestors of these men have been warriors through all recorded history, fighting for the French against the Germans, in the Civil War in Spain, and long before in the Roman legions of Augustus and Pompey. In the bazaars of Marrakech they show themselves a physically strong, friendly, gay people like most humans who live close to nature under a hot sun.

But the differences between the north and the south, the coast and the interior, do not mean that Morocco is a divided country. As in all of Islam there is here the binding cement of the Mohammedan faith, as well as a strange atmospheric unity.

That July of 1941, however, our interest in Morocco was neither atmospheric, historical nor geographic. What concerned us all was what the enemy would do next. I began to ask questions around Casablanca. I soon learned that there was no unusual German or Italian excitement, and that, contrary to the reports in Washington, there were no German "tourists" in Morocco. The Germans had an Armistice Commission, composed of about two hundred Germans, both officers and men. Their official function was to check on all French military installations, equipment, and personnel, and see that the North African Army made no attempt to rearm. An Italian Armistice Commission had originally had charge of this work but some months after the British-de Gaullist attempt on Dakar, the Germans had taken the job over from their allies, in the early spring of 1941, not trusting Italian efficiency. There were also some Axis representatives with a not too clear diplomatic status in North Africa. Their main job was to remind the highest authorities that France was a beaten country and to keep an eye on the place generally.

None of the Axis authorities seemed to be particularly excited about the presence of a handful of new American vice consuls, and there were no other Germans or Italians in evidence anywhere. The local French authorities, I learned too, had had no protests yet about us from the head German Armistice authorities at Wiesbaden. Obviously, they intended to let the Weygand-Murphy agreements be implemented. In spite of this French officials implored us to stay out of sight. Our knuckling under to these timid French bureaucrats seemed even more unnecessary than I had thought. We grew restive and anxious to begin our work. Time, we thought, was short. We little dreamed we had years not months ahead of us and we lived under the fear of a sudden German crackdown.

Under this sense of strain, everyone's temper grew short, and we began our diplomatic career ignominiously with one of those childish and utterly unnecessary office brawls, in which the amateur group of control officers got itself hopelessly and absurdly involved in a pointless warfare with one of the professional diplomats. North Africa's climate is intense, and the atmosphere there is quasi-oriental. The place produces an unexpected gift for gossip and intrigue in the most normally sensible Americans, who find themselves acting like Arabs in no time at all. By the time poor Robert Murphy turned up in Casa-

blanca from his main headquarters in Algiers, things had reached a
state in which we were communicating pompously by note and generally behaving like a group of burnoused Arab politicians in the
couloirs of the Sultan's palace.

It must have been a dismaying moment for Murphy, arriving to
take command of his little underground army of diplomatic sleuths,
only to find us behaving like the inept amateurs we were. We could
hardly have looked like people with whom you could do a job of
checking on the simplest shipments, let alone setting up a spy system
and gathering military information. Murphy proved at once his enormous flair for handling people. He was relaxed, friendly, witty and
efficient. Without taking sides, without hurting any feelings, he managed to let us see how childishly we had behaved, and we resolved
our differences in a sort of mutual shame. Never, by a word or a look,
did he let us know what he must surely have thought about our initial
performances as the representatives of a great power. Our morale
miraculously revived. We also discovered that, thanks to Murphy, we
could now come out of hiding and go to work.

I got to know Robert Murphy very well indeed over the next two
years and my liking for him never wavered. He was already a center
of press criticism at home, so I had been curious to meet him. I suppose I had visualized a cold, impeccably, correct character, the Talleyrand of all this dealing with Vichy. I saw a tall, thin, strongly-made,
but loosely put-together man, who looked younger than his age, which
must have been fiftyish at this time. He was clean shaven, with the
peculiarly white Irish skin, and a shock of blonde hair over clear, blue
eyes. In personality, he was anything but the "stuffed shirt" he was
pictured in the press. He had a gaiety that brought out gaiety in others,
a tremendous gift for friendship, affections that were almost too easy-
going and warm. He wanted to, and inclined to, believe the best of
everybody. He was, I found, a devout Roman Catholic, and something
of his deep faith seemed to be reflected in the loyalty and liking he
showed toward acquaintances, colleagues and even the men with
whom he negotiated.

The things for which Murphy was criticized in the liberal press were,
paradoxically, almost the opposite of the few faults people on the
scene might have found in him. They pictured him as one of the

"cookie-pushers," a socially elegant reactionary, even a fascist. He was none of these things. Born in Milwaukee, Wisconsin, he came from a family which was sod, rather than lace curtain, Irish, and his successful career in the Foreign Service was based on sheer merit, not on social connection. He would have done equally well in any field he chose. His father had worked on the railroad, and Murphy himself earned his education in very humble and American ways. He served long years of apprenticeship in the prosaic and far from social consular service. He was called into the diplomatic end of the Foreign Service by our then Ambassador to France, William Bullitt, who handpicked him as Counselor of Embassy in Paris. Far from being pro-Nazi, he had good personal reason to detest them, aside from any ideological aversion. His wife had been rudely treated by some arrogant Nazis when he was stationed in Germany, and the resulting dispute had caused the German government to ask for his recall.

On the other hand, Murphy's faults passed equally unrealized by his critics. There was no question in the mind of some of his warmest admirers that his very gift for friendship sometimes betrayed him. Though he had a hot Irish temper, which came in occasional lightning-like flashes, he was in general too indulgent, too loyal, too fair-minded, in a way, for a diplomat, whose main job is, after all, to sell a national bill of goods. Sometimes some of us wished that the lightning of his Irish temper would flash oftener when he had to deal with particularly slippery Vichy characters, and that he would be more tough-minded with the people who eluded, outwitted, or betrayed us after the landings in North Africa. His qualities of charm, generosity and friendliness were undeniably useful, however, as we planned and organized our African underground. His likeable personality, his gift for making friends, his executive skill, and his great capacity for hard work, were invaluable at a delicate time, and he served his country well and showed great judgment at a time when thousands of American lives might have been lost by fumbling diplomacy. The storm of criticism that raged around him in the American press was equally surprising and painful to Murphy, conscious of his own sincere and successful attempt to execute our official prelanding policy.

When he had quieted the tempest in the teapot of the Casablanca Consulate, Murphy set to give us our special assignments. We were, as I have said before, an oddly assorted group for such a crucial military job. Harry Woodruff and John Utter, two bankers who had lived in Paris many years, went off to Tunisia, the easternmost outpost of French North Africa. (Utter was, I think, the bravest man in Africa: he suffered an interminable series of boils, sheer torture in that humid climate, and no one ever heard him complain.) Woodruff, dark and poised, spoke French like a Parisian, which counted for a great deal with the expatriates with whom we negotiated. In Algiers, Murphy placed John Boyd and John Knox. Boyd was a richly accented Mississippian who had managed the Coca-Cola branch in Marseilles before the war, a man with great humor and a gift for friendship. Knox, slim and greying, had followed schooling at Groton with a most unusual education for an American—some years at St. Cyr, the French equivalent of West Point. Two businessmen, Ridgeway Knight, brought up in France, an ex-Cartier salesman and wine merchant, and Leland Rounds, went to Oran. A sophisticated yet sincere, witty and rather Elizabethan adventurer named David King; a construction expert from New York, Stafford Reid; a California oil man, Sidney Bartlett; and a young, energetic lawyer, Franklin Canfield, remained in Morocco. Frederick Culbert, an Annapolis graduate, and long an American expatriate in France, joined us later from Dakar, after Canfield resigned.

All these men played a major role in our North African activities, with the exception of Canfield, who shortly resigned, and Sidney Bartlett, who left somewhat before the landings. With all our inexperience, we had some early successes as well as making more than our quota of mistakes; and we had adventures enough to satisfy anyone. Some of our mistakes were political, and therefore dangerous; some were personal, and merely food for the constantly grinding mill of North African gossip. They were all miniature examples of the way the human element will frustrate the shrewdest international plans.

One of us, for instance, fell madly in love with a singularly flamboyant young French woman who passed herself off as an innocent young girl. He proposed to marry her on the spot, over the articulate protests of almost every American in sight. It was revealed, at the last moment, that the lady had not only some connections with members of the German Armistice Commission, but was already married to a Frenchman at Dakar, who arrived in the nick of time to save her from bigamy.

Such romantic complications, fortunately, were rare, and we never, incredibly enough, ran into personal violence or had valuable papers stolen. One reason for this immunity was that Mr. Murphy insisted that we work in pairs. He didn't want us to have to leave the diplomatic pouch if a car broke down, or put ourselves in a position to be framed either by the Germans or the Vichyites. But we did find ourselves, throughout our North African experience, in a spider's web of espionage and counter-espionage. Our wires were always tapped; we learned to talk in an elaborate conversational code, and often filled in gaps with American slang. We had nicknames for the main characters with whom we had to deal. We learned that everything we said not only circulated by conversational grapevine all over North Africa, but ended up, carefully itemized, and usually totally inaccurate, in the *dossiers* kept on us by the Vichy secret service. At first, especially, we said much too much. It seems to be hard for Americans, the most outspoken people in the world, to realize that the spoken word can be as dangerous as the written word.

By the time Mr. Murphy sat down with us to assign a special job to each, I knew exactly what I wanted to do. I wanted to work directly with the Arabs, rather than the French. I was already fascinated by the drifting, shifting Arab world I saw even in the modern city of Casablanca, an eternal human tide flowing endlessly around the precise little islands of French civilization, and seeming wholly indifferent to it. Part of our consular control job was to check in the jostling bazaars (or *souks* as they are called in Morocco) on the way in which our goods reached the ultimate Arab consumer. Part of our political job was to sound them out, as we sounded out the French military men in their lonely inland posts, and the French bureaucrats in their offices. This didn't mean, of course, that we proposed to play politics with the Arabs. We had no intention of making trouble for the French. Whatever our private opinions, as Americans, about imperialism, we were in North Africa as guests and really as allies of the French people in all but name. We were not there to preach democracy or independence. We were there to find out what the Arabs really thought about the Axis and about the democratic nations, what sort of propaganda swayed them, how much the Axis infiltrated and corrupted the Arab world, and how receptive that world would be if American action were ever necessary in Africa. As I watched Arabs ride endlessly by, their dark faces looking withdrawn under their voluminous headdresses, or peeked through gateways into Arab palaces, I was consumed with interest in these people and curiosity about their thoughts and ways.

When I asked Mr. Murphy if I could have the Arab assignment, he was delighted. "I've been waiting for someone to offer to do that particular job," he said. "If you can persuade one of the other control officers to go with you, go ahead."

After some argument, I finally convinced Canfield that working with the Arabs would be even more interesting than working in the French world, and we started out on the most fascinating assignment I can imagine. With Canfield, for two months, until he left, and then alone, I drove through nearly every village in Morocco, chatted in the *souks* with all sorts and kinds of Arabs and Berbers, visited the medieval mountain castles, called *kasbahs*, in the Atlas Mountains, and drank endless cups of mint tea with Arab princes in their palaces. It would have been interesting in peacetime. It was intensely so, as we crossed and recrossed the path of the German Armistice Commission, and tried to elude the watchful eyes of the Vichy secret service. We knew almost nothing about the Arab life, little enough about Morocco itself, when we started. But slowly, like a negative in a chemical bath, the picture of that strange world filled in before our eyes.

CHAPTER III

French Morocco—The Shadow of Lyautey

Our whole diplomatic drama with the French was played out against this exotic and little-known background in North Africa. I have always felt that many of the complications we got into there, complications which affected our historic relationship with France, were due to the sultry, intriguing, socially backward atmosphere of Morocco and Algeria. It was an atmosphere which made personalities seem over-important, which produced fantastic plots, and led to petty personal bickering of all kinds. And the extremely Tory flavor of the French colonials had another untoward effect. It made it necessary for us to deal with people who were politically and even personally unpalatable to the American and British public and to us as well. This seemed inexplicable to the people at home, largely unaware of the ingrown, conservative, plot-ridden *milieu* of North Africa.

For these reasons, the Arabs and the colonial French, and the North African land itself, are important to any understanding of the way in which we suffered our diplomatic defeat with France. We were ill prepared to deal with them because of our general American ignorance of this strange part of the world.

Morocco was a peculiarly interesting place in which to observe French colonial techniques. As we make the postwar world, we shall hear much debate about British and French imperialism and about colonial trusteeships. I had always read and heard a great deal about the British colonial methods, but French ones, as far as I know, have been much less publicized. The French approach is quite different from the British. It has its own virtues and its own faults. Like the political and social atmosphere in North Africa, French imperialism also affected our whole diplomatic history with France.

I was surprised, at first, as I set out to explore the native world, by the ease with which France seemed to be controlling Morocco. There was a nationalist group there, calling for independence, to be sure, and many Arabs were flirting with or actually in the pay of Germany and even of Japan. But, there was no real revolt, and this seemed amazing in view of France's utter prostration in 1941.

I soon discovered that this quiescence, like the remarkable calm during the first World War, was due to two things: to certain traits in the French and Moroccans themselves, and to the heritage left by Marshal Lyautey, one of the greatest of all colonizers.

Modern Morocco *is* Marshal Lyautey. His great figure, his proud head and magnificent mustachios and his resplendent uniforms, will dominate that land for years to come. Lyautey conceived his "drop of oil" policy when stationed as a young officer in Algeria. Under this adroit policy the armed French built a fort and established themselves in hostile Arab country. Then they laid in great supplies of green tea, sugar, white cotton cloth, lamp oil, candles, and the like. The fort soon became the best trading station for the natives. Now, Arabs would rather trade than eat, and the Arabs near the fort soon grew accustomed to dealing with Frenchmen and came to depend upon them. When relations were firmly established, a military column would go on to establish another post deep in unconquered territory. In other words, French influence spread like a drop of oil on water. From time to time, it was met by resistance from mountain tribesmen aroused to action by some half mystic, half warrior *marabout*, or saint, but these episodes were unimportant compared to the smooth, continuous, civilizing, infiltration of the French.

Politically, Lyautey believed French power should be exercised within the framework of Moorish civilization. He had a deep and genuine respect for Moroccan traditions and the Moslem religion from which they spring. He understood better than anyone the Moor's tremendous nationalistic pride, and the paradox of his strong democratic spirit yet accepting a feudalism darker than anything in the European Middle Ages.

To the Moors, the sovereignty of the Sultan is supreme from a religious as well as a temporal point of view. Under him, in the shape of a pyramid, is a feudal organization made up of the Grand Vizier and lesser Viziers controlling the judiciary, the schools and other branches of the government. The pashas administer the government in the cities; the *caïds* in the country districts. As an instrument of political control, the Marshal simply kept this Moorish government, or *Makh-zen*, intact. Over and above it, he placed the French Residency, as arbitrator and controller. The Resident General signs all the *dahirs*, or edicts, of the Sultan, and, in practice, of course, is the absolute power in Morocco. Still, the Sultan remains in apparent dignity and in genuine magnificence. On all levels of the native administration there are corresponding French ones that aid, supervise and control. This system, while it might seem a mockery to us, somehow satisfies Arab pride.

Another astute political move of the French Government was to see to it that the businesslike, sedentary Arabic-speaking people on the Moroccan plains should keep their own system of laws and customs, while the wild Berber tribes in the mountains keep their entirely different one. This policy of *divide et impera* infuriates the nationalists but serves its purpose with the mass of the people.

Marshal Lyautey's perception of Arab feeling was both delicate and profound. He refused, for instance, to allow any Christian to set foot in a Mohammedan mosque, and Morocco is the only North African country in which this rule is still scrupulously observed today.

Lyautey also believed that the French should govern largely through the Army. The Moors are traditionally warriors; they respect and understand Army minds and ways. The Office of Native Affairs is still almost entirely made up of young French Army officers. Army control had another advantage: it made it possible for Lyautey to rebuild Morocco using Army funds, which were not under the direct supervision of the *Chambre des Députés*. Strangely enough, France's most successful empire building has been carried out almost in spite of the Government at Paris.

Everywhere, as Lyautey pacified, he rebuilt. "A workshop," he said, "is worth a battalion." As he subdued each feudal chieftain in turn, he built roads in that district, ploughed fields, and encouraged native industry. Matting from Salé, embroidery from Fez and Marrakech, rugs from Rabat and the south, began to find markets in Paris. All ancient buildings and monuments were classified, studied and restored. Schools, clinics and hospitals opened; the old Moslem universities were rebuilt, and new ones founded.

Lyautey died in 1934, but the French administrators who have followed him have been careful to follow the trail he blazed.

Unfortunately, the French leaders in North Africa today reflect the basic tragedy of France: her lack of competent leadership. For France, as General de Gaulle and Marshal Pétain have agreed, lacks men, in quantity as well as quality. Her population began to drop more than a century ago, long before the rest of Europe. Her whole economy was thrown out of gear by the defeat of 1870. World War I bled the country of her best leadership. The French who remained had less urge than ever to colonize. This accounted in large measure, I felt, for the slackening of integrity, the decline in ideas and creativeness, of the French Moroccan administration after Lyautey. The pervading influence of the *Banque de Paris et des Pays-Bas*, one of the great "interests" in France; the sly intrigues and timidity of the Residency, produced a situation that called for the best in diplomacy.

Yet the French administrators in North Africa kept some of Lyautey's admirable qualities. In the first place, the French are freer than any great nation of all traces of snobbery about "natives." There is no trace of condescension in their interest in Moroccan art and architecture, and they mingle with the Moors without that consciously broad-minded air that Anglo-Saxons and Germans cannot help using. The Moors feel and appreciate this. In the second place, the French are civilized enough to enjoy other people's civilization. They never, for instance, ruined native towns with chain stores or cinemas. Their own modern, gleaming cities were built at a discreet distance from the native towns, which were left intact. They paid native buildings like native customs, the tribute of respect. The French sense of style, too, appealed to the Arabs who love pomp, show, ceremony and riches.

A few incidents early in my Moroccan experience brought home to me the tenderness with which the French preserved Moroccan culture and the easy friendliness with which they treated the natives. They made me realize the strength of the French Empire. I was on a trip with two French officer friends in the Sous Valley. We had left Taroudant, lying at the head of this valley, and were on our way to Agadir. There is no more beautiful drive imaginable than from Taroudant to Agadir between the two snow-capped mountain ranges of the Great Atlas and the Anti-Atlas, in a valley so rich it produces four and five crops each year. The Sous River region, after the war, will certainly be developed by irrigation. In Elizabethan times it must have been even more fertile than it is today, because the entire sugar supply for the British Isles once came from this relatively small region.

It was late in the afternoon, and we stopped in the shade of some olive trees to make tea and have some sandwiches from our tea basket. I had always heard of the cobras that lived in these woods in the Sous Valley; the Arabs catch them and charm them in the squares of the Moroccan towns, and I looked everywhere for them, with no success. While we were having our tea some Arabs came along on camels and stopped to chat with us. The two officers with me could speak Berber and asked them to join us at tea. As we did not have enough cups to go around the Arabs produced their own from their camel bags along with odd, mealy cakes and walnuts to add to our tea party. Some young boys, brothers or sons of our guests, who watched the camels, began to play acrobatic games, and I joined them to demonstrate, to their delight, how to walk on one's hands. Finally, after an hour or two of conversation, the little caravan packed up and started off up the valley. One of my officer friends turned to me and said, "Now those Arabs will go all over southern Morocco spreading the startling news that they have met an American and that Americans must be civilized like the French because they also drink tea in the afternoon shade and like to chat and gossip with friends. The news will spread north over the Atlas Mountains, and all Morocco will know that Americans enjoy Arab talk and walk on their hands."

In and around Agadir, which I also visited early, southern Moroccan life can be seen at its purest. In the future, Agadir will be one of the great ports of this country, since it lies at the mouth of the fertile Sous Valley between the rich mineral deposits of the Great and Anti-Atlas Mountains. I am told that the word *agadir* means castle or storehouse, and modern Agadir is dominated by a formidable citadel-rock on top of which is an ancient Arab fortress. The coastline is made up of miles of shining beaches, which we later carefully surveyed as possible landing points for the American Army. (They were finally crossed off the list, one reason being: the ocean at this point produces a strange kind of tidal swell which would make landings dangerous.)

South from Agadir the road leads a bit inland to the beautiful oasis of Tiznit and further on, to the last oasis to be reached by modern road, Goulimine. In this town you still see caravans of traders from the

Sahara Desert. These Touaregs or nomads are known as the Blue Men, because of their indigo blue turbans and robes. Men of great stature, they are often veiled with the same blue material against the desert sun and sands.

Tiznit was a delight to me. Here I found a miniature Marrakech without one vestige of European life, a pure Moroccan oasis built around a cool spring and clear pool. The French had preserved it as carefully as a French antiquity. One evening in Tiznit, French friends took me to hear the music and see the dances of the famous dancing girls, or *Cherats*, of Tiznit.

I was ushered into a small room with red walls, opening into a court-yard. We sat on a low couch facing four handsome Chleuh girls dressed in black robes belted at the waist, with a *djellabah*, or flowing robe, of thin white cotton material over the black. On their olive-skinned foreheads hung silver coins and around their necks were dog collars of blue, green, and pink enameled silver beads. Their heads were wrapped in many-colored turbans over which they draped a short white shawl. On each side hanging from their shoulders over their breasts were large triangular plaques of silver, jeweled and ornamented, that served to hold in place the thin white *djellabahs*. One candle lit the room and threw strange shadows on the walls. A negro slave brought us mint tea to drink. As we sat facing the girls they would look shyly at us but we could never catch their eyes. They were always downcast when one tried. They held their heads high with great pride and dignity as they sat against the red wall, and there was never a trace of a vulgar gesture.

Suddenly the leader began to play on a curious primitive stringed instrument. As the strings squeaked under the motion of her bow the sound, strangely, was more that of a wind instrument than of a stringed one. One girl began to beat a copper kettle drum with two metal sticks. Suddenly two of the girls stood up and, adjusting their belts, began to dance. Their movements seemed slowly to breathe life into the music. The dancing was done almost entirely with their feet and their clapping hands, their heads and torsos remaining motionless. They faced each other like two little twin sisters and then turned quickly back to back, all the time beating the earth with their bare feet. The heads hardly moved but the feet persistently beat out the time and the motionless bodies swayed as they moved back to back, face to face, and then without any warning made a quick-moving symmetrical procession of two around the narrow confines of the little room.

As they danced the leader playing the stringed instrument and the girl beating the copper drum sang. The sound of the bare feet beating on the floor was like two more instruments added to this strange orchestra and the clapping of their hands accentuated the monotonous beat. Then, suddenly, the whole tempo of the music changed and became faster, almost like our swing music. The beating on the floor grew more persistent, the turns quicker, but still, in spite of the accelerated speed, the lack of movement in the bodies gave an oddly static quality to this otherwise animated dance. One had the impression of great dignity hiding passionate emotion. The room became almost oppressive with the beating of the drum and the feet, with the clapping of the hands and the singing, as the tempo was forever quickening in these strange Chleuh dances.

After several hours of this music and dancing it paradoxically grew less monotonous. I had an odd sensation, like a vision, that here in the *Quartier Réservé* in this little oasis of Tiznit, was the shred, the tail end, of some ancient mystic tradition. Very distinctly the dancing more than the music seemed to have a ceremonial religious origin. The extraordinary dignity of these little Chleuh harlots with their flute-like voices made a lasting impression on me.

Outside in the dark street under the brilliant stars with the palm trees rustling in a cool breeze, I heard the music of their last dance. Standing there alone with all this space around me, the sounds of the music and the singing seemed to take on another meaning. Within four walls it had been too oppressive, but heard through the courtyard out in the street it seemed that this music had originally been born on the desert, under the sky, where its vibrations and the persistence of its ever-quickening tempo could move off horizontally across the sands into limitless space with no walls to change its direction and intensify its monotonous beat.

I saw these Cherats again, much later after the Allied landings, when General Mark Clark, Mr. Murphy and I went down to Tiznit with Resident General Noguès on an inspection tour of southern Morocco.

General Noguès who was to play a big part in our dealings with the French in North Africa, was an ambiguous and interesting figure. He was trained by the great Lyautey himself, though he did not immediately succeed him as Resident General. He was an outstanding character in Morocco with his erect, trim, St. Cyrian figure (which local gossip insisted was actually as well-corseted as it looked), his manner, which was crisply military in business hours and utterly charming in a *salon*, and his face, burned olive by the brilliant African sun, with its glancing eyes and its sudden, delightful smile. Noguès was an extremely able administrator, and a hard worker, keeping French prestige and influence high with his constant visits to every Arab leader in every town in Morocco. But he was more than politician-soldier. He was, in fact, a sort of African Vicar of Bray, holding to his job regardless of changes of administration. He had originally been appointed by Léon Blum's liberal *Front Populaire* government and yet stayed on very happily under the reactionary Pétain.

On the surface, in spite of this, Noguès seemed to be one of the Frenchmen upon whom we could count. He was far from popular with the intensely Tory landowners in North Africa, who loathed Léon Blum and anyone connected with him, and General Weygand himself had told a friend of mine a year or so after the armistice, "When the moment arrives, you can count on Noguès." At the time of France's defeat, Noguès came nearer to continuing the war against Germany from French North Africa than any other colonial figure. He was unquestionably able. Yet there was something about his supple personality that should have warned any American not to trust him.

Noguès was our first example of how fatally easy it is for Americans to ticket people, especially foreigners, into "good" and "bad," of our national tendency to divide the world into Our Team and the other team. Actually, the world, especially the diplomatic world, is full of people like Noguès who are not on any team but who play their own obscure game. Noguès was very human, and very African. In that shadowy land, full of complicated plots and undercurrents, we shortly discovered that most of the whirlpools seem to center around the Residency.

From the moment our delegation of control officers dropped into Casablanca, Noguès was uneasy and irritated. He was annoyed at our mere existence, so inconvenient, so hard to explain to the Germans. He asked us to remain inconspicuous. He was afraid of demands from the German Armistice Commission to counteract this arrival of Americans. We, in turn, took to watching him. We saw him constantly play off the German Armistice Commission against the American Mission, and vice versa. One day, he would use the threat of Arab uprisings to get special privileges from Vichy; the next day, he would demand more food from the Arabs with dark murmurs about German pressure on Vichy.

During Vichy's shameful period of anti-Semitism, he constantly exaggerated the Jewish problem in Morocco. The Arabs and the Jews have lived together in Morocco for centuries, and have worked out their form of a *modus vivendi*, a pleasant business relation tempered by an occasional Arab uprising, when the Arabs think the Jews have taken too high a percentage and look too unbearably prosperous. The rare cases of French persecution of Jews in Morocco brought no wave of approval from the Arabs who conveniently forget their own intermittent sins in that direction: on the contrary, they were contemptuous and angry. Actually, Noguès, like many Arabs, had intrigued so long that he had often lost view of his goal and seemed merely to practice his art for art's sake. Before and after our landings, we were to see him try to make trouble among the Americans, and between the British and ourselves—and sometimes successfully.

The atmosphere of the French world around Noguès was one of strange unreality. Casablanca is a white modern town, glistening under an African sun. In 1941, it also had a flavor of Lisbon. Morocco was crowded to overflowing with refugees. Many of them, the tragic ones, were Spanish Republicans, and German Jews and Central European refugees, living miserable lives under the long arm of the Vichy government in Africa—lives that horrified us and many good French men and women I knew there, it was in such contrast to their country's liberal tradition. (We tried to remember, however, that that same France had taken these poor creatures in when the United States and other countries had refused them.) Then there were Belgian and Dutch refugees, faring better; and a large number of French men and women from occupied France, most of whom fared very well indeed.

Almost all these latter people had some reason for being in Morocco. They owned property there, or had relatives who did, or men in their family who had been soldiers in Morocco. Financial pressure brought them there, too; French currency at home was rapidly sliding to the brink of ruin. Liquid capital, from the world market point of view, decreased daily in value. Anyone who had capital, therefore, felt an irresistible impulse to buy some land in North Africa. The sum result was a sort of boom town atmosphere in Morocco, crowded trains and restaurants, great activity and an appearance of prosperity. Many of these French men and women were seeing their Empire for the first time; they were struck and fascinated by it, but they did not add any stability to the world with which we had to deal.

The men with whom we worked regularly, as Americans, were the French officials, Army and civilian, the permanent population in Morocco. Like most colonials and military men, they were conservative, intensely nationalistic, intensely parochial. People back home wondered audibly why we didn't find de Gaullists or "liberals" with whom to work. We worked, like everyone else, with what we had, and what we had were people who were French and patriotic to their fingertips but politically the equivalent of any group of stockbrokers in an exclusive Long Island club.

In June, 1941, as anyone who was there can testify, North Africa was passionately loyal to Marshal Pétain. There were a few former intimates of Marshal Lyautey who knew of the disloyal way Pétain had behaved toward him at the time of the Riff War, but Lyautey had concealed Pétain's ignoble role from the public with a dignity true to the best traditions of the Marshals of France. Pétain, to North Africa, was the spirit of France, carrying on in an hour of darkness, mystically imbued with leadership, waiting his time to restore France. Just before we arrived, Pétain had forced Laval out of his Cabinet under dramatic circumstances, with the help of that very Marcel Peyrouton who was to be a storm center after our landings. A story flew around North Africa that the Marshal had said: "At last I have rid myself of that treacherous Laval! And now I can sleep at night." The North African French hugged that remark to themselves: it seemed to prove that the Marshal was fundamentally true to the best in France and forceful enough to protect her. It was unfortunately to be his last such action; by the time we went to work in Africa, President Roosevelt had written a clear and explicit letter to Admiral Leahy, the American Ambassador in Vichy, explaining American policy: "In his (Pétain's) decrees he uses the royal 'we' and I have gathered he intends to rule." [3] The truth about Pétain, however, had not percolated through to North Africa. He remained a hero to most of the local French.

The French with whom we had to work, both as control officers and in setting up our military contacts were not only pro-Vichy: they were definitely anti-British. Universally they admired British courage during those terrible months of 1940–41, and the fact that Britain, after the fall of France, "held the middle watch alone." But three things conspired to keep anti-British feeling at fever heat. First, came the unceasing and adroit German propaganda, aided by Vichy collaborationists, over the radio and in the press. This had a great effect. All the traditional differences and misunderstandings between France and England were emphasized and restated. Second, came the still open and bleeding wound of the British attack at Mers-el-Kébir of July 3, 1940. A year later I saw a memorial service for the French sailors killed by British action at Mers-el-Kébir. *La Légion des Ancients Combattants* (a fascist-tinged Vichy organization) pulled out all the stops on the anti-British organ and gave it full value. Widows and families swathed in black were thrust into the foreground, wreaths of flowers were tossed onto the sea, and press and radio men were on hand to bring out every overtone and every painful implication in the ceremony.

The third item in this tragic anti-British feeling in North Africa was a parallel feeling against de Gaulle whom they considered a British puppet. I was amazed, when I began to work in North Africa, to discover the violence of the anti-de Gaulle feeling there. Back in America, I had taken it for granted that all anti-Nazi Frenchmen must be pro-de Gaulle. In Morocco, I found the men who could most help us in any military action, men of the highest character and devoted patriotism, were more anti-de Gaullist than they were anti-British. They never could forget that de Gaulle, a Frenchman, had taken up arms against his own countrymen.

The center of de Gaulle's propaganda in Africa was, of course, Brazzaville, in French Equatorial Africa, where he had his radio station. From it, he made his first important public statement—the famous Brazzaville Declaration of November 16, 1940. [4] Though this statement was couched (significantly, as we realized later) in rather grandiose terms, using the royal "we," it contained some admirable ideas. It promised, for instance, to uphold the French Constitution of 1875 incorporating the Treveneuc Law of 1872. This law, which became a key point in the whole battle that raged later around de Gaullism, was framed by the National Assembly to safeguard French constitutional government should France ever be occupied by an enemy. It set forth a definite plan to preserve French sovereignty for the people, and to restore democratic methods as rapidly as possible after any such occupation.[5] This Brazzaville Declaration had very little effect in North Africa at the time, though it was later discussed a great deal when de Gaulle repudiated not only the Treveneuc Law but the French Constitution.

The item that most weighed against de Gaulle in North Africa was the Dakar episode. It made such an impression on North Africa, and therefore on American plans there, that it is worth reviewing briefly. It colored French thinking for years, and made it necessary, when we dealt with the North African French, to keep the role of our British allies completely in the background.

In the autumn of 1940, the British were looking desperately for almost any military adventure that might divert the Germans from the British Isles. General de Gaulle suggested an expedition to Dakar. Unfortunately, he based his plans on completely erroneous military information. He assured the British that Dakar was full of Germans. This was not true; there were no Germans at Dakar.* De Gaulle also assured the British that he would be welcome in the port, even though Admiral Muselier, head of de Gaulle's naval forces, was justifiably afraid of and opposed to the expedition. At this point an element of detective story mystery comes into the whole episode. In the first place, the Dakar adventure was not protected by the usual military security; either through over-optimism or incompetence it was freely canvassed. In the second place, when the fleet reached Dakar, General de Gaulle instead of landing himself, in the full panoply of his prestige, sent underlings into the harbor to negotiate with the French Governor. Why? No one knows.

In any case, Governor Boisson refused to treat, and the expedition fizzled out. Whatever the reasons for the debacle, it was the first of

---

* One exception was a German business man travelling on a French passport as "M. Martin" who turned up there on the very eve of our own landings.

many episodes that produced a growing British uneasiness about de Gaulle. Said a British Cabinet Minister to a friend of mine: "If General de Gaulle had been dealing with any other people than the British, he would never have returned from Dakar alive."

Dakar had many evil results. The first was that it made the Germans much more aware of the possibility of Allied action in North Africa. Shortly before the Murphy mission arrived, they had removed the original Italian Armistice Commission in Morocco and replaced it by a more efficient German one, which set to work systematically to undermine the Allied cause and which progressively demanded more and more military concessions in Morocco. This, in turn, set the North African French even more against the British and de Gaulle, the inadvertent cause of the increased German pressure. All through North Africa, too, Dakar gave Frenchmen a horror of what they called "commando raids." They were afraid that when Allied landings came—as they suspected some day they would—we would not come in sufficient force. Any such abortive action would mean, they feared, that the Germans would move in completely on North Africa. Then their underlying, nightmare dread might come true, and Frenchmen might be found fighting as allies of the Germans, hopelessly and forever divided. It was a direct result of the attack on Dakar that Frenchmen were arrested in North Africa when suspected of being too actively pro-ally, for fear they might encourage another Dakar. And it was Dakar that made many Frenchmen, still haunted by the idea of an unsuccessful "commando raid" resist our final landings.

This, then, was the political atmosphere of the French world in Morocco: anti-British, anti-de Gaullist, mystically believing in the old Marshal at Vichy, and yet, incredibly as it seemed to our American eyes, patriotic, anti-Nazi and largely willing and even anxious to cooperate with us as we began to build an American underground in North Africa. It was a lesson to us, as Americans, in the complexity of the European psychology, in the danger of dismissing international affairs in terms of large generalities. It was also depressing and yet challenging to discover that we could not work, as we had hoped, with an anti-Vichy, pro-de Gaullist underground. That underground, as de Gaulle's Washington representative was later to inform the State Department, simply did not exist.

In the meantime, as we made French contacts we also made Arab ones. The Arab world was quite separate from this stormy French one. Slow, secret and persistent, it led its own life in *souk* and shadowy street, undisturbed, except economically, by the troubles of its European masters.

CHAPTER IV

Into the Moslem World

AFTER Mr. Murphy had assigned each of us our part in the North African adventure, Canfield and I set off at once to explore this Moslem world of Morocco. Our assignment, we soon discovered, was the most interesting we could possibly have picked. We had to do what we wanted to do anyway—crisscross the little-known country, get to know the dark faces under the softly draped burnouses, dine in the town houses of pashas and *caïds*, and visit their *kasbahs* set like medieval castles on the lofty heights of the Atlas Mountains. Through our Arab contacts we found we could learn much about Axis operations in North Africa. Through them, too, we discovered many interesting things about the relations between the European and the Moslem world. Later, our Arab friends were to be most useful to us in setting up our pre-landing underground and building a secret communications system that could have been useful had the German Armies beaten us into North Africa.

One cargo of goods from America had already arrived before we set out on our first two-month swing around Morocco. As we drove, we inspected village markets and gossiped with native chiefs. We carried with us lists of our imports; white cotton cloth (for shrouds, as it turned out—the Arabs said the quality was too poor for clothing), green tea, the national drink of Morocco, sugar, condensed milk for children, coal, gasoline, fuel oil, binding twine, and sacks for the rich Moroccan harvest. All these products, but especially the gasoline and oil, were as I have noted before, severely frowned upon by the British Board of Economic Warfare which was convinced that we could not keep them out of German hands. They worried us, too, but we felt—and rightly, as it turned out—that the gamble was worth taking because of the hope of keeping French and Arabs alike on our side.

Our journeys into the dark background of Africa soon taught us a surprising thing: that the natives knew much more about us than we knew about them. They knew all about us, in fact. Moors are natural spies. They spend whole days moving around the bazaars exchanging news and gossiping. Long before we started checking our first invoice, each *souk* knew just what goods had arrived and where they were headed. Arabs who unloaded them started the underground telegraph system working, and word spread to the Atlas Mountains themselves as fast as the little Arab mules could trot. This native trait was a fine thing for our purpose: we used it later for our own pre-landing signal system, and it was invaluable in checking on enemy activities.

Canfield resigned a few months after we began this work and returned to Washington. By then Mr. Murphy evidently considered I knew my way around enough to work alone, instead of with a partner as originally planned. I was deeply grateful for this trust because I did not want to discontinue my association with the Moors, and there was no one else who wanted to do this sort of work.

Arab psychology is a fascinating study to an American or European interested in the whole pattern of European empire building. Much of what goes on in places like Syria or North Africa must seem utterly confusing to anyone who has not lived with Arabs and been in close contact with their subtle and indirect ways of thought. At first I was completely baffled by some of the conversations I had with them. As I carefully recorded my notes afterwards, I would find that my written record of the conversation was quite different from the *impression* I had of it. Sometimes it seemed exactly the opposite. I soon learned that this was because conversation with Mohammedans takes place on a series of different planes. There is an upper stratum, a surface, which to the casual observer seems the subject of conversation. Under this surface, there are often as many as four or five different planes, or subjects, on which the Mohammedan is communicating with you. They appear, glance, and retreat, or are only felt, like lights in a prism. It is on these planes that the real exchange of ideas is made. Communication with all Moslems takes place largely through the antennae of the mind. Again and again I found that I was right in my *feeling* of what some *caïd* was saying rather than in his actual words.

This love of communicating in a sort of mental chess game probably helps to account for the political inefficiency we constantly found among the Arabs. They talked politics a lot, and they seemed restive under French rule. They loved America and, like most unsophisticated foreigners, had a touching idea that we were all-good and all-powerful. They were critical of Europeans of all kinds. And yet they obviously were making no concerted effort to throw off the European yoke, even when Europe was so preoccupied. Unlike the Hindus, their resistance movement was limited and not too important. Relative prosperity, of course, helped account for this fact: most powerful Arabs and Berbers were doing nicely in the wartime Moroccan boom. But their incurable tendency to dissect instead of implement their dissatisfaction seemed to me one of the main reasons why, since their final military eruptions under Abdul Krim in the Twenties, they had been so passive under French control. I always liked the remark of an English friend of mine, Jessie Green, who had spent a good deal of her life being kind to the poor Arabs in Tangier. "I could have more respect for them," she said, "if they would walk right into my house and cut my throat."

Another trait that kept the Arabs relatively docile under French control was their indifference to yesterday and tomorrow. Though they cling to traditional ways of doing things, they neither remember nor plan consistently. The French colonizers soon discovered, for instance, that while the Moroccans are always building, they build out of the most impermanent materials and pay no further attention to a building once it is done. It was Edith Wharton who said that the Arabs and Berbers have a collective form of the artist's indifference to the finished product. Morocco is always crumbling into decay, like the sand castles of a careless child, and it is built with the same divine negligence. Once I saw a Moroccan constructing an elaborate doorway for what was apparently to be a house. "What sort of a house are you building?" I asked him. "How should I know?" he answered. "I haven't finished it yet." The immediate past does not exist to a Moroccan, and the future is unforeseeable. If the national motto of Mexico is *mañana*, that of Morocco is *inch Allah*—if God is willing.

One of our main jobs among the Arabs was a study of the political influences being brought to bear on them. This was obviously important to us in any evaluation of North Africa from a military point of view.

Riding up to Fez one day on the train, I caught a glimpse of the amount of political pressure that was being brought to bear in this curious Arab world.

Sitting beside me in the train was a young Moor absorbed in an elaborately printed and illustrated book, written in Arabic. The printing looked conventional enough, but there was something very odd about the flavor of the pictures I could see. As Father Brown would have said, they were the Wrong Shape. I fell into conversation with the young man and learned that he was a professor in an Arab school at Casablanca. The book he was reading was a gift from the Japanese consul there. It was a history of the Japanese Empire, illustrated with magnificent pictures of the emperors and state ceremonies, in a power and glory to delight the heart of any Arab. The young professor found the book intensely interesting, and said he had a profound admiration for the Japanese. In Mohammedan fashion, he was attracted by the long, unbroken tradition of the imperial house, and above all by what he told me was "a happy synchronization of religious ritual, governmental protocol, national habits, and the evolution of the individual." I could see that in this case, at least, the Japanese were showing a very shrewd feeling for Arab psychology: for their love of tradition, ritual and power. The Japanese were obviously exporting more than cotton goods to Barbary.

German influence, too, was evident among the natives throughout Morocco, but here the happy Moslem habit of taking the cash and letting the ideology go was quite evident.

In Marrakech, for instance, I met an extremely intelligent Moroccan who held high office in the local government. I saw him constantly, and enjoyed his friendship very much. He was the enormous, very dark son of a prince of the royal house of Morocco and a Senegalese slave. Through his father, he was a direct descendant of the Prophet and therefore bore the title of Sherif or *Moulay*. This fusion of negro and Arab blood is rather common and produces some remarkable results in Morocco. My princely friend was a delightful companion and always kind to me, but I had no illusions about his activities. With me, he always professed a touching loyalty to the Allied cause. His wife's family had played a very important role in Moroccan history and his father-in-law had been knighted by Queen Victoria. This fact he used to dwell on to me, as a proof of his deep fondness for England. By habit and education he was indisputably pro-French, and would remain so as long as France held the Protectorate power. At the same time, he was deeply attached to the imperial family and Islamic traditions, and in his youth had been an ardent Nationalist.

I soon learned from the Arab grapevine that he was in close contact with the German Armistice Commission and received large sums of money from them. This gave me another reason for seeing him, and I was always interested in his eloquent condemnation of the Nazi ideology, methods and practices. He especially criticized German anti-Semitism because he knew they held the negro in equal scorn. I could always tell what the Germans were up to and what form their propaganda was taking from a talk with him: not so much from what he said, of course, as from what he left unsaid, from his method of approaching a subject and from all those subtleties of Moslem conversation I have already mentioned. I knew, of course, that he went back hotfoot to the Germans with reports on me, and that fact had its uses when I wanted to fire a shot on my own small sector of psychological warfare. I realized, too, that he always believed that I was on the point of out-bidding the Germans and offering him a sum of money appropriate to American power. I let him think so but, needless to say, never involved the United States in this exotic form of Lend Lease.

Nowhere in the world, I believe, is this sort of opportunism and lack of principle as prevalent as it is in the Arab countries. It is the quality that most disintegrates and destroys government, and I think it helps to account for the backwardness of Mohammedan countries, and their inability to play the part in the world to which their resources and density of population entitle them.

Like so many Arab faults, this opportunism actually was a help to us. It kept the Germans in a state of frustration as they futilely bribed and corrupted Arab leaders and then watched them pleasantly accepting the British gold that all Europe knows as "the cavalry of St. George," from the horse of St. George stamped on the sovereign. As a matter of fact, we were the only people who never bribed the Arabs—and never had to. They freely gave us information and help. I had never fully realized before the extent of our prestige and popularity among the underprivileged of the world, the way in which the most ignorant and unlettered natives somehow knew that Americans were kindly people who asked nothing from them and would never join the long list of their exploiters. I saw the soundness of their feeling beautifully symbolized after our landings, when, on a lonely, dusty road, I found two Frenchwomen whose car had broken down. A jeep full of doughboys had stopped to fix the car, and I heard the Frenchwomen thank them profusely in broken English. "Gee, Ladies," said one soldier with a friendly smile, "that's nothing. We're Americans, and we *love* to help people." Before the landings, the humblest Arabs were sure of that.

With all their opportunism, the Moroccans were strongly attracted by anything ideal, anything wide and general and couched in spiritual terms. They are a curious combination of tough materialism and a constant yearning for the sublime. I had some missionary friends, for instance, in the little town of Demnat, in the foothills of the Middle Atlas. They were a young English couple named Kingston. Mrs. Kingston had Bible classes, in which she read out loud from the New Testament to groups of Arab women, simple women who understood only their native tongue. (Even today, no Moorish woman can read or write.) She told me a remarkable fact: that during her reading the women would apparently pay no attention, gossiping and giggling together over their tea. Yet the moment she came to the actual words of our Saviour, they would stop talking, turn to each other and say with deep solemnity: "That is the truth. Those are true words." Like all the missionaries I ever talked to, the Kingstons were totally unable to make any Arab converts but they were encouraged by Arab response to spiritual truths.

The Atlantic Charter struck this same chord of idealism in the Arab mind. It made a truly profound impression on them, and for months they hardly talked of anything else. I imagine they still discuss it today. The effect it had on the Arabs, the way it helped win them to our cause, cannot be too highly emphasized.

The Arabs also admired our apparently boundless power. This power clung like an invisible halo even to the lowly control officers. I could soon see why our small American group worried the Germans, the collaborationist French and even the competitive British so much. As we moved around the *souks*, or tracked down Black Markets, or gathered news of shipments to Germany, we attracted as much attention as if we had been a thousand times as many Americans driving jeeps and tanks. The worried Germans and collaborationists thought we were disguised Naval officers, and the British feared that we had Singer Sewing Machine and Standard Oil contracts in our pockets.

Actually, we stuck close to our three jobs. We kept an eye on American goods; we gathered all the information we could; and we began to lay the plan for a very nice pre-landing Arab underground, in case the Germans took over Morocco first.

Fortunately for my work with the Arabs, I was able to live in the sort of quasi-oriental splendor they enjoy and respect. When I went to live in Marrakech, the winter of 1941–42, I was lent one of the show-places of the world, a magnificent and famous villa called La Saadia. It was one of the very few American properties in Morocco and be-· longed to the estate of a rich American. His widow very kindly allowed me to live there in her absence. Before this, I had always stayed at lovely Hotel Mamounia, but numerous members of the German Armistice Commission stayed there, too, and made trouble for any Frenchman seen with me. Marrakech, by this time, was overflowing with refugees, not only from France but Indo-China and Syria. Housing was difficult to find, so I was doubly grateful for a chance to live in the inimitable La Saadia.

Since President Roosevelt and Mr. Churchill, as well as countless other war leaders, stayed there with me, a note on La Saadia might have some historical interest. It is a stylized, modernized version of a south Moroccan *kasbah*, or castle. The thick walls are of pinky-red plaster; the single, spreading main story is dominated by a high sloping tower some six stories high—a tower from which Prime Minister Churchill liked to watch and paint the Atlas Mountains. The two inner courtyards held famous gardens of orange trees, geraniums and bougainvillea around black marble fountains, all indirectly lit at night to give a magical, undersea effect.

Inside the house, the rooms were panelled and painted in mint green, yellow and blue, with elaborate Moorish carvings and decorations, low couches, small tables and a vast baronial dining table. The bedrooms, each with its own huge marble bath, all different colors, were highly decorated with intricate panelling and low, wide beds. The one Prime Minister Churchill favored had a blue-tinted arched recess for the bed, and I am told that the sight of that rubicund great man, working over his papers against that medieval and ornate background, was something unforgettable. Outside, and around the villa, the grounds spread out in banks of violets, petunias and other flowers around fountains and rivulets and a pool which, from the tower, sparkled like a square cut emerald in the Moroccan sun. A vast terrace overlooked this Arabian Nights scene.

My head man in this enchanted castle, when I lived there, was a most extraordinary head-servant who later followed Mr. Murphy to his European post. Louis was one of the best known characters in North Africa, and generals, ambassadors and admirals always remembered him and asked for him. The son of a Syrian father and an Indo-Chinese mother, he was an oriental Admirable Crichton, efficient, imaginative and a czar in his own kingdom. No occasion was too much for him, and he basked in great occasions and the reflected glory of great men. When Archbishop Spellman arrived, Louis genuflected and kissed his ring as smoothly as a Roman; when the President and the Prime Minister visited he was the smoothly functioning (but humanly happy) *maître d'hôtel* behind the scenes. Educated at the Sorbonne, and veteran of the Foreign Legion, he was an intellectual as well as military snob, and read enormously. He spoke perfect French, correct if stilted English and German, and a little Arabic. He had a large collection of birds in his room, where he could talk to them, was constantly getting engaged but never married, and had been the ping pong champion of France. When I found him, he was a waiter in a cafeteria in Casablanca. Thanks to him, and the caretakers, La Saadia functioned smoothly through all the long procession of foreign agents, spies, American soldiers and aviators, visiting dignitaries and heads of states.

As I drove around Morocco, or entertained Arab and French figures with Louis' help at La Saadia, I began to suffer from the disease that afflicts all Europeans in North Africa. It is a disease that accounted for much of the trouble we had later in our diplomatic negotiations with the French and in the manoeuverings around de Gaulle in Algiers in 1943. Something about those hot blue skies, the secret, gossiping Arab world, the sense of being far removed from northern civilization, makes Europeans and Americans as touchy and personal as the Arabs themselves. People soon become more important than issues; petty gossip takes the place of policy. The French historian, Taine, produced the theory of the influence on history of *le temps, le climat,* and *le milieu*. Both the climate and the environment in North Africa helped to distort our own diplomatic history there. We moved in an atmosphere of intrigue and plot, spies and secret agents. Some of these intrigues and plots were merely curious, even fantastic, to American eyes. Some of the later ones, like the dark manoeuverings around Darlan, had their effect on history. Before many months had passed in Morocco, I learned that the most Hollywood melodrama could actually take place in North Africa. Like everyone else, I began to think in terms of personalities and I became intensely conscious of the miniature power politics in the African world.

CHAPTER V

North African Plots

ALL through these early days in North Africa we learned the lesson that
is so hard for Americans: that neither countries nor individuals are
wholly black or white but some human, personal shade of gray. We
could seldom classify people as wholly on our side and "good" or wholly
on the other side and "bad." Some of the people most passionately
on the American side and most useful to us in our undercover work
were very dubious characters by any personal standard, or indeed by
even French political standards. Some of the most Vichyite characters
in Morocco were fine, patriotic people. In the same way, our own representatives on the scene made some very dubious political choices, and
our allies often took paths that were not only different from ours but
cut right across our policies. We never sufficiently classified or enforced
our policies either among our own representatives or with our friends
on the scene.

Perhaps the most fantastic plot we ran across in North Africa, for
instance, was produced by the British. This episode was the attempt of
the Prime Minister in the spring of 1941, to have the Comte de Paris
—the Orléans-Bourbon pretender to the throne of France—issue a
manifesto and rally the French to the royalist standard with British
backing. The Comte de Paris was living a curious, semi-royal life at the
time, in a large rented villa eight kilometers outside Rabat, surrounded
by his numerous children, his blonde, royal Brazilian wife, and the
remnants of a small court. We used to meet him frequently, an active,
wiry little man, riding his bicycle around Rabat.

The British invited him to Lisbon in March, 1941, where he went
into conference with their Ambassador, Sir Noel Charles. A French
agent had gone to London beforehand to establish a basis for negotiations with the Prime Minister. Luckily, the Comte de Paris discussed
the project with a Frenchman who had a basic knowledge of the situation, and realized the danger of the plan. He persuaded the Comte

to return to Morocco and abandon the undertaking. The British, however, didn't give up all hopes of a restoration, and the "Pretender" again emerged from Moroccan obscurity at the time of Darlan's assassination at Algiers. This manoeuvering interested us because it proved something we already suspected: that the British were not wholly convinced that de Gaulle, who was not informed of this episode, would prove to be the best possible leader for France.

At this time, of course, we were more preoccupied with the Germans in Morocco than with de Gaulle and French politics. We didn't even realize yet what an overwhelming part de Gaullists were to play in our final diplomatic defeat with France in 1943. The Germans were enough to absorb our interest in 1941. Like everyone else in North Africa, they intrigued, but they did it in the German manner—with a nervous sense of inferiority and a heavy hand, suspecting each other, apparently, as much as anyone else.

Herr Theodore Auer, the German diplomatic agent in Morocco (an illegal position to begin with under the terms of the Armistice), was a professional German diplomat. He acted unofficially through the German Armistice Commission, about 200 Army men in civilian clothes. While they toured and inspected military installations he handled the political warfare. A man with a rather flushed face and sandy hair, he was the son of the great Auer chemical works in Cologne. Like many of the Nazis, he secretly admired the English, spoke English everywhere, wore fine English tweeds, and was obviously delighted when people took him for an Englishman. As usual, the German Government sent a sort of super-spy to spy on their own spy—a Prussian aristocrat who knew entirely too much about North Africa as a whole, but whose only mission, apparently, was to take a villa and keep a discreet eye on the Armistice Commission in general and Auer in particular.

The Germans, as it happened, were quite right in keeping an eye on Auer. He used to draw some of our diplomats aside and tell them in a whisper that he represented the "better part" of Germany and regretted being forced to associate with the Nazi scum. Couldn't they, he suggested, arrange a passport for him when the inevitable moment came, help him disassociate himself from the Armistice Commission? Running across Murphy one day in Rabat, he seized him by both hands and recalled the days when they were colleagues in Paris before the war.

He also kept trying to meet me—why, I never knew, except that he hoped, no doubt, to glean some information from such an inexperienced American vice consul. One day, a collaborationist Frenchman gave me a startling message from Auer. "Herr Auer," he said, "wants you to know, M. Pendar, he is a friend of yours, and regrets, because your two countries are enemies, he can not see you. But he asked me to tell you, when the time comes, as man to man you can count on him." I hear he was later beheaded by his Nazi overlords for his failures and indiscretions.

All this manoeuvering, typically North African, ended in an almost incredible lack of coöperation between American groups abroad. Herr Auer invited a young American career vice consul to dine, and this vice consul, after a pleasant meal, dutifully drew up a report of his dinner conversation for the State Department. When we read it, we could hardly believe our eyes. Herr Auer, it seemed, had said: "These new vice consuls of yours now, Mr. X, they do not look like diplomats. To me, they look more like some of your Army and Navy officers in civilian clothes than consular officers." To this our fledgling diplomat had replied, according to his own report: "Well, Herr Auer, one thing I can tell you is that they certainly don't know the *first thing* about consular work."

This episode was only one instance of the unnecessary trouble we Americans made for each other by a lack of coördination from Washington and our own lack of training and, perhaps, of basic sense of international self-preservation. The State Department couldn't be blamed for the many *naïvetés* and blunders of myself and my control officer colleagues: we had been picked by the War and Navy Departments and more or less thrust upon State. But I felt that a Department more on its toes would have had men of its own with adequate knowledge of the French and of French colonies, trained and ready; or would at least have given our little group some indoctrination and talks with experienced Foreign Service officers. As it was, our whole effort was unbusinesslike and half-baked, and didn't merit the fair success we had. In a less friendly or more organized country than Morocco we would have been forced to leave.

Some of the trouble we Americans made for each other would have been funny in a less serious situation. We control officers, for instance, were so anxious to be capable international sleuths that we produced many of the prize rumors in that rumor-rich land, and it was a poor week when we didn't turn in at least one report of an imminent German invasion. (French and Americans alike had, as a matter of fact, a justifiable fear of a simultaneous Axis attack through Spain and Morocco to Dakar.) We also turned in lists of pro-Germans and collaborators, most of whom later proved to be among our closest well-wishers and friends. Then we suffered from an absurd sense of rivalry among ourselves, like cub reporters on their first beats. We jealously watched each other's pipelines among the French and natives, and were hair-raisingly indiscreet. A control officer would often, in conversation with a foreigner, repeat something that the foreigner had said in confidence to a second control officer. This rapidly brought us a bad reputation for talking too freely, and panicked some of our best contacts into silence. Most of this was due, I felt, to bad indoctrination and also to our old-fashioned American sense of careless power—the feeling we still have but must lose soon, that we are so much top dog that we can do and say anything we like.

We also, like the French themselves, suffered from a confusion of idealogies. There was certainly no agreement among us politically—a good thing, needless to say, in the representatives of a democracy—but there was unfortunately little discipline and little agreement on the reasons for the war and the way in which it should be fought. This came poignantly home to me in an episode with a young man and his wife, Jewish refugees.

They were, it is true, wealthy refugees with that name synonymous with Croesus in Europe, Rothschild. The wife had been married to a German and had managed to get out of Germany after her first husband's death by taking most of her large fortune, as the Nazi laws then demanded, converting it into cash, and pouring it bodily on to the desk of a top Nazi official. The remainder she left as a trust fund for family retainers, some of them very old at the time. One day, these refugees were obliged to go from Rabat to Algiers; the wife was so ill that the doctor forbade her to go by the small African train, more crowded than any wartime trains in America. I offered to drive them, as it so happened I was motoring there with some colleagues in a caravan of three cars. To my amazement, two of these colleagues pleaded with me not to do it. "You know," they said, "how anti-Semitic many of the French are. It would be *extremely* tactless." I knew, of course, many of the more social North Africans actually would not dine at a house when these Jewish refugee friends of mine were present. I made the trip, nevertheless. It produced one curious episode, typical of those tragic Nazi years.

At a restaurant where we dined, I suddenly saw the wife pale. She asked if she might change places with me. I discovered why when I sat down in her place and realized that I was looking directly at a table full of Nazis, only a few feet away. The one facing me had a singularly cruel, pasty face, the face of a "movie" villain. Early the next morning, the husband came in my room. "Alix could not sleep all night," he said, "because she was haunted by that Nazi's face, and this morning she suddenly remembered who he is. He is a dangerous Nazi, the son of a footman who worked for her mother for years and whom Alix is still supporting in Germany. Her family sent that man we saw last night through college."

The French added their own element of confusion to this clouded North African scene. Soon after our arrival we found that General Noguès and his official family were extremely nervous about our presence. Part of our agreement with Vichy was that full publicity should be given to our shipments, both among the Arabs and the local French. Unfortunately, Germany by that time completely controlled the press back in Vichy, and Vichy in turn controlled Morocco. Noguès made less than the minimum effort to publicize the facts about the arrival of American goods. (This, of course, was a slap in the face for Germany, and one which the Arabs fully appreciated as they sent the news around by grapevine. Germany had asserted that she could take care of all needs. Actually, her total exports to Morocco while I was there consisted of a small shipment of nails, used to close the crates in which oranges were shipped to France and thence to Germany. And those nails weren't German; they were Swedish.)

We could understand why Noguès couldn't make the press cover the news of American shipments, but it was irritating to find, as Canfield and I did on our first trip around Morocco, that American cotton goods were not even marked "Made in the U.S.A." and that the local

French had never been told of their origin. They believed the shipments were brought from Spain, or drawn out of old stocks already in Morocco. These cotton goods were particularly precious to the Arabs, since they lacked even the necessary minimum of clothing.

Noguès, as a matter of fact, hadn't wanted us to make our inspection trips at all, even though the goods had been sent upon definite assurances that they would be carefully controlled. When Canfield and I applied for permission to make our first trip, Noguès first wanted to forbid it altogether and then tried to delay it. There were, he said, entirely too many American vice consuls travelling around Morocco. It invited the attention of the German Armistice Commission.

Yet Noguès was not pro-Nazi. French officialdom in North Africa was not all black, from our standpoint, any more than it was all white. The government took immediate and ingenious action against collaborationists, French or native. An agent of the French G2, for instance, lurked near the beaches around Casablanca where important Arabs used to meet secretly with members of the German Armistice Commission. He photographed them with a camera fitted with a telescopic lense. When the pictures were enlarged and the men identified, these Arabs were quietly removed to southern Morocco, where they would be out of touch with the Germans.

Yet, while we appreciated this adroit French resistance, it was irritating to have Noguès unwilling to go farther in living up to the Weygand agreements with us. Legally, no American citizen has to ask permission to go anywhere in Morocco because of the extra-territorial rights already mentioned. We asked permission of Noguès only because Murphy wanted to demonstrate our good-will.

We were finally forced to use the peremptory tone that American diplomacy seldom—all too seldom—employs. When Murphy told Noguès that we intended to invoke our capitulatory rights if necessary, Noguès shrugged and yielded, sending word to his agents in the towns on our itinerary that we were to be received, but that they were not to hold any political conversations with us. Incidentally, these men at the same time received the only official word they ever had that American goods were coming into the country, and this was done only when General Noguès had checked our itinerary. Later I found that those officials who were not on our route were never told.

The importance of all our American shipments was, of course, largely in their propaganda effect, which was decisive, and in the excuse they gave us for making friends with the Arabs. If all the goods had been transshipped *en masse* to the Germans, they wouldn't have made that mighty war machine grind perceptibly faster. Actually, I feel safe in asserting that none of these particular goods ever got out of North Africa. Plenty of Moroccan goods, however, did get exported. The German Armistice Commission, throughout the Russian campaign, used their military inspection trips to do some military marketing. They bought out native bazaars of every scrap of wool, in cloth or rugs, as well as of leather, copper and brass, in a desperate effort to supply their strained war machine.

Throughout our own control trips we checked railroad stations, docks, and warehouses. We saw evidence of the great amount of foodstuffs that were being requisitioned and shipped out of North Africa, and French officers and officials were always ready to tell us of shipments we didn't see with our own eyes. Cobalt from the Atlas mines, used in making steel for armaments manufacture, and phosphates from the plains near Casablanca were also being exported. We ran across shipments of rubber on their way to France, and thence Germany, from Madagascar. (Vice Consuls David King and Stafford Reid discovered these important shipments in the course of their inspection trips to the port of Casablanca.) The United States hadn't yet started preclusive buying. The French sabotaged this trade by loading, reloading and delaying the shipments in every way possible.

Though our own goods weren't transshipped, they did sometimes, inevitably, end up in the enormous African Black Market. Some French officials were corrupt, and many Arab civil servants; they often released goods through illegitimate channels. But the Arab purchasers themselves were responsible for most of our trouble. They would genuinely and even desperately need five yards of cotton goods for clothing, go to the bazaar and buy it, and then discover that it could be resold for several times the original price to a Black Market purchaser. This discovery was too much for human, or at least Arab, nature to bear. They would rather trade than be clad. Fez was the center of this traffic, and as we threaded our way through its seething streets we used to wonder how much olive oil, how many yards of cotton goods, were hidden away in the walled houses of the merchants we passed. It was obviously impossible to check on such an intricate Black Market superimposed on an intricate oriental native life, and we finally had to tolerate it as one of the many native evils we could deplore but not correct.

When we got back from our first two-month inspection trip, Canfield and I were full of ideas for improving our work in Morocco. We wanted our government to force more publicity on the economic aid we were giving North Africa. We even cut stencils to be sent to the United States for marking goods and crates in both Arabic and French. We wanted more funds for propaganda work. But we ran at once into the dissension on policy within the State Department at home. Some of this dissension was inevitable. The economic experts in charge of the shipments couldn't be told our ultimate plans because of military security. They were the butt of constant criticism from their colleagues while their superiors ordered the shipments to continue without explanation. While the top leaders in both England and America were whole-heartedly behind our North African policy, most of the British, influenced by de Gaullist propaganda, were vociferously against our dealings with the Vichy French, and the State Department, under violent attack from the American press, had great difficulty keeping up the shipments at all, let alone backing us with propaganda or economic weapons. We were left to operate in a sort of half-world of our own.

As 1941 wore on, the political situation in North Africa grew darker and more difficult. The British and de Gaullist action in Syria in June and July, 1941, coming only ten months after Dakar, caused still more division between the French in France and the French in exile. The Syrian invasion was so distorted by the Axis radio and the German-controlled Vichy press that the North Africans thought it was a grossly unwarranted attack on France's sovereignty, an attempt on de Gaulle's part to hand over a piece of the empire to the British and to a small clique of pro-British Frenchmen. Some of them could see the urgency of the British need for air bases, but none of them could understand de Gaulle's participation. They could understand a call to fight the Germans, but not to fire on other Frenchmen, whatever their politics. De Gaulle had, in fact, signed an agreement with Mr. Churchill soon after he reached London, stating:

"Article I—General de Gaulle will proceed to constitute a French force composed of volunteers . . .

"Article II—This force will never be permitted to bear arms against France."

Yet he had insisted that his soldiers should go into Syria with the British. The troubles the British and French forces had there among themselves were one of the major causes, as I later learned in Algiers and London, of the growing British suspicion of de Gaulle.

Oddly enough, as de Gaulle and British popularity waned, ours actually increased. At first, the French had naturally associated us with the British. We were backing the British, we seemed unable to understand why France could not continue the war, our press was violently de Gaullist. At the start of our first inspection trip, we found both French officials and civilians a little touchy with us. Later, as the German oppression grew worse, and the French got used to the idea that we were working with them rather than undermining them in North Africa, they became increasingly friendly, even in the most Vichyite circles. But they continued to hate de Gaulle, believing more and more that de Gaullism was a political rather than a purely anti-Nazi movement. Paradoxically many of de Gaulle's most violent enemies in North Africa came to be labelled "de Gaullist" merely because they were pro-British and pro-resistance. This fact was later very confusing to Americans coming to North Africa.

Over in Algiers, General Weygand, General Delegate of the French Government in North Africa, began to have increasing difficulties with the Germans. This energetic man had secretly been helping us, and the Germans began to suspect as much. He had also rallied all the strange and sometimes shabby areas of North African French together, electrified the natives with his military dash and magnetism, and given all Barbary a new, strong devotion to France; a devotion the Germans didn't like at all. And it was at his command that the Intelligence Division of the French Army performed the really remarkable feat of photographing every document sent out or received by the German and Italian Armistice Commissions. This was done with the approval of General Noguès and probably explains in part why Weygand so misguidedly thought we could count on him.

Watching from Morocco, we were already afraid that Weygand would be recalled, particularly when General Huntzinger arrived, in the fall of 1941, on his famous trip of inspection on behalf of Vichy. There is no question but that Huntzinger's plane was deliberately sabotaged by anti-Vichy Frenchmen. Unfortunately, his briefcase was found intact in the wreckage of the plane in which he met his death, and in the briefcase was the documentary evidence that Weygand had been secretly on our side.

Our collaboration with Weygand had been bitterly criticized in the democratic world. It did not, of course, imply any approval of his role in the 1940 armistice. The fact was that he held all French North African interests in his hands and was the only man we had to deal with in our negotiations. Unlike other Vichyites, too, he never wavered in his anti-German feeling or his belief in eventual Allied victory. The proof of this was the way in which he held fast against the Germans during the tragic Greek, Yugo-Slavian and early Russian campaigns, when Europe seemed ready to fall completely into German hands.

While all these intrigues and manoeuvers went on, we continued our day-to-day job of inspecting shipments and gathering information, driving from market to market, talking to *caïds* and pashas, French officers and French bureaucrats, Arab fruit growers and Berber shepherds. War clouds were darker all the time. As the fall wore on, more and more of our native friends would say, matter of factly, "After Ramadan * when the Americans land in North Africa. . . ." "But," I would say, "where do you get these silly rumors? You know surely that North Africa is always full of rumors you cannot believe. We are not even at war." "Ah," they would say, smiling, "that is true. Now, *when* the Americans land in North Africa. . . ."

* The Moslems' period of fast like the Christians' Lent.

CHAPTER VI

Moors and Frenchmen

By the fall of 1941, we had many good Moorish friends, and I was beginning to feel at home in the town houses with their veiled, oriental facades. I never quite got over, though, each time I visited one, that feeling I had of living in a Pierre Loti world. It seemed fantastic to be discussing German radio propaganda with dark figures in perfumed courtyards. We should have been gossiping over the latest crusade, or a batch of Christian captives.

The whole atmosphere of Morocco is theatrical, but you live close to nature there: ocean, sand, the mighty Atlas Mountains, rich plains and desert are your companions. The atmosphere is very clear, with almost constant sunshine. Even the Arab world, backward and often diseased as it is, has vivacity. Everywhere you see Arabs on mules, on camels, on foot, in buses, in trains, in broken down cars, going and coming from the *souks*, sitting in doorways, endlessly talking, trading, laughing, joking. They are almost always dressed in white or grey, but they have a fantastic sense of color. In the midst of a burnt out desert waste, you suddenly see a man or woman dressed in sky blue, light pink, brilliant orange, bitter lemon yellow, or mint green, like an unexpected exotic flower in barren land.

I saw a great deal of some of the key men in this Arab world as 1941 went on and we began to develop a large network of French and Arab contacts.

Perhaps the most important and interesting was Hadj Thami el Glaoui, Pasha of Marrakech, and head of the tribe of Glaoua, a fierce band of Berbers in the Great Atlas Mountains. When the French took over North Africa, there were three great southern Moroccan families, the M'tougi, the Goundafi and the Glaoui. Only the Glaoui were shrewd enough to realize the inevitability of French control. Today, El Glaoui, who, by a sort of osmosis, absorbed the wealth of the rest of his family, is a quasi-independent feudal lord of southern Morocco, a satrap for the French. El Glaoui's dark, aquiline face used to be a familiar sight in Paris, where he had a superb house on the Avenue Foch; and he kept a wonderful combination of European and Moorish sophistication. He was equally fond of golf and of boar hunting, and served cocktails and champagne to his guests along with Moorish dinners of wild magnificence. Like all Moors, he loved to build, and often I would find he had added a garden house or a pavilion to his palace between my frequent visits.

I first met El Glaoui soon after my arrival in Marrakech. I had already fallen in love with the town itself, the archetype of all medieval Moroccan cities. Into its great Place Djemaa El Fna pour thousands of Berbers from the Great Atlas and Anti-Atlas Mountains, nomads from the deserts to the south, Arab farmers from the fertile plains nearby. They exchange ideas, bits of news and gossip; they have their heads shaved under the wicker canopies of the itinerant barbers; they have scribes take down any writing they wish done, applaud the young Berber dancing boys, listen to stories from the Koran, watch snake charmers, laugh at clowns and tumblers, eat hardboiled eggs and *couscous* and drink mint tea, and barter the goods they have brought. Every Moroccan town has a central meeting place like this, but none with the character and flavor of the Place Djemaa El Fna.

At sunset, my first day in Marrakech, I drove in a carriage to the great Aguedal gardens of olive, pomegranate and orange groves, in the Park of the Sultan's palace. In the midst of these gardens are two vast reservoirs, like lakes, filled with precious water from the mountains. The water flows into canals under the trees, and keeps the Sultan's park perpetually green. From the balustrade around these lakes, you can look across the fragrant gardens to the white peaks of the high Atlas, and guess at the heart of Africa beyond. Marrakech is an outpost of North Africa, a gate to the dark continent to the south. As I watched the mountains bleach out in the gathering dark, that first evening, I saw a black, horse-drawn brougham roll by with most of the shades lowered. Through the one open window, I could see two Arab soldiers with two veiled Arab women, their black eyes gleaming under the hoods of their *djellabahs*. As they passed, I heard the tinkling of some guitarlike instrument and the notes of strange singing. They stopped a minute, eyed me, chatted and laughed, and then went on deep into the garden, strumming their guitars and singing in the fragrance of the darkening night. This carriage passing me, like a ship at sea, so strange, so far away, so removed from anything I knew, made me feel the gulf between our life and this outpost of the Orient.

That night, I dined with El Glaoui for the first time. He sent guards and slaves to my hotel to lead me through the maze of streets to his palace. Like all Moroccans, he followed the Koran which urges the faithful to keep the facade of their house simple and unpretentious, so as not to excite the envy of their fellow men. The reddish brown, rather ugly, facade of El Glaoui's palace gave no hint of the incredible luxury and magnificence of the rooms, courtyards, gardens and pavilions beyond. We were six at the *diffa* or dinner, sitting on deep cushions and eating course after course of exquisitely cooked food from a single plate with our fingers. From the alcove where we dined, we could hear a fountain splashing and smell fragrant flowers and shrubs. The whole courtyard was flooded with moonlight, and the deep blue black sky overhead studded with stars. Around the edge of the courtyard, sat slaves and servants, their eyes gleaming under white turbans or red fezes, ready when the Pasha gave the sign, to bring more food, chickens cooked in olives or oranges, succulent roast lamb with spices or pitchers of milk flavored with rose leaves or almonds, or orange juice tasting of cinnamon.

From the first, I had a feeling that El Glaoui was sincerely loyal to the Allied cause. Naturally, being a Moroccan and my host, he expressed sympathy for America; but it was not his polite phrases that gave me this feeling. It was the few but highly pertinent remarks he made about British and American war potentialities. He had a shrewd and informed knowledge of our sea power, our industrial capacity, and the strategic geographical positions we held in the coming battles. He spoke not merely as a mountain tribesman, bred to war, but as a world strategist, a soldier well aware of the international picture.

But as we discussed the war, I had a mounting and most peculiar sensation that something strange was going on in the Pasha's palace. The atmosphere seemed more and more charged; palace functionaries whispered in corners, and the majordomo, each time he went by the Pasha, would very softly say something in his ear. I studied the Pasha's face, but saw not a trace of concern or preoccupation. It was a mask of composure, dignity and calm, he and his manners remained those of the perfect host, seeing to the pleasure of his guests.

After dinner, as we walked around the palace and listened to musicians, I felt even more tension in the air. As we turned corners in the winding high ceilinged corridors, we would come upon groups of slaves whispering together. They would fall back silently against the white walls, their black eyes following us as we passed. One of the guests would occasionally, apparently by accident, drop a little behind us, and then there would be a hissing whisper of "*Monsieur le contrôleur, Monsieur*" and a Moor would slip up, whisper a few words in the man's ear, and then, with a masklike face, fall back again beside the wall.

Finally, we said goodnight and left, only to find even more tension outside the palace. There are always crowds of Arabs at the Pasha's door, but this night the whole street was teeming with excitement. I saw an Arab friend waiting for us, obviously because he wanted to discuss the affair with one of the Pasha's guests. He told us what had happened. While we were at dinner, El Glaoui had sent his men to raid the palace of his first Khalifa, El Biaz. El Biaz, it seemed, though he owed his fortune to the Pasha, had been plotting against him. Without any warning, the Pasha had surprised El Biaz and thrown him into jail this very evening. His riches, wives, and slaves, were taken away from him and he was later banished to the Atlas Mountains. This, I soon found, was in the best Moroccan tradition and was a sample of the fear and uncertainty under which rich and poor alike live.

Other chieftains did not give me the same impression that El Glaoui did of belief in our cause, or at least in our victory. I knew a son of the powerful Caïd Layadi, for instance. Caïd Layadi is the head of an Arab tribe (the Glaoua belong to the more vigorous and intelligent Berber stock) on the barren plains between Marrakech and Settat, halfway to Casablanca. Like El Glaoui, he had had the good sense to side with the French when they were taking over Morocco, and he was profiting from that worldly wisdom.

The young Layadi I knew took me to my first Arab wedding. It was, like El Glaoui's dinners, pure Arabian Nights. A servant was sent to my hotel to lead me to the place in the street where Layadi was waiting for me, and together we watched the procession of gifts from the Pasha to the groom and bride. The street was jammed with people, who were pushed out of the way by the Pasha's guards. Back of them came scores of slaves carrying enormous rugs rolled up and laid on their shoulders. Back of them, again, were other slaves, trays on their heads with pyramid covers over tea leaves and perfumes, or with great jars of honey and precious oils. Layadi told me that he had also, that afternoon, sent over a truly royal present: forty Swiss cows. While the procession wound through the streets by torchlight, the *fatimas* (Arab women) made the night quiver with a strange high-pitched noise called the *yoyo*, a sort of quavering yodel they use for moments of great excitement. Finally Layadi said: "Now, we shall go into the palace." With that, he called his servants who went before us with whips and mercilessly beat a path for us through the crowd. We followed them to the palace among screaming, stampeding children, veiled women and turbaned men. Inside, the vast inner courts were filled with hundreds of the Caïd's tribesmen. The light welled up from below and cast a sort of submarine glow on the scores of Arab women who sat, swathed in white, watching the party from the roofs.

The big event this evening was the presence of the old Caïd, receiving and welcoming the guests assembled in honor of the wedding. The next day, and succeeding days (a rich Arab's wedding often lasts two or three weeks) the bridegroom and his friends spent their time in a gaily colored tent in a garden, eating and watching clowns and dancers. About midnight, each night, the whole party would make a procession back to the palace and deliver the bridegroom to the bridal chamber door before which, on a chair, were placed the wedding robe and golden *babouch*, or shoes, of his bride.

Layadi, I think, felt a genuine friendship for me. He assured me that he and his father admired the United States. Yet when he went on to say that his father believed in the Allied cause and disliked the Germans, I did not have the same feeling of conviction that I gathered from the conversation of El Glaoui. In the months that followed, I learned that Caïd Layadi, was, as a matter of fact, the most important of the native chiefs in German pay.

This spying and counterspying in North Africa was extremely complicated even among Europeans. While Americans diplomats abroad seldom lead the exotic life sketched out for them by Hollywood, they do, in wartime at least, come in contact with a good deal of international intrigue and even violence. Some of our North African experiences were interesting to anyone concerned with the day-to-day job our Foreign Service must do.

One of our functions as control officers, was to act as couriers between Tunis and Algiers, Algiers and Oran, Oran and Casablanca, Casablanca and Tangier. Most of these trips could be made on the excellent civilian air lines of Air France. This company did a remarkable job considering its shortages of gasoline and repair parts, but our trips were watchful ones. German and Italian agents often made the flights with us and when we saw one of their familiar faces on the plane we had to keep especially close guard on the baggage compartment where the padlocked canvas diplomatic pouches were kept. (In those days, these pouches were filled with maps for future use, reports on the North African political situation, and military data on topics like beaches and airports. Later, we also carried heavy and secret cargoes of radios and more dangerous equipment in them.) The Air France personnel were all, as far as we could see, on our side, and made special efforts to protect us and our papers.

Each time the Casablanca-Algiers plane stopped at Oran our faithful colleagues, Knight and Rounds, were at the airport to give us their pouch and their news. One day, at the dusty Oran airport, during the usual twenty-minute stopover, I was sitting talking with my colleagues in their car when suddenly, a few minutes before the time for departure, two little men rushed up with a couple of red and white awning-striped canvas diplomatic bags. "If you please, sirs," said the most harassed looking of the pair, "will you be so kind as to leave these bags for us at the Italian Consulate in Oran? We have been expecting a car but it hasn't yet shown up and the plane is due to leave." We couldn't help smiling as we looked at the two nervous, hot Italians. Knight said, "You evidently don't realize we are American vice consuls." They paled visibly under their layer of dust, gave us a sickly smile and melted away.

The trip from Casablanca to the international madhouse of Tangier was more difficult, because the one inadequate night train was finally cut to two trips a week. We often had to make the trip by car, two of us together, so that the diplomatic pouches would never be left alone in case of accident. Accidents were frequent with our battered old cars, and we often walked miles along deserted Moroccan roads in search of help.

In those pre-landing days, the only official contact we had with the British was at Tangier; their consulates and diplomatic representatives left French-dominated territory when diplomatic relations were broken after the British attack on the French fleet, and the British nationals left in French Morocco were mostly Jews from Gibraltar and Malta. The British, like other powers, had many secret agents in French Morocco, but communication with them was difficult, partly because of censorship, partly because of the numerous spy systems.

Naturally we helped the British in their war effort in any way we could. One of our jobs at the Consulate was to act as liaison for them and also to hand on information that we collected, particularly on shipping. We kept them posted on the French naval units and noted any merchant ships that came by Morocco on their way to Marseilles with, for instance, cargoes of rubber.

We came in close contact with British intelligence work. The British were in an almost desperate situation at that time. Gibraltar was their last bastion in the western Mediterranean, and only Malta, Egypt and the extreme eastern Mediterranean coastline were free from enemy control. British officials sat helplessly in Gibraltar and Tangier, watching ship after ship of the French merchant marine carrying supplies from the empire to metropolitan France. They knew that only 20% of this material remained in France, while 80% was divided, very unequally, between Germany and Italy. Any agents they could get to impede this traffic, any act of sabotage against it, was a military victory.

We understood this, and sympathized with it, but we deplored what we thought was a lack of comprehension of a bigger stake to be won on the diplomatic level. In the first place, the British bribed the worst elements in the population; most of their information was paid for. This practice of paying for information is, many American diplomats believe, expensive, dangerous, and politically almost useless. Anyone who will receive money to give information obviously has his price, and is merely waiting to get more money from your enemies. I never used money at any time, and yet found a great many Frenchmen ready, for purely patriotic reasons, to give us any information we wanted.

In the second place, the British used violent sabotage. We objected to this on policy grounds, and our differences with the British here reflected, of course, the differences on a higher level on the whole policy with France. Our idea throughout was to work *with* the French, even the Pétainist French, in the belief that they were basically honest and patriotic. The British had despaired of the Pétainists and washed them out as possible allies. They worked in French territory as if it were enemy territory. When they involved us in their more drastic moves, it naturally undercut our whole influence in North Africa.

I remember one episode particularly which illustrates this difference in policy in those early, troubled days. One day, on a courier trip to Tangier, I was approached in the Minzah hotel lobby by an Englishman of the Intelligence Service who had recently arrived from London. He asked me if I would take a small package and a letter to one of his secret agents in Casablanca on my return trip. I said that I would, and asked him to give me the package and letter. "Oh, no," he said, looking around the crowded lobby, "we will bring it to your room if you will set an hour." At 9:30 the next morning, he showed up with a young assistant. I said to them, "I shall have to ask you to open the package and the letter so I can see what I am taking before I assume the responsibility of carrying them into French Morocco on my diplomatic visa."

"Oh, there's nothing important in the package," the secret agent said negligently. "Just hand it over to our man in Casablanca."

I looked at the address, and saw it was being sent to a man who lived not far from my apartment. "Well," I said, "if you don't want to open the package I shall have to."

Unwrapping it as I spoke, I found that it contained two bombs. "I'm very sorry," I said, somewhat taken aback, "but I shall be unable to deliver these for you."

The agent reached into his pocket and drew out an enormous roll of bills, saying as he did so, "Perhaps this would come in handy." "No, thank you," I said, "I don't need the money. But don't worry. On second thought, I think I can manage the errand for you."

I realized at once that the bombs were to be used to sabotage a stock of rubber that was lying, at the time, near the Casablanca harbor. When I later opened the letter, on the way back to Casa, this hunch was confirmed; the letter named the day for carrying out such a plan. I was much concerned, because I feared that if any such blatant piece of sabotage took place while we Americans were circulating around Morocco, we would be blamed, perhaps expelled, and our whole overall plans for the future jeopardized. So I quietly jettisoned the bombs in the Atlantic and deposited the letter in my strong box at the Consulate.

This sort of thing happened time and time again between the British Intelligence Service and ourselves, until finally the top men in London and Washington worked policies out better, the British were more convinced of the good results of the American approach in North Africa, and the overall directions from both capitals were straightened out.

All was not sweetness and light, of course, in the handling of the American policy, and we had increasing trouble with Vichy officials, especially after the recall of Weygand.

Weygand was so passionately attacked and defended in the American press that a note on him, as we saw him on the spot, might be a useful footnote to history. I do not know the whole Weygand story in detail, but I know enough to hope that one day the State Department will release the missing facts in it.

Weygand was heavily involved in a question that will always be a bitter one to Frenchmen: the question of whether or not an armistice was necessary, and whether or not the government could have been moved to North Africa. Weygand's recommendations on both scores were purely military ones. The political decisions were made by Reynaud, Pétain and others. All were wrong from our point of view. When Mr. Churchill made his generous offer of joint citizenship to the French, Weygand again took a purely military view of it. It was not a question, he said, of fusing the two empires in the future, but of how many troops and airplanes Britain could immediately supply. All in all, he was an acute example of the unhappy relations that always exist between the military forces of defeated allies.

In Africa Weygand was in charge and served his country well. We had no other person to deal with there. Once faced with French defeat, and with the fact that his fears over England's chances for resistance had proved false, he set to work, as a general virtually without armaments, to use the only weapons left to him: ingenuity and patriotism. He was a man of extraordinary personality, and it was easy to believe that one of the many rumors about his royal, foreign birth might be true. Weygand had certainly been entered at St. Cyr as of "unknown parentage," and his appearance was both distinguished and foreign. He was very small and wiry, with high cheek bones and deepset eyes. Though he was seventy-four years old at the time of his service in Algiers, he was incredibly young and active, giving a feeling of inexhaustible nervous energy under an iron control. I remember the young wife of a French diplomat who had to take to her bed after a half-day of sightseeing on foot with Weygand, while he kept on working the rest of the day and evening. Unlike most Frenchmen, he took good care of himself, and followed a strict regime, even eating "sensible" food.

In Africa, he traveled incessantly, and did the most important thing necessary in fusing the countries together and giving them strength to resist German propaganda; his magnetism, the quality the French call *rayonnement*, produced in them a real fire of devotion to the idea of France. He held the Army together, even though it was unarmed. As noted before, he kept careful tabs on the Germans and was useful in many ways to us. Though he was a Tory of the deepest dye, had fought the Russians and distrusted the intelligence of the English, he had always firmly believed, for the security of his country, in alliance with both Russia and Great Britain. During this war, however, he thought only the United States could help France. (He estimated it would take us two years.) His Toryism actually made him more useful to us in North Africa, where we had to deal with feudal and reactionary people, used to living under a military dictatorship.

Weygand has been criticized for not coming over from southern France to North Africa at the time of our landings. From accounts of people close to him, I think that when the whole story is known it will be found that he expected at that time the Allied landings in France itself that both the British and ourselves let the French think would be made. He stayed in France, to assist us there, on the undefended southern coast.

When the Germans, who had thought he was a "safe" man, saw him flying from Tunisia to Algeria to Morocco to Dakar and West Africa, when they saw the way in which his gift for military drama appealed to the natives, when they saw the way Africa united behind Weygand, and when they saw Americans begin to appreciate him, they knew it was time to send him home. Huntzinger's spying confirmed their worst suspicions, and Weygand went back sadly to France. The Nazis so thoroughly distrusted Weygand by this time that they would not allow him, or his son, to return to Algiers long enough to pack their luggage. Their action was a tribute to our wisdom in working with Weygand.

In December, 1941, shortly before the beginning of General Rommel's terrible, and almost decisive, drive across Libya that nearly reached Alexandria, our diplomatic work became more difficult. French cries for gasoline and oil were piercing. The whole economy of North Africa, the very life of the country, depended on gasoline and oil for transportation, irrigation and farm machinery. This was a very grave problem indeed, and although the arrival in the summer and autumn of 1941 of the French tankers *Frimaire*, *Schéhérezade* and *Lorraine* had made a great impression, the fact that no more tankers followed their single voyage caused a great deal of criticism. Wherever we went, we met Frenchmen who either asked with strained politeness why we sent no more, or sneered openly at the inadequacies of our aid. The former attitude was annoying enough, but the latter was particularly difficult to take. For we had learned—not from Vichy, but from obscure and unwilling Frenchmen who were forced to handle the work—that the Vichyites led by Darlan had sent Rommel, in November and December, 1941, 1,000 trucks, 100,000 tons of wheat, and 8,000,000 liters of gasoline.* Under the Weygand-Murphy agreements, no product originating in the United States, or *any similar* commodity, could be sent out of North Africa; so the supplies that reached Rommel were a breach in spirit if not in fact of our agreement. By that time, however, we were in the war and our military needs in North Africa were so urgent that it became more vital than ever for us to remain there. We swallowed a good deal of our annoyance and went on with our work.

Pétain, by that time, as I have heard from people who worked with him, had only a few morning hours of energy or even lucidity. By afternoon those of his advisors plotting for closer collaboration with Germany found it increasingly easy to get his signature on dubious agreements. At this point, down in North Africa, we began to hear

---

* The gasoline, as a matter of fact, did not come from North Africa but was shipped from France in French boats.

more and more about Admiral Darlan, who was to play such a big role in our landings and the political drama immediately afterwards.

Darlan was perhaps the most interesting case history in the whole question of our wartime diplomatic dealings with the French. Our contacts with him, our final decision to work with him, were bitterly criticized. In microcosm, they represent a basic issue in our foreign policy and in our diplomacy—the issue of expediency versus principle, of being "practical" or of holding out, even at the cost of American blood and resources, for American ideals. As will be seen later, most people in North Africa, liberal as well as conservative, finally agreed that our dealings with Darlan were justified in the final balance.

Everything we heard about him in 1941 was, however, unfavorable. He was the real father of Vichy collaboration, constantly working the old Marshal around to his point of view. Yet he was not a "traitor" to France. He worked with the Nazis in the belief that only through their friendship could France survive. After Pearl Harbor and German reverses in Russia, he suddenly realized, with his knowledge of seapower, that while the war would be long it would eventually end in Allied victory. In December, 1941, though he remained a passionate anglophobe, he found it wise to change sides again.

Unfortunately, before this final switch Darlan was committed by two visits to Hitler in March and May, 1941, to a substantial amount of collaboration: The first meeting was to establish the principle of coöperation, the second to plan details, such as giving the Germans the "right of passage" on Syrian airfields. In these agreements, Darlan fatally committed his country to a policy of helping Germany. Although seven months later his belief in German victory wavered, he was in no position by that time to force Hitler to release France from her commitments. When Admiral Darlan was confronted by the American Embassy in Vichy with the help he had given the Axis, he said it was a question of giving the Germans supplies or of handing over Bizerta as a base. "I picked the lesser of two evils," he insisted.

While Darlan swung slowly to our side, we Americans hung on by a thread in North Africa. We were at last in the war but in no position then to take over Algeria, Morocco or any other place. Our problem was to survive in North Africa even though the Weygand-Murphy agreements were being constantly violated in spirit by Darlan's collaboration policies. Our career diplomats in Vichy and Mr. Murphy in Africa deserve every credit for their ingenuity in staying on. They used Weygand's removal ingeniously to meet the situation. "Very well," they said, "Weygand is gone and Darlan has violated our trade agreements; therefore we stop everything or renegotiate with some better assurance this will never happen again."

Shortly after this, on New Year's Eve in Marrakech, I met Commandant Bataille, a former naval officer who was in charge of rationing in Morocco, and one of General Noguès' confidants. As we chatted over the champagne, he made several sneering remarks about American aid, claiming it was worthless, and asking why we wouldn't send more gasoline. I gave him our reasons, mentioning the fact that Admiral Darlan had broken our agreement by sending gasoline to Rommel. Commandant Bataille became literally livid with rage at what I said, either because he knew it and had thought I did not, or because he thought I was lying. There was tremendous excitement next day throughout Marrakech over this conversational episode.

We had many reasons to resent any talk of this kind in Morocco. The Weygand-Murphy agreements were to be based on reciprocal trade. Cork and tartar, as well as products of lesser importance, were to be shipped to the United States, and we were especially anxious for olive oil. Tunisia and Morocco were the greatest producers, and Moroccan oil was far more available than Tunisian because of transportation difficulties. General Noguès, however, in spite of Weygand's request, refused to allow a drop of Moroccan olive oil to leave for the United States. There were two reasons for this; the fact that Noguès was bitterly jealous of Weygand—a feeling that dated far back in their military careers, and the fact that Noguès, ever fearful for his job, thought that Weygand was running too great a risk in dealing so freely with us.

Yet during the black hour of Pearl Harbor, and after, I felt again how right our policy was in Africa. As we entered the war, letters and visitors poured into American houses in Morocco. All were sad and sympathetic, because all the French knew the full horror of war. Yet they were hopeful because they knew that with America in the war, the end, however long delayed, was certain. All 'through North Africa, for months afterwards, I met those same spontaneous, unmistakably sincere, feelings of liking and sympathy. Only a few officials had a reaction which left a bad taste in our mouths. In a rather patronizing way, they would say: "*Now* you will understand what war is, and can't go on with your rich Yankee attitude of 'business as usual.' " This patronizing reaction, however, came from wounded pride and a sense of inferiority. It was not that they wished America ill, but that they felt we had never suffered enough to understand the suffering that had humiliated and defeated them.

CHAPTER VII

Black Months

THE months after Weygand's recall, and especially after Pearl Harbor,
were dark for us, as for everyone else. We had the special sense of fa-
tality that everyone far from the front lines had, even when their job
was intimately connected with winning the war; and the French officials around the Residency did not make our lives happier. Weygand's
recall signalled the beginning of much heavier German pressure on the
French authorities, and Noguès knuckled under. Americans in Morocco were more and more on the index. We thought at first that the
orders came from Vichy, but our pipe lines soon let us know that they
came direct from the Resident General at Rabat.

Most of our French friends, however, remained courageous and sympathetic. In April of 1942, for instance, when Mrs. Leahy, wife of our
Ambassador and a much beloved figure in France, died at Vichy, I received no fewer than thirty letters of condolence simply as an American
representative, many of them from total strangers. There were some
French, of course, who had a much less sympathetic point of view
toward Americans. They were not pro-German. I heard of very few out
and out pro-German French, anywhere in North Africa. They were
simply xenophobic. They hated everybody. They thought France's role
should be to stay neutral and let the Germans and Allies exhaust themselves in the war, as France exhausted herself in 1914–18. Then they
believed that France would start even, so to speak, in the world race
again. This xenophobia was hard to distinguish from anti-American-
ism at times, and it strained diplomatic patience to the limit.

Our isolation as Americans, and particularly mine, which was the
most extreme, soon became a topic of conversation not only among the
French but among the Moroccans. One day, I was told that the Pasha
of Marrakech, my friend El Glaoui, would like to see me. At his palace,
he gave me the usual warm welcome, with ceremonial mint tea and
elaborate Arab cakes. We spoke of many things until, in the glancing

Moroccan way, he mentioned the real reason he had sent for me. "I want you always to feel free to come here, or to go to any of my *kasbahs*," he said. "My sons live in many of them, and will also be glad to welcome you." I told him how grateful I was, and he continued: "I know of the order from the French Residency about you, but as long as you remain in my city of Marrakech, among us Moroccans, I want you to know we are glad you are here. I have never hidden from you my belief in the Allied cause." At that point, with another charming smile, he adroitly changed the conversation again, and earnestly discussed horses and farming. Mehdi Glaoui, El Glaoui's son, remained a faithful friend of mine too. He was a true believer in our cause, as well as a close personal friend. I was doubly unhappy to hear that he had been killed, fighting heroically as our ally in Italy in 1944.

During this period political events in France had immediate repercutions in North Africa. One began on February 19, 1942, at Riom in France with the trials of the French leaders judged responsible for France's defeat. With their mistaken psychology the Germans were encouraging these trials, believing the evidence brought out would further anti-Semitism, Nazism, and generally aid the cause of French collaboration with Germany that they pretended was so close to their heart. The effect was quite the contrary. News from the courtroom at Riom acted as a stimulus to true French patriotism all over France and in the empire. Finally the Germans were obliged to order these trials stopped.

When Laval came to power, the xenophobic Frenchmen in North Africa, particularly the ones close to the Residency, became even more out-and-out anti-American. The United States was grouped with Great Britain for the first time in anti-Allied propaganda. Laval's return was a dreadful shock and disillusionment to a great many North African French. Those who had sincerely believed Pétain was working for the best interests of France were horrified to see the Marshal welcome Laval back into his government. But many of them still held to their mystic, blind faith in Pétain no matter what he did. I remember running into a Frenchwoman I knew, an intelligent, cultivated person. She had always assured me that Pétain's ousting of Laval in December 1940 proved that he was forceful enough not to become a German puppet. Yet when Laval returned to power she merely said: "Ah well, no matter: everything will be all right as long as we still have our Marshal."

The worst result of Laval's return, from our own standpoint in Morocco, was the effect it had on Noguès. In spite of Noguès' coldness to us, the Germans had recently asked Pétain to recall him. The reason they gave Vichy was that there was too much American influence in Morocco, and that Noguès was surrounded by officials of whose politics they were not "sure." (The real reason, as we knew on the spot, was that Noguès, with all his faults, was an integrating force in Morocco, a good administrator who tried to keep French sentiment vigorous throughout the land.) Noguès was called to Vichy for "consultations" in the spring of 1942. He flew there posthaste.

We heard later that Herr Auer, the German diplomatic agent in Morocco, happened to be sitting in Laval's waiting room when Noguès turned up. Noguès begged Auer to take up his cause with the Germans and even pleaded with him to intercede with Laval. Auer did so, and Laval and the Germans restored Noguès to favor. But the episode left Noguès more afraid of American friendship than ever. As far as America was concerned, Noguès was useless from then on.

With Allied resistance continuing, Vichy's old nightmare of an abortive commando raid on the Moroccan coast was revived. As a preventative measure, the Vichy authorities one day ordered every British subject living on the coast to move at least 50 kilometers inland. The majority of these were Gibraltarian and Maltese Jews who had lived for generations in Morocco and knew not one word of English. This action had a contrary effect to what Vichy wanted. The few hundred refugees immediately began learning English and overnight became more conscious of their nationality than they had ever been before.

As the black months of 1942 drew on, it was harder and harder to persuade the Arabs, especially, of our ultimate victory. This was particularly true from the time of Rommel's hair-raising drive in December, 1941, until the magnificent stand of the British Eighth at Mersa Matru the following June. Defeat followed defeat on every front, especially on the North African one of which the Arabs, naturally, were most conscious. The very day Tobruk fell with 30,000 British taken prisoner, Auer arrived in Fez, called together the most important Arab leaders, and said, "You see, German victory is inevitable. Soon we will be supreme in Africa, as in all Europe."

All we had to counteract his undeniable facts were our arguments about the moral superiority of our cause, especially because of the German race philosophy, and the military fact that our potential production and size was so much greater than theirs that time was on our side. It seems amazing in retrospect that most Arabs remained on our side, and that the majority of the French never lost faith in spite of the pessimism around the Residency. The blacker things looked, the more Frenchmen came quietly to us to tell us that they remained loyal and would help us to the end. During this time, we helped many Frenchmen to escape from North Africa to join the Fighting French outside, though we had to be careful, of course, to help only the Frenchmen we knew personally to be sincere, eager to fight, and already in danger from Vichy reprisals because of their sympathy with us. Too many were soldiers of fortune, tossed up by the tides of war in North Africa and trying to escape Moroccan debts—or worse.

Propaganda from all sides reached a new frenzy during early 1942. It was interesting to study the propaganda of the different countries from the receiving end in Africa. The Arabs seemed to agree that the German propaganda was well handled, even though they paradoxically didn't believe much of it, because they knew too much about the Germans. Even during the last war, the Germans had left agents in the South of Morocco to stir up the Arabs; and Moroccan soldiers taken prisoner during that war were used to teach German agents the various Moroccan dialects. During World War II Germans did the same thing. They also bribed, corrupted, and trained some of the Moorish prisoners and sent them back to Morocco to act as spies.

From Rome and Berlin, Arab leaders * chosen for their eloquence, radioed a stream of speeches on the evils of French control, the vices of British imperialism, and the support Pan-Islam would receive from the Germans after Nazi victory. They told the Arabs that the French had favored the Jews at the expense of the Arabs, and that this would be even worse under British "Jewish-Free-Mason" influence. Through their agents, they painted a picture of commercial advantages in dealing with the Germans: Arabs are shrewd business men.

Sometimes the Nazis with more adroitness, made the French Pro-

* Notably Hadj Anim El Husseini, The Grand Mufti of Jerusalem.

tectorate announce some pro-Arab measure and then forbade it to be put into effect, confusing and irritating the Arabs. In Marrakech in 1940, and in Tangier in 1942, they used the favorite Nazi method of training small groups of agitators who could be turned loose at the proper moment to start riots by breaking windows, pillaging, even throwing bombs in the *souks*. The Arabs knew all this, and rather enjoyed all the attention they were getting. Many of them admired Germany, especially as Rommel swept across Libya, as Moors always admire power and great warriors. Yet they discounted German propaganda. Like the millions of pro-Roosevelt Americans who read the violently anti-Roosevelt press, they listened eagerly to the Axis speeches and agents, discussed them interminably, and believed them little if at all.

The Italians got nowhere in North Africa with their propaganda. Moors, especially, simply disdained the Fascists, both for their reputed physical cowardice and for their cruelties, widely reported, toward the natives of Libya, Abyssinia and Albania.

British propaganda the Arabs considered much less interesting than the German. The de Gaullists were a handicap to the British here as elsewhere in North Africa, because the official de Gaullist line was that Morocco would be returned to its pre-war regime. Since the Arabs had won some concessions from the French during the war,* this didn't go down well. The British also suffered from what the Moors considered her pro-Jewish attitude in Palestine.

The French worked with their usual adroitness to counteract German propaganda. Instead of openly refuting it, they had their secret agents photograph a report of Herr Auer's in which he said that the Moors were a degenerate people, unworthy of consideration by the *herrenvolk*, and that the French were degenerate, too, for associating with them. The French, he added, as Germans have frequently said, were not stamping their influence on Africa, instead they were allowing "the Africanization of the French." This report was spread from *souk* to *souk* through Morocco and had a great effect.

* The French set aside certain new districts for exclusively Arab colonization, gave native authorities some purely theoretical powers, admitted Arabs into the official French Legion of War Veterans and enforced anti-Jewish laws.

As for us, we made little propaganda.* Our job was two-fold, to counteract German propaganda among the French themselves, by emphasizing our strength, and to counteract it among the Arabs by emphasizing not only our strength but our ideals. British propaganda among the Arabs actually made our job with the French more difficult. For some reason, they sent in tracts from Tangier which could be interpreted as rousing the Arabs against the French. De Gaulle propaganda, too, was far from helpful. It came over the BBC in a flood of vituperation against Vichy, with no word of even halfway understanding for the millions of Frenchmen who, rightly or wrongly, felt they were sincerely patriotic in following the Marshal. Our job with the Arabs was simpler on the political plane, partly because of the influence of the Atlantic Charter and the fact that we had never exploited an Islamic country, partly because of the solid argument of American cotton and milk. Moors have a human tendency to like the material evidence of good will.

During the spring of 1942, we also did more and more underground military work. By this time, the landings in North Africa were openly speculated on at home and abroad, though only a few, of course, knew that they were actually definitely planned. We went about Morocco with a secret and growing excitement.

Among the most loyal and important figures we began to work with in 1942 were General Béthouart and his Chief of Staff, Colonel Pierre Magnan. Béthouart, known as "The Hero of Narvik," was a soldierly figure who was sincerely and passionately anti-German though he later proved to be disappointingly ineffectual in aiding us during the landings. Like our other military contacts, this relationship with Béthouart was handled in a very careful way. Our Casablanca staff kept touch with him and the others not directly, but through intermediaries. In addition, the French military underground from France was in direct contact with them via their agents in Algiers.

As early as July, 1941, the military attaché at Tangier, Colonel William Bentley, had told us what would be needed in Washington in

---

* Some O.W.I. pamphlets actually arrived, but they were so misdirected that we unanimously agreed to burn them. We found photographs of bombers, ships and factories much more effective.

the way of military information. We soon began to collect the best
French military maps. Some of them came from our friends in the
French Army, who would bring them secretly to our homes. Others we
bought at a Casablanca bookstore where the proprietor, a handsome,
dark-eyed Frenchwoman, would hide them for us in the cellar. (She
always told the German Armistice Commission, which also tried to
buy them, that she was out of stock.) We also gradually accumulated,
throughout the next year, a mass of information of all kinds: the depth
of ports, the best beaches for landings, the position of coastal defenses,
the tides, the treacherous Moroccan currents, the strength and disposition of French warships, the position and sizes of Army regiments, the
condition and direction of roads, the location of bridges, tunnel and
railroads.

Finally, we had to have secret communication systems, ready to go
into action if the Germans beat us to the draw in North Africa. We
placed radios with carefully selected French and Arab friends, and put
them in touch with the proper people in Gibraltar and Tangier, and
we also set up a native courier system to function as a second string.
Both systems reached from the Mediterranean and Atlantic coasts
deep into the interior of Morocco.

The Arab courier system used the native grapevine which was extraordinary. I once, for instance, took a trip to Tetuan, in Spanish
Morocco. There I learned of the arrival of some new important German agents. I came back at once with the news to Marrakech and
waited for my Arab friends to give me this information. Within four
days after I had heard the news in Tetuan, several of my Arab friends in
Marrakech reported to me accurately the Germans' arrival, their work,
and names, yet Tetuan is ten days from Marrakech by mule or camel
back.

During these black 1942 months in Morocco, we had one bright
piece of French military news: The fine action of General Leclerc and
General Koenig in the wars in the Libyan desert. This gave North African Frenchmen great heart. They were enormously proud that Frenchmen at last were with their allies, fighting Germans. Oddly enough, it
didn't increase de Gaulle's personal popularity at all. "He should be on
the battlefields of Libya," they said, "instead of making propaganda
from London and Brazzaville." Stories about de Gaulle's political

manoeuvering were also beginning to be reported to North Africa from London. We heard, for instance, of the way in which he had forbidden French fliers to become part of the RAF, as the Poles and Norwegians did, and of his stubborn refusal to coöperate with his own allies, or even with violently anti-German Frenchmen who would not swear blind allegiance to him. Frenchmen commented bitterly that he never made one anti-Nazi speech: his speeches were directed solely against other French factions.

We also heard rumors from London regarding de Gaulle's belief in personal leadership. In *Le Fil de L'Epée,** his book on the revival of French Army power, for instance, he had long before emphasized the idea that a great military leader should seize any opportunity to stamp his own mark on history. The masses, he added, "can only be moved by elementary feelings, by violent images, by brutal invocations." "Force is the law of nations and settles their destinies." The man of character, de Gaulle said "moves to impose his stamp upon action, to take it over for his own account and to make of it his business. He has the passion of will power and the jealousy of making decisions." "The passion of acting by himself is evidently accomplished by a certain roughness in the means employed. . . . Such a chief is distant. . . . Below him there are murmurings. . . . (But) when the crisis arises, it is he who is followed." Politicians and soldiers alike, he concludes, must be "haunted with this ardor (to) see in life no other meaning than that they should impress their stamp upon events. . . . There exists no illustrious career in arms that has not served a vast political aim, nor any great glory of a statesman that has not been gilded by the brilliant light of national defense." Though de Gaulle also added, almost as an afterthought, that these Carlyle Hero-Men should also be kind to the people they dominated, the whole book gave its few French readers ** a heart-sickening impression of a man who thought only in terms of power, of nationalism and of militarism: a man, in fact, indistinguishable from the militarists he was fighting. No one who knew the inside stories about de Gaulle was surprised when he began trying to play

---

* Paris, Editions Berger-Levrault, 1932. The volume, incidentally, is glowingly dedicated to Pétain, who, the author says, is his source of inspiration.

** It passed almost unnoticed in France and evidently didn't reach the de Gaullists in America at all.

the Americans against the British as early as the summer of 1941, angling for the best offer he could get. In spite of the gallantry of the Free French, de Gaullism was another dark question mark in our minds in North Africa in 1942.

My own personal life changed at this time. In the late spring of 1942, our Chargé d'Affaires ad interim in Tangier, under whom the Casablanca Consulate functioned, asked for my recall to Washington. I was, he said, unfair to General Noguès and I was making trouble for the French among the Arabs. He himself was strongly pro-Noguès and believed in him up to the very moment at which Noguès resisted us during the landings. Needless to say, I was disturbed to discover that my work had not been approved by my immediate superiors, though I realized that the difficulty was due to a genuine difference of opinion and perhaps to an unavoidable clash of personalities. Washington, although I had had commendations from the State Department, issued the order for my recall, but Robert Murphy got through to them and I was transferred instead to Algiers to be with him. In June, I very regretfully left Morocco.

CHAPTER VIII

Under Cover Days

ALGERIA has an entirely different flavor from Morocco, even in peacetime. It had an especially different flavor for us, as Americans, that summer of 1942. For here preparations for our invasion—now only a few months away—were even more urgent, secret and dangerous than in Morocco. The capital city, Algiers, was the GHQ of our underground. Here we were directly in touch with our key agents, rather than with the French sympathizers (mostly Army men) we used in Morocco. Here we saw agents direct from France and later the top British and American military men. Algeria was a network of intrigue, the scene of an international melodrama that was all the more exciting because it took place entirely beneath the surface of that sultry, strange North African land.

It is a less attractive land, in many ways, than Morocco. Lying rich and exposed on the Mediterranean shore, it has been an imperial highway for many hundreds of years. Algerians seem softer, more Levantine than the Moroccans. The poorer ones, dressed in filthy European-style clothes, topped with fezzes, swarmed in homeless thousands through the streets of Algiers that summer of 1942. They slept in doorways and alleys, leaving a trail of stench and human filth wherever they went. The prevailing atmosphere was one of degradation, lack of ambition and sheer dirt.

Algiers had lost the romantic quality it apparently had before the first World War. The famous Casbah district had been almost destroyed, for sanitary reasons. Where once lay the incredible tangle of an Arab seaport, there rose an enormous, vital European city, a fake French town but a magnificent one. An esplanade, with a row of fine classical white apartment houses and shops, ran parallel to but above the waterfront, hiding the untidy but interesting life of the port from view. Behind it, on steep streets and endless steps, rose the shining white city. The Admiralty section of town was entirely different:

crooked and African, it projected into the sea on the first of the tiny islands that encircle the port and that, christened by the Spanish conquerors of long ago, have given their name to the city. Most of the magnificent, snowy villas that at the time of the French conquest used to gleam among the pine trees above the harbor, had given way to mammoth white apartment houses of a more modern architecture. Motor transport had completely broken down in the city; only a few diplomats, high ranking French and German and Italian Armistice Commission members still had cars, only a few buses still ran; and Arabs, cruelly flogging their bony horses, drove carts and wagons up and down the steep streets between the shining buildings.

The French Government had grown more and more inefficient in Algiers, and the general atmosphere of dirt and disintegration among the natives, the breakdown of communications and the lack of morale I soon encountered were all made worse by a growing clothing and food crisis. Clothing was so scarce that the Berber women living in the nearby Kabyle mountains often had to wait at home until their husbands' return, and then borrow the men's *burnooses* to go and fetch water. As far as food went, conditions were not, of course, as desperate as in France—it was touching to see the joy with which French refugees crowded into the restaurants—but they were bad enough to make you start thinking inadvertently about lunch an hour or so after you finished breakfast. The standard meal, in good restaurants, was a watery soup, noodles or spaghetti, an occasional lamb stew, lettuce with an anemic tomato, and water ice. Everything was cooked, for unfathomable reasons, in oil which had been shipped in kerosene cans; and everything had an unique and far from palatable flavor. Those who could, drove frequently to the Black Market restaurants which flourished in the country outside Algiers. The most famous was at Bouserea, run by a beldame who deeply admired Americans and Mr. Murphy in particular and refused to allow any German or Italian to set foot in her Hotel Celeste.

The climate of Algiers, I soon felt, accounted for a lot of its atmosphere of opportunism and amorality, and left its stamp on all our dealings there. Morocco is hot, but it is an Atlantic country; there are sea winds, and the air inland is dry. Algeria is bathed in heat like a Turkish bath, humid, clinging, suffocating, except for the dry magnificent date-producing oases of the inland. The moisture over the rich land around the coast produced, of course, great riches of citrus fruits, grains, and above all grapes. But it also produced hot tempers, indolence and a pervading atmosphere of indifference to ideas or ideals.

Our offices, as control officers, were next to Mr. Murphy's in the old British Consulate opposite the Admiralty. We were on the top floor, and the view from our windows was one of the loveliest imaginable, with small pleasure and fishing boats dotting the blue of the little Yacht Club harbor below us. Beyond it, we could see the main port, sparkling blue, too, but strangely empty except for an occasional sleek looking French submarine or a bristling destroyer. From time to time, a single steamer made a round trip, to intense excitement, from Marseilles; two or three others lay permanently docked in the harbor and became landmarks. The French used them as barracks after the landings. Beyond this big bay again, to the east, lay the Kabyle mountains, washed with still another shade of blue, beautiful but tame after the mighty Atlas range of Marrakech.

The European atmosphere in Algiers was international in flavor, and yet provincial. Gossip was local and petty; personalities loomed bigger than life. The city boasted a university, a museum, a library, concerts, even an occasional play. No dancing was allowed publicly nor alcohol to be drunk on certain days, on orders from Pétain, who wanted France to consider herself more or less in mourning, but there was incessant gambling at the Hotel Aletti casino. Rich Algerian Arabs, in their high white headdresses and pongee suits, played there with Europeans of all stripes, and huge sums of the inflated French currency changed hands over the green tables.

The Aletti, where I lived, was an African version of Grand Hotel, pillaged by Arabs until it had only one questionably clean linen sheet per bed, and so low on supplies of all kinds that hot water was turned on only an hour daily, and finally not at all. Its sidewalk café and bar produced the wildest rumors in Algeria. It was jammed every afternoon with business men marketing date and wine crops, most of which found their way to Germany. (The local story was that the wine was made into industrial alcohol.) In the crowd were adventurers, secret agents for all countries, Armistice Commission dignitaries, demimondes and rich natives. Down near the railroad and bus stations, you sometimes saw refugees just out of France. You could always spot them; their faces were thin, the men's collars too big for them. The better dressed women almost invariably wore a great deal of gold jewelry; this was because gold was their only security against the terrific inflation.

In the evenings, as the heat lifted, Algiers promenaded along the esplanade, or collected in the Place Bugeaud, near the harbor, to listen to the military band under the palm trees. Then it seemed, except for the Arabs, more like Nice or Marseilles than ever. Outside the city, a rich and seclusive life went on in the villas and great country estates of the landowners. We never saw that life. The so-called aristocracy of Algeria was in part afraid to be seen with us and in part simply didn't like Americans. They kept equally aloof from the French refugees in Algiers. Beyond, far beyond, lay the desert, to the south, and the Kabyle mountains, to the east. These mountains are unique and have a civilization of their own: I loved the strange villages, built on the top of mountains, where the women must climb down to the valley daily to get water. Here, as everywhere, I found English women missionaries patiently working at their monumental and apparently hopeless task of converting the Mohammedan natives. This peace and idealism was far distant, however, from the seething, spy-infested city of Algiers.

The blowsy Algerian atmosphere is important to an understanding of our actions there. We were criticized at the time for not finding more acceptable collaborators for our landing. We often, God knows, wished for a better organized underground there, for agents with more moral conviction, for larger groups of liberal minded, pro-democratic Frenchmen in Algiers. They were, unfortunately, simply non-existent. We did deal with what small left-wing groups were available, with some patriotic Army men, with the Jewish minority, with some intellectuals. But most of the men who could actually help us in our dangerous military venture were not men we would have picked for a political one. They were useful to us for their own reasons, and those reasons were varied; some personal, some political, some creditable, some not. All were sincerely anti-German, and not one betrayed us or our cause. They were the only human weapons available, and we were probably fortunate to find them.

For the truth of the Algerian situation was that the country was intensely conservative, anti-Semitic, even feudal. The landowners who form the dominant class came largely from Alsace-Lorraine, after the Franco-Prussian war. Able pioneers, they soon grew prosperous; their descendants conserved their gains and became enormously rich. The country, almost exclusively agrarian, was divided into vast, self-sufficient estates, empires within an empire, and the landowners themselves gradually became Algerian rather than French, insulated against all the social turmoil and liberal thought of France. Recent arrivals from metropolitan France were much more sincere patriots. They sensed and disliked, with us, the unwelcoming and rather hostile atmosphere created by their North African compatriots, so long transplanted from the soil of France. Algeria, they soon realized, was commercial-minded, a money-making country; and the whole tone among the Algerian French was set by the tory, backward economic structure.

Most of Algiers, however, was pro-American, but pro-American in a passive way. Most Frenchmen we met there hoped that the United States would some day help France to rise up and drive the enemy out, but were unwilling to do much to speed her deliverance. The English were far from popular and neither was de Gaulle. A sizeable minority of Algerian Frenchmen were simply apathetic; they believed France's relative position in Europe would be strengthened by remaining passive while the other big powers exhausted themselves. (This was one of Marshal Pétain's most shocking and devitalizing contributions to French thought.) A small, but very active, minority were ardent collaborationists, though, oddly enough, they were not pro-German. (No one was. In spite of the moral sleaziness in Algiers, I never saw a French girl with a German. I did see one beautiful and rich Algerian French blonde with an Italian from the Armistice Commission: infuriated patriots promptly shaved her lovely head.) All three kinds of Frenchmen—hopeful, neutral and collaborationist— looked to Pétain as head of the state, mystic leader, and symbol of eternal France. Pétain filled and played up to the fullest the role of supreme patriarch over a Roman Catholic State, the role which is today being more and more simulated by de Gaulle.

There was a genuine if unpublicized underground in Algiers. Most of this underground was in the Army, then demobilized and in civilian clothes, but still kept in a cohesive group by secret directions and guidance from France. It had no political or party flavor: it was purely anti-German and pro-French. If this underground had a hero, it was General Giraud. Giraud had written a letter to his children from his prison at Koenigstein, Germany, in which he outlined his plan and dream for the future of France.[6] It was remarkable to see how this letter kindled hope in the discouraged French. Copies of it were circulated all over France. Even in Morocco, French men and women constantly borrowed my typewriters to make copies of the letter for distribution in North Africa. The fact that Giraud had refused to buy his release from the Germans, as many others did, the fact that he had escaped from Koenigstein and returned to France under breath-taking circumstances, and the fact that he had a brillant military record in North Africa as well as in France, soon made us realize that he might be a good choice of a French military leader with whom to negotiate for the coming landings.

Through secret agents, Giraud then sent word to many officers in the French North African Army, asking them to join him in collaborating with the Americans. We worked with numbers of these officers. One of our earliest and most important collaborators was small, thin General Mast, of the Region of Algiers, known in our secret code as "Flagpole." He represented Giraud later at the secret Cherchell meeting with General Clark. General Alphonse Juin was commander-in-chief of all the French forces in North Africa but because of his allegiance to Pétain and the fact that he had been released from prison in Germany only after giving his word of honor that he would never take up arms again against the Germans we did not feel as sure of him as of Giraud.

De Gaulle's followers criticized us bitterly for not using their General or the de Gaullists groups in our landings. We actually tried to do so, but when our State Department asked André Philip, the head of de Gaulle's underground, if he could put us in touch with de Gaullist groups in North Africa, Philip was forced to answer that they did not have a single "cell" there. There was no de Gaullist movement in Algiers or Morocco, though anybody who was pro-ally was popularly called a "de Gaullist." Many resistance forces did later join with the de Gaullists, after our landings, but in 1942 they were simply anti-

Vichy, pro-ally, and above all pro-American.

The men who were most useful to us had only this simple common denominator: they were anti-German and for us. Some of them— Algerian Jews and brave Frenchmen who had lost their jobs because they had defied Vichy in some way—had deep, emotional reasons as well for loathing Vichy. Unfortunately, the Jews, though they were eager to help us and did help us at the time of the landing, were almost useless in reaching the men we needed most; the men who could see to it that we did not meet heavy military resistance when we landed. They had little influence in the Army to begin with, and their feeling was so intense that it made them extremely indiscreet and frightened would-be collaborators away from us.

We had other minorities of a wide variety helping us, too; some of our most earnest workers paradoxically, were royalists; some headed strange youth movements or the like. All in all, we had such strange breeds and stripes of people in our odd but successful underground, that it was hard to remember them all. I remember once, for instance, seeing a hauntingly familiar face at the Hotel Aletti bar and half bowing with the feeling that this must be one of our agents, only to realize suddenly with inner amusement, that it was a member of the German Armistice Commission in Morocco who tried to have me expelled from North Africa.

The agents we used most were men who were in touch both with the French underground and with the all-important military leaders in Algiers and Morocco. Four of them, especially useful to us were widely and sometimes rightly attacked at the time. They were strange and interesting figures and I will have reason to mention them again in discussing the French political situation after our landings. For the record, here they are.

The first was Jacques Lemaigre Dubreuil, a powerful, aggressive business man who brought his family to Algiers shortly after the fall of France. Our code name for him was "Robinson Crusoe." Though he was unquestionably reactionary, he was anti-German and a patriot. He was also a shrewd and subtle operator, who made the Germans believe that he was a collaborator and got them to let him move much of his Dunkirk factory to North Africa. His relations with the Germans were invaluable to us; they meant that he could travel freely from

North Africa into both Unoccupied and Occupied France, keeping us in touch with various elements of the French Army in both places. A thickset man in his mid-forties, with piercing eyes and an oddly husky voice, he was a dynamo of energy more in the American than the classic French style. He had married Simone Le Sueur, daughter of one of the "200 Families" which reputedly controlled France before the war, and as a result had practically a monopoly on French cooking oil through Le Sueur and Company. His business, which was founded on the olive oil of North Africa and the peanut oil of Dakar, gave him an excellent excuse to see us in Algiers.

Working with Lemaigre Dubreuil, theoretically as a business employee, was a most extraordinary character, Jean Rigault, known in our code as his man, "Friday." Actually, Rigault did no business for Le Sueur and Company: his only activities were as an agent for us. A thin, almost emaciated little man, he seemed all mind and no physique, but he demonstrated tremendous endurance during all the landing period and after, and was invaluable to us. He had a strange history: a period of political study while he was in a tuberculosis sanitarium; a period as a journalist; and a short career as an adviser to a French bank. He had also, at one time, belonged to that violent and semi-Fascist organization, the Cagoule, but, I understand, to a dissident minority which broke away. This rather unsavory background made him suspect to many; yet the curious fact is that he served our interests loyally, risked his life for us, worked harder than anyone I have ever known for the cause, and after the landings, urged Giraud toward a democratic, liberal policy which the General unfortunately adopted too late. He was another example of the danger of classifying human beings into "good" and "bad."

Jacques de St. Hardouin, another of our original key men in Algiers, was a career diplomat with the rank of Counselor of Embassy in the French Foreign Service. Bald, shiny headed, with a long, pointed nose, he had a delightful sense of humor. Since he refused to have anything to do with Laval or Vichy, he was on leave of absence from the Foreign Service, and he showed a most undiplomatic willingness to take chances and expose himself before the landings.

Henri d'Astier de la Vigerie, our fourth key agent in Algiers, was an important leader in the local youth movement—the *Chantier de la*

Jeunesse. That was his cover for underground work. Slim, good looking, fanatically royalist and devoutly Catholic, he had an almost hypnotic effect on young people, both Catholic and Jewish. They called him "Chief" and had a blind and mystic faith in him. His assistant and shadow, the Abbé Cordier, was a younger but equally fervent royalist, as well as a Jesuit priest. Both men, I realize in retrospect, were dangerous; both had a very odd reputation of political and even bloody intrigue back of them; both, used by the de Gaullists after the landings, turned against their former American friends. At the time, I didn't realize that men of that type, straight from the Florence of the Medicis, could exist today. It was only at the time of the Darlan assassination, in which they were deeply involved, that I came to understand their potentialities.

At this point, in view of the violent criticism the United States Government received for not having used de Gaulle in the North African adventure, our position with the de Gaullists must be carefully reviewed. First of all, we had a declared policy of helping anyone who was willing to oppose the Nazis. This had been our policy even before we were in the war. We had already given de Gaulle and his forces Lend-Lease by re-transfer from Great Britain under an agreement of November, 1941. But in North Africa, we were looking for people with influence, and de Gaulle's unpopularity there was enough by itself to make it impossible to use him. But there were also other reasons, episodes that took place in Washington itself, that made the government resolve, by 1942, to use some reserve with the de Gaullist group. De Gaulle's attitude toward the United States at the time of the St. Pierre and Miquelon episode, his anti-American broadcasts from Brazzaville, his lack of coöperation with us in New Caledonia in the Pacific, in fact the increasingly anti-American tone de Gaulle began to use generally caused trouble within the de Gaullist mission itself in Washington that spring of 1942, just as the State Department was making its plans for North Africa.

The de Gaulle mission at Washington was made up of Etienne Boegner, Raoul de Roussy de Sales and Adrien Tixier. Roussy de Sales' and Boegner's attempts to make de Gaulle understand his responsibilities toward France and her allies were soon well known to the United States Government. Tixier, however, was the *homme de confiance* of de Gaulle. He returned from a trip to London in April 1942 expressing such violent anti-American sentiments that it undid the good that Roussy de Sales and Boegner had been able to achieve. Boegner went to London at the end of May, 1942, in a final effort to persuade de Gaulle to see the American point of view. Boegner hoped to avoid a rupture between the French National Committee in London and the United States Government before the North African landing. But all his attempts at conciliation were received by de Gaulle with total misunderstanding. The General even spoke insultingly of the American people and their war leaders. After several futile interviews, Boegner, who felt de Gaulle was fatally betraying French interests in this anti-American policy, actually resigned from the de Gaulle mission.

By this time Roussy de Sales, the second member, was fatally ill, and only the blindly loyal Tixier was left to represent the French National Committee of London in Washington.* Episodes like these left the administration convinced, by the summer of 1942, that de Gaulle and his followers were deeply anti-American and could not be used in any operation as delicate as the North African landings.

Yet, not withstanding de Gaulle's attitude, the State Department wished to leave no stone unturned to bring about some sort of *modus vivendi* with him. They therefore invited him to come to the United States during the summer of 1942. The invitation was transmitted through his close friend Henri de Kerillis, a distinguished journalist and politician, who was at that time one of de Gaulle's staunchest supporters through the medium of the French newspaper *Pour La Victoire* in New York. De Gaulle refused to come unless he was to be received as the sole representative of France. This we obviously could not do because of our vital and complicated dealings with Vichy. Later in the year, yet still before our landings in North Africa, the United States government further augmented its assistance to de Gaulle and the Free French under a new Lend-Lease agreement of September 3, 1942, by which we sent direct Lend-Lease aid to the French National Committee at London.

---

* In April, 1945, Tixier, then Minister of the Interior in the de Gaulle Government, forbade the Paris Municipal Council to hold a special meeting to honor the memory of President Roosevelt.

As late as the summer of 1942, many agencies back in Washington did not realize the full meaning of our North African adventure. Our economic warfare people, like their British counterparts, still talked in terms of disorganizing North African economic life in order to frustrate the Germans; there was still argument and dissension during economic meetings at the State Department. These were finally quelled on a direct, handwritten order signed "FDR," as the Army began to hasten preparations for the landing. Only then did we begin to have whole-hearted backing in our work in Africa.

That work swung into high toward the end of that summer of 1942. In spite of the sordid atmosphere in Algiers, it was good to be there as the time for the landings drew near. For one thing, we felt closer to France, to the underground there, and to the war itself: this increasingly rugged life in Algiers gave us at least a small sense of participating in the French struggle. For another, it was encouraging to work in close contact with Robert Murphy. Though his policies after the landing have been much debated, and were certainly debatable, no one can ever deny the lives he saved us by his skillful work before our landings, and no one who worked with him there can ever forget his steady, good humoured piloting of our small and troubled underground. All the man's innate kindness, level-headedness and friendliness came out at a time when he had to deal with inexperienced and over-anxious Americans on the one hand and a series of Frenchmen who were too often experienced in the wrong way on the other.

CHAPTER IX

Make Ready for the Landing

THE first hint we had that the landings were imminent came one August day when I was helping out in the code room. We were "unbuckling," as we called it, what seemed to me just one more of hundreds of such coded cablegrams. Suddenly I read a cable asking Mr. Murphy to return immediately to Washington. No more boredom in the code room; it became a passionately interesting place. No more monotony to the armistice stagnation of North Africa. Our work swung into high. Action we had always dreamed of but had never dared mention seemed imminent.

It wouldn't be easy: we knew that. In Morocco, Noguès, for instance, would be a tough proposition under any circumstances but particularly now after his attempt to curry favor with Laval. Murphy told me after his return of his last pre-landing talks with Noguès. These did not occur during a routine call: they were a foreshadowing of real action. But Noguès wouldn't take them seriously, he was so convinced that we weren't ready to move. Murphy asked Monsieur Chevereux, the ex-Préfet of Clermont-Ferrand, and a sincere friend of the Allied cause, to use his influence, based on long friendship, with Noguès. Madame Chevereux too, a remarkable woman of even sharper intelligence than her husband, undertook to persuade both General and Madame Noguès of the importance of coöperating with American forces. They failed utterly; in fact, the Noguès broke the long tie of friendship they had with the Chevereux family. Noguès considered that any American landings in North Africa would be disastrous. In Morocco, we realized then we should have to work directly with Béthouart and our many contacts in the lower echelons of the French Army.

In Algiers, Rigault, d'Astier de la Vigerie and Lemaigre Dubreuil, the men described in the last chapter, were already in touch with General Giraud, as well as with French Army men in Africa. We established a radio system with Gibraltar as its contact. The transmitter was hidden in the house of an agent of ours down near the port. If we wanted to send a message, we hung a typewriter cover out on a balcony outside our office. Our agent had an assistant ride his bicycle by our office building three or four times a day. If the cover was there, he dropped in and we gave him a message in code.

Rumors flew hotter and faster than ever as the autumn drew on. One evening, in the fall of 1942, three members of the Murphy mission suddenly and quietly left North Africa. Culbert left Casablanca, Rounds departed from Oran, and Knox from Algiers. They returned to those same posts on the night of November 8, with the Allied fleets from England and the United States. One day Admiral Darlan himself came out, theoretically on an inspection trip of the whole North African Empire. Actually, I suspect, he wanted to investigate the very conflicting rumors of our landings, and of German demands to take over the defense of the French Empire. Most Aletti rumors now said we would land at Dakar. Talk of American action wasn't just an Aletti rumor, either. One day Commandant d'Orange, General Juin's *aide de camp* told me he would like to call on Mr. Murphy and have a talk with him. He wanted to know if I thought a visit to his office could be made without being detected. A few days later d'Orange appeared, inconspicuous in civilian clothes. This visit was certainly made with General Juin's full knowledge and instigation. It was a feeler to test out the force of American intentions. However it was made very late in the game, almost on the eve of our landings. It would have suited us admirably to start plotting with Juin if our landings had been scheduled for the spring of 1943 instead of November 1942. As it was we didn't dare take any more risks; we were obliged to take the Juin elements in the North African Army by surprise.

With the German difficulties in Russia, the political climate in Algiers, made up of allegiance to Vichy and general apathy, began to change. Resistance began to burn brighter even in the more resigned hearts. This growing attitude symbolized by the noble letter that Herriot and Jeannenay wrote to Pétain on September 9, 1942, protesting his usurpation of power and the dissolution of parliamentary government in France.[7] Herriot, head of the Chambre des Députés, and Jeannenay, head of the Senate, were both in France: their letter was an act of considerable courage. De Gaulle's official newspaper, *La Marseillaise*, [8] promptly attacked both men in terms of abuse that were almost embarrassing, and that had definite anti-democratic overtones.[9] On September 14, 1942, the five French Deputies in exile in the United States wrote an open letter in praise of Herriot's and Jeannenay's courageous republican stand.[10] On October 3, Herriot was arrested by the Vichy authorities. Immediately, Under Secretary of State Sumner Welles, in a press conference in Washington, praised Herriot's courage at length and said "I wish him well." Finally de Gaulle after weeks of silence since the article in his official paper criticizing Herriot's action, was forced by this strong reaction of sympathy for Herriot to praise him, too, which he did in a short statement to the British press.[11] The whole episode left our diplomats worried by such deep French disunity on the very eve of our landings.

When Mr. Murphy came back from Washington, I went on a 48-hour courier trip to Casablanca and motored down to Marrakech to keep in touch with my contacts there and to pick up some warm clothes for the autumn. Driving by the Hotel Mamounia, I was surprised to see a long line of cars turning in there: cars were conspicuous by their absence in North Africa in those days. I followed them, and, as I got out of my car, a man walked up and asked me a question in German. I answered him in French, and he said, still in German: "Aren't you one of our Mission?" "No," I answered, "I am an American vice consul." He looked startled, but made a correct little bow and turned away. I dropped into the hotel office where the staff were friends of mine and asked what went on. I was told that a high-ranking German General, with a large staff, was touring Morocco. "I think," one man added, "that the Germans intend to take over the defense of North Africa this winter."

After dinner that night, I called on my friend, Mehdi Glaoui. He told me that he and his father, the Pasha, El Glaoui, had just entertained Noguès and Darlan, both of whom had come to Marrakech incognito and had been dressed in civilian clothes. "Something is going on," he said. "Both men seemed so tense. I think they expect Allied action. What do you think?" I told him I thought both Darlan and Noguès had been worried about a possible Allied invasion for months, and that, after all, autumn didn't seem quite the time for it. As he spoke, I was most interested in the fact of Darlan's presence, which hadn't yet been announced in any way. Next day, I ran into the Pasha who put both hands on my shoulders and said earnestly, but with a smile: "My friend, last night Admiral Darlan dined with me. I think we shall soon see the events which you and I have awaited so long." I stood silent as he got into his car, wondering how much he knew. Darlan went on south, I discovered, and when he reached Dakar, it was for the first time announced that he was making a tour of the African empire.

A later courier trip back to Algiers had an exciting touch. Final arrangements had been made, at the beginning of October, for the secret meeting of General Clark and the French General Mast, General of the Region of Algiers, at that town with the wonderfully confusing name, Cherchell. In the best Bulldog Drummond tradition, M. Rigault and M. d'Astier de la Vigerie had chosen for the meeting an isolated house seventeen kilometers west of Cherchell hung high over the Mediterranean at a spot where the sea was deep enough for a submarine. Secret cables fixed every detail ahead of time, and I knew the hour, the place, and the fact that General Clark was to come by submarine. As I flew back to Algiers on October 22, the day set for the meeting, the plane, instead of flying inland from Oran to Algiers, as it always did, flew a hundred yards or so off the coast. The change of schedule seemed strange and suspicious to my secret-weighted mind, especially since there were two Germans and two Italians sharing the plane. I didn't dare doze off, as I usually did in an airplane, for fear of talking in my sleep. As we approached the house near a lighthouse where the meeting was taking place at that moment, I looked down at the Mediterranean with a hair-raising feeling that I (and the Axis men on the plane) would see the outline of a submarine just off shore. Nothing, of course, looked unusual, and the French airline personnel, who always served us loyally, had not been tipped off. The change of route was sheer accident, and the Germans unsuspicious. When we reached Algiers, I checked in at once with Felix Cole, our Consul General in Algiers, where I learned the Cherchell meeting was still going on, there having been a delay of one day due to misunderstandings.

All of the "plotters," as we rather romantically called ourselves, gathered at Cole's villa the night of October 24, to wait, with Mr. Cole himself, for Murphy and Knight to return from Cherchell. Cole was, as usual, calm and sensible in the midst of the tense atmosphere. He was a tower of strength in Algiers: tough-talking but kind-hearted, loyal always to subordinates and to our collaborators, and full of an unusual brand of common sense. I remember his saying, about this time, when we felt a little nervous about working with such oddly-assorted French contacts: "Why not? Just use them; don't let them use you."

On this October 24, Lemaigre Dubreuil, Rigault, de St. Hardouin, d'Astier de la Vigerie, John Boyd, and Miss Hardy, Murphy's secretary, were gathered in Cole's hospitable living room. Typewriters and notebooks were ready on tables to make a record as soon as possible, both for Washington and for General Giraud. The next morning, Lemaigre Dubreuil was going to take this report by plane to Giraud, who was staying near Lyons. There was an ominous absence of news: midnight came, and one o'clock. Three or four times, we started to drive to Cherchell, and each time we were afraid that a trip late at night might attract attention.

As the hours marched by and Murphy and Knight still didn't appear, we realized no precise report of the Cherchell meeting for Giraud could be prepared in time for the airplane taking Lemaigre Dubreuil to France. Consequently, a hasty, innocuous form of code to be used over the regular French telegraph system was prepared by the "plotters." Lemaigre had to take his place on the Air France plane and contact with him had to be maintained. Madame Rigault, a few days later, went over by the regular boat service between Marseilles and Algiers with more definite information for Giraud. Finally, Murphy and Knight turned up, white from mingled emotion and fatigue, and we learned in detail about their clandestine meeting.

On October 17, General Eisenhower had picked General Mark Clark to act as his deputy at this secret *rendez-vous*. Captain Jerauld Wright of the United States Navy, Colonel Julius Holmes, who spoke French fluently, Colonel Arch Hamblen, and General Lyman Leminitzer of G3 were chosen to go with Clark. At 7:30 A. M. they set out by plane from England and joined up at Gibraltar with the British submarine under the command of Lieutenant N. L. A. Jewell already standing by on orders from London. At once they set out for the African coast.

It had been arranged that a light would be in the window of the isolated house if all were well. At 4:00 A. M. October 21 the submarine sighted the light but with only a few hours until dawn, stayed submerged until 11:10 P. M. the next evening when once again the light shone in the window. Then the party put ashore in small kiaks accompanied by three British Commando officers. Holmes landed first and promptly met up with Knight on the rocky beach, the others landed, the kiaks were hidden, and the meeting got under way. At 7:00 A. M. on the morning of October 22 General Mast, acting as Giraud's deputy, and his party arrived. Immediately General Clark set to work. The tonnage capacity of the ports of Casablanca, Algiers, Oran, Tunis, the plans of the French Navy in case of landings, the estimated capacity of French Army resistance, details on airplane runways and the like were given.

The owner of the house had previously given money to the Arab farmers living on his property and sent them away. The Arabs, always unpredictable, returned before they were expected and were again sent away. They became suspicious and reported to the local police that they thought strange things like smuggling or Black Market activities were going on in the house. Then the night was passed between police visits, forced hiding in the cellar for the military men, a pretended drunken party on the part of Murphy and Knight as an excuse for their presence there, and finally a fight with a high wind and an angry sea that almost prevented the departure of Clark and his party in the flimsy kiaks back to the submarine. Murphy returned at 8:00 A. M. on the 24th and the next day General Clark arrived in London minus a pair of trousers he had lost when his kiak had capsized. We sent him a coded message the next day that we had his trousers, cleaned, pressed, and waiting for him. Then with almost breathless activity we awaited D-Day.

This all-important Cherchell meeting had been arranged to prove to the French that we meant business. Unfortunately, during all these last weeks, before the landings, misunderstandings, which left their scars, arose; and some of them, anyway, were connected with this meeting.

First, the French were left believing that our landing was to take place at the end of November. No one in North Africa but Mr. Murphy knew the real date and hour of the landing, and he was under orders from the War Department to reveal it to no one until a few days before the event.

Second, Giraud and others had been led to believe all along that there would be simultaneous landings in the south of France and North Africa. The secret French High Command, working with General Giraud, believed that it was of paramount importance to land at once in the south of France. The Germans had not yet prepared an adequate coastal defense there, and the French maintained that their military underground was strong enough to hold back the enemy until our landings were well established. By this manoeuver they believed we could take over the French fleet. They had, so the French assured us, hidden considerable stocks of arms and ammunition, and clandestinely manufactured three hundred modern tanks. Manpower was efficiently organized in hundreds of cells. I shall never forget the wires that reached us from Giraud via our Vichy Embassy just before the landings. He begged us to make the south of France the spearhead of our attack, to let France give her soil again as a battlefield to wipe out the shame of her defeat. Unfortunately, we were not yet ready to undertake this major military venture. But, French leaders were so desperately concentrated on the deliverance of France itself, so sure of the strength of their underground, that we let them think until the last moment that there was a possibility of action there.

Third, Giraud sincerely believed he was to be commander-in-chief of all Allied forces once they were on French North African soil.

At the same time General Weygand, in southern France, was also an unsuspecting victim of false information. He was in touch with Giraud as well as with British agents who assured him that landings would be made in France to coincide with North African action. Although Weygand has been severely criticized for not coming to North Africa the moment we landed there (his son is supposed to have given him bad advice on this point), there are many unknown facts that may some day prove that he felt his presence was needed in southern France.

It seems incredible in retrospect that such grave misunderstandings could have existed between us and the French, but two points must never be forgotten: first, the incredible difficulties we were working under; and, second, the inevitable mistrust that had grown up because of lack of contact and association between two groups fundamentally conservative both by force of circumstances and tradition—the Anglo-American and the French High Commands.

It was because of these misunderstandings that Giraud and the men around him deputized Mast to participate in what they thought was the planning of a subordinate, coördinated action in North Africa. Giraud himself waited in France until he was told, at the last minute, of our real military program. He had already given his chosen agents, Lemaigre Dubreuil and Rigault, letters to certain key Army men in Africa who, he felt, could be counted upon to break the armistice terms with him. Giraud had a great reputation as a soldier in North Africa, particularly in the campaign that had led to the conquest of southern Morocco. Even the Arabs said he had the *baraka*, an almost untranslatable word for mystic quality around certain individuals. Many of the men to whom he wrote came over gladly to our side.

It was the very end of October before Giraud's agent, Rigault, decided it was time for him to deliver Giraud's messages to Army personnel in Morocco. He had to cover all the posts rapidly, an impossible job without a car, and we were afraid that it might attract attention if he used one of ours. Our own men in Morocco had worked very little with Rigault, whom I saw often in Algiers, so I asked Mr. Murphy if I might fly to Casablanca on Monday, November 2, and use my own car to drive Rigault around. He agreed.

Shortly before the first of November, messages from President Roosevelt had arrived by cable for the Sultan of Morocco, Resident General Noguès, the Governor General Chatel of Algiers, as well as the Resident General Estéva and the Bey of Tunis, explaining our coming actions and the motives back of them. Helping to decode them, still with a strange sensation of unreality, I knew at last that our landings were definitely scheduled for that fall. But, I still thought, like the French themselves, that it would take place at the end of November.

Early on the morning of November 2, before taking the plane to Casablanca, I learned the truth. I was living then at Consul Cole's house with Mr. Murphy, who joined me at an early breakfast. He seemed to be under such tension beneath his calm and pleasant exterior that I said suddenly: "Bob, am I wrong when I believe our landing will take place toward the end of November?" He nodded. I asked more questions, most of which he answered wordlessly, by nodding, and I left for the airport knowing beyond question of doubt that the landing would come the following Saturday night: at one A. M. in Algiers and Oran on the Mediterranean, and at four A. M. in Morocco at Safi, Fedala (next door to Casablanca) and Port Lyautey on the Atlantic.

When I reached our Consulate in Casablanca, before joining up with Rigault, I found everyone in intense activity. Their greatest worry was trying to perfect the radio system between Casa, Tangier and Gibraltar, to be used in communicating with our fleet. In the late afternoon, as I sat in on a meeting between Vice Consul King and Rigault, I realized from their conversation that neither knew the exact date of the landing. Rigault had already seen General Béthouart and learned his detailed plan for placing the troops he counted on to help us during the landing: from the way he described the arrangements, it was obvious that they were planning for action at the end of November.

As we started out in my car, Rigault and I, with a letter from Giraud to General Martin of Marrakech, I worried inwardly about whether or not I should tell Rigault that these plans would have to be changed. I knew that of all the Allied landings, the one in Algiers was the most important. It was the one nearest Tunisia and our eventual battlefield—unless, as we sometimes feared, the German airborne troops arrived swiftly from Sicily, France and even Spanish Morocco, and made all North Africa a battlefield. Chances were that Algiers would be the crucial point, leaving Morocco more or less behind the lines, and obliged to coöperate with us. Even so, I knew Mr. Murphy felt that we could not trust Noguès. If Noguès were to order or allow vigorous resistance in Morocco, our whole plan could be delayed and even jeopardized. It would be safer if Rigault knew the exact date of the landing in order to lay plans with Giraud's military contacts in Morocco, and counteract any resistance from Noguès and the Residency. Finally, after seventy-five miles of balancing these factors, I turned to Rigault and said: "I'm afraid you will have to change your plans with Béthouart and the other Generals. The landing in Morocco is scheduled for the early morning of November 8."

Rigault, in all the crises in which I saw him, never revealed any emotion. This time, he asked me to stop the car while he got out, stretched, as if he had to let his emotions come out somehow, and then climbed back in. "*Ce chameau*, Bob," he said smiling, "why didn't he tell me? This changes everything, everything." Then, suddenly, he looked very grave. "*Mon Dieu!* My wife will be caught in France." I suggested he arrange for some third party to telegraph her to take an earlier boat. He replied, "No, I'll never do that—the risk is too great. I am certainly suspect, and she, as my wife, may be too. She knows the risks involved and will certainly understand."

We went on to Marrakech, where Rigault delivered his letter to General Martin and stayed very late discussing plans with him. Just before dawn, we started back to Casablanca, and, without pausing for sleep, Rigault spent the next day changing his plans with Béthouart. I gave Vice Consul Mayer the messages from President Roosevelt to the Sultan and the Resident General and told him Mr. Murphy would let him know the day to deliver them. Then I discovered that some of my colleagues were planning to be away at Tangier on the date of the landing. I felt I couldn't tell anyone but Rigault the actual time of the landing, so I merely told them that Mr. Murphy wanted them to stay in Casablanca as he planned to come over to hold an important meeting with them.

After dinner, Rigault, King and I composed and coded a wire for Gibraltar, to be sent on to the fleet, which was by this time steaming toward Morocco. In it, we asked the American forces to be sure to send a detachment to Rabat the minute they landed, to reinforce General Béthouart and Colonel Magnan who planned to have Noguès either with them there or their prisoner. (This inside tip was never acted upon, unfortunately, by our landing forces. Perhaps it was never received.)

In the early morning, still without sleep, Rigault and I started for Rabat, Fez, Taza, Oujda, Oran and Algiers. Just before we started, it began to pour. The rain lasted for three days—an unheard of thing at that time of year—and the roads were so flooded that the car stopped three times, its hood completely under water. As we drove, our excitement grew, but so did our worry over the rain. We were afraid that the airfields might still be flooded and useless the following Saturday.

Before we left Casablanca, a member of the Intelligence Bureau of the French Army warned Rigault that the Germans had heard that he was in Morocco, and that two members of the Vichy police had been sent out to look for him and arrest him. We didn't dare stop anywhere except at the houses of friends we could trust implicitly. From Monday morning, the second, therefore, until we got back to Algiers at two A. M., Friday morning, we never took off our clothes or even lay down; and we drove the entire time at top speed, stopping only to contact military leaders at different garrison towns. We ate as we drove, using a basket of food a friend gave us in Rabat. As we neared Algeria, the rain stopped, and the sun began to beat down with intense fiery heat.

I never knew until that day that heat could literally make your eyeballs burn. Fifty miles from Algiers, coming down a series of hairpin bends from the mountains onto the coastal plain, I had so little strength left from struggling against sleep that I couldn't make the car take a sharp turn. It piled into the ditch looking as tired as we felt. Our luck held! At that very moment, we heard a train whistle, jumped from the car, and ran down the hill along a little road in the direction of the sound. There we found a tiny station, and at that moment, in came the twice-a-week train from Morocco to Algiers. Rigault hopped on, and I telephoned for help, and then went back to guard our papers until the Consulate sent a car for me.

All during our trip, Rigault had kept saying, "Well, Ken, in less than a week, these long hot deserted roads will be teeming with endless military traffic. Can you believe it?" I couldn't then, but, in the months to follow, as I looked down from the air during the innumerable flights I made between Algiers and Morocco and watched hundreds of miles of endless American convoys, I often thought of Jean Rigault's remark.

As I waited, far too keyed up to sleep, in my car, for another one to come and fetch me, all the past long dreary months went through my mind in a sort of kaleidoscopic review—the endless courier trips by air and car with diplomatic pouches, first filled with reports, then maps, and, finally, heavy with radios and other more practical objects.

Then suddenly, I was seized with apprehension. Three quarters of the last convoy to Malta had been sunk by Axis submarines and airplanes. The last air attack on that heroic island had been carried out by an enemy force of nearly a thousand planes. Would our landing have the tragic consequences of just another commando raid? Was Spain really filled with Germans ready to swarm into Morocco? By the time the car came to my rescue, I had more or less relaxed into a fatalistic attitude. Whatever happened to me, I hoped I would be able to sleep, even in a German or North African prison. I had my little store of gold pieces, bought from the money lenders of Tangier—pesetas, francs, marks, dollars, and two gold watches that somehow or other I hoped to take to my imaginary prison and then, after a restful sleep, to use in bribing my way out.

The next day, Friday, and all day Saturday, the last before the landing, we burned endless papers, destroyed codes, hid records, wound up endless details. We made very sure that, in case the Germans did forestall us, and we were made prisoners, none of our friends' names would be found in our possession. Late Saturday afternoon, Murphy, Woodruff and I tried to decide where to hide three small packages of personal papers and valuables. Finally, we took them cautiously down the street to the headquarters of a group of French women ambulance drivers. They had done magnificent work during the war in 1940, and later with prisoners. They had come to North Africa with Weygand, to await the day when they could return and help in the liberation. We handed the packages to Nicole de Brignac, the gallant leader of these women, and asked her if she could look after them for us. "*Certainement*," she said. She took them in her hand to the window and stood there a moment looking north over the bay of Algiers. "I don't intend to leave this window the rest of the night," she said, smiling up at us. "I think at last I am going to see the thing for which I have lived and prayed these last terrible years."

CHAPTER X

This Is It

GREAT events are seldom bigger than life. Instead, they are a mosaic of small, odd, humorous or irritating details: the heel off the shoe, the missed appointment, the cup of coffee while waiting for the next thing to happen. The Landing—the great event we had looked forward to, dreamed of, worked for during the past year and a half—had this confused, rushed, episodic quality for our underground on shore.

Murphy and a few of us dined at Felix Cole's apartment the night of November 7, going over all the things that might, and probably would, go wrong. We didn't realize that many, perhaps most, of the Vichyite forces were going to resist the landings, in spite of our carefully spotted collaborators. And, yet, we already knew their psychology. They had authoritarian minds, to begin with, ready to follow the "head of the state," whoever he might be. Many of them, in addition, shared the genuine devotion of so many Frenchmen to Pétain, the blind faith that he was doing what was best for France, that he would somehow bring her battered ship of state through this engulfing storm. Many had an almost neurotic fear of commando raids, of Anglo-American hit-and-run actions, without sufficient strength, which would simply bring the Germans in full force into North Africa. Most of the top men had given a soldier's oath of honor to the Germans in return for their freedom, an oath that they would not bear arms against Germany. Juin had given this oath, but we believed he would not feel held by it. (Giraud, of course, had refused to do this and was a free agent.)

The vast majority loathed the Nazis and longed for an Allied victory; but equally, it must be admitted they were politically timid, afraid to climb out on any limb until they were sure it would bear their official strength. All this combination of Pétainist feeling, anti-German feeling, rigidity, and rather unattractive caution, produced exactly what could be expected: a night of unexampled, sometimes funny, and sometimes tragic, confusion.

About ten-thirty that night we went down to our secret headquarters for the landing: the apartment of a distinguished Jewish doctor, Professor Henri Aboulker, at 26, Rue Michelet, the main street of Algiers. We were surprised, with the secret on our minds, to see the usual Saturday night crowds streaming down Rue Michelet on their way to the movies (American movies, of course, were forbidden) or waiting in line for the infrequent buses. There had been a lot of talk in Vichy papers and radios about the vast convoy that had been observed at Gibraltar, supposedly preparing for Malta, but most people believed our first action would be in Dakar. Algiers looked calm and normal.

At 26, Rue Michelet, crowds of young men from our underground and from the *Chantier de la Jeunesse* groups under d'Astier de la Vigerie milled around the Aboulker apartment, in a very French setting of crowded fumed oak (dining room) and crowded gilt-and-tapestry (living room). In a bathroom off one of the bedrooms, full of lacework and curly maple, stood our secret wireless system. Some of these younger civilians had formed part of the original resistance group of North Africa, starting in Oran: they were the action wing for the group of older anti-Nazis headed by Abbé Cordier and d'Astier de la Vigerie and other less known men. Some of them, mostly Jewish, belonged to a group which used to meet secretly with Vice Consuls Boyd and Knox at Guy Cohen's clothing store on Rue Michelet: a fierily resistant group including José Aboulker, René Brunel, André Achiary, Bernard Karsenty and Pierre Alexandre as leaders. Few of these men gathered in Aboulker's apartment had taken part in the larger military planning: they were coming on the scene now for their own special job: taking over key points in Algiers and acting as guides as we landed. Vice Consuls Woodruff, Boyd and Laroux, a career man, waited with them for final assignment to spots like the power station, the telephone offices, and the landing beaches. Two doors down, at 30, Rue Michelet, in Pierre Alexandre's apartment, our Army and over-all agents, like Lemaigre Dubreuil, waited to discuss last minute details with Murphy.

About midnight, the young men who were to seize key points in Algiers left, and later, the others went off with Woodruff, Boyd and Laroux to the various landing beaches to act as guides for the debarking forces. Toward twelve-thirty, Murphy asked me to go with him to the *Villa des Oliviers*, above Algiers at El Biar. In this ancient, square, yellow Arab palace lived General Juin, the powerful, physically courageous but politically timid head of the entire French Forces in North Africa. Murphy got into a car with Colonel Crétien, the quiet-mannered, cautious head of Juin's *Deuxieme Bureau*, or Intelligence Section. I followed in Murphy's own car with a bodyguard who had been assigned to Murphy for the evening by the resistance forces of 26, Rue Michelet. When the first car drove past the sentry boxes, with their huge black Senegalese guards, and into the graveled courtyard, as prearranged I waited outside, ready to notify our friends if things went wrong. As I had had little sleep since Monday, I closed my eyes on the dimly seen flower gardens, the view of *Fort l'Empereur* with its great obelisk, and asked the guard to let me know if anyone went in or out of the villa. I must have slept about twenty minutes when Colonel Crétien himself awakened me (the guard, who had the mind as well as the physique of a gorilla, had been placidly enjoying the view) and called me in to Mr. Murphy. Murphy asked me to drive over to the Victorian villa of Admiral Fenard, the man who had handled many negotiations with us after Weygand was pulled back to France. (He is now head of the French Naval Mission in Washington.) I was to pick up Darlan who was staying there, and Admiral Battet, his intimate friend.

Darlan and Battet ran down the steps of the villa soon after I got there, and climbed into Murphy's Buick with me. Darlan evidently feared no plot at this time—he hardly looked at me and never even glanced at our gorilla, who was sitting beside me, armed to the teeth. I dropped them at the door of Juin's villa and, this time waited at the door in case I was needed. Soon after Darlan went in, the house was surrounded by guards from our own underground. I knew nothing of this until General Sevez, Chief of Staff to Juin, tried to leave the villa. A young man armed with a rifle told him he could not go farther than the car where I sat. Sevez, startled and angry, went back into the villa, and then I could see, looking around the shrubbery by the house, that the place was alive with armed civilians commanded by a reservist, a Lieutenant Pauphilet, in uniform.

The over-all commander of these amateur troops I learned later was Henri d'Astier, who was to be intimately involved in the post-landing intrigues around Darlan. They surged forward under the half light from the villa entrance, pointing their guns from the waist. In a moment, Colonel Crétien, Juin, Madame Juin, and Murphy, himself, appeared at the villa door, with Darlan and Battet behind them in the hall. All looked surprised and disturbed. Crétien commanded the officer in charge to step forward, but he refused. They called to each other from a distance through the dark: the officer said no one and nothing could leave the house except Mr. Pendar in the car he was driving. Everyone retired in good order into the villa, and after a hurried conference, Murphy came back and told me to drive to town, find out who had placed the watch dogs and have them called off—or at least get permission for one of the French officers at Juin's villa to leave in a car with me. Murphy was obviously playing for time. At this juncture, Crétien turned to Murphy and said pompously: "If these are your friends, they are behaving in a *most* disgusting way."

I drove back to 26, Rue Michelet and tried to see General Mast or Colonel Jousse to ask them if they were responsible for the guard around Juin's house. (At this point, I also got rid of my gun and the guard, both more of a liability than an asset.) I found our secret headquarters in a terrific state of excitement. Reports poured in from the young men we had sent out to take the Post Office, radio station, electric power station, telegraph office and the *Préfecture*. The entire town of Algiers was actually in our hands without the people realizing that anything had happened. Now everyone was waiting to hear from our landings. Everyone asked me if Crétien was with us: as head of Juin's Intelligence Bureau, he was a key man, and he had played an elusive game with both sides.

At headquarters, I found my old friend Rigault, paler and tighter-mouthed than ever. He got into the car with me and drove back to Juin's villa. Darlan asked him for permission to return to Admiral Fenard's to sleep, but Rigault refused. Murphy drew me aside and told me to go back to town and not to hurry. He was stalling for time until we actually landed, he said: then, his bargaining power would, of course, be much greater. Darlan was beginning to talk politics, he added, and it looked as if both Darlan himself, the officers who recognized his authority, and the vital French fleet, might all fall into our hands. Juin, it seemed, wanted to help us but felt obliged to defer to Darlan as his superior officer.

I dropped Rigault at 30, Rue Michelet, where de Saint Hardouin was waiting for him. We decided that it was now time to tell Admiral Fenard that our underground had seized every key point in Algiers. We drove up to his villa. On the way, we had to refuse a lift to a young sailor running up the road with a dog. Something about him made me uneasy, and we learned later that he was a messenger who had been sent by Naval Headquarters at the Hotel St. George to warn the authorities against us.

When we reached Fenard's villa, we found him fully dressed and puffing on his pipe. Half-dressed sailors, on night duty, were wandering in and out of the house in considerable confusion. As we talked, Madame Fenard's anxious face, above a black kimono, peered through the portieres from the hall. We told Fenard what had happened, that Algiers had been taken over by our underground, and that the Americans were landing along the Moroccan and Algerian coasts. Fenard shifted his pipe in his mouth two or three times, looked at us intently, and then slowly broke into a smile and said: "*Rudement bien joué.*" Then, thinking of the man who was his superior and to whom he owed his career, he laid his hand earnestly on my arm and added: "But don't let anything happen to Darlan."

We drove Fenard back to Juin's villa, and he and de Saint Hardouin joined the conference inside. Darlan, obviously suffering from great emotion, was still pacing the floor and debating what he should do. Murphy reminded him that he had promised Admiral Leahy in 1941 that if the Americans ever came in great strength we could count on him. Darlan came back again and again to the fact that he had sworn a solemn oath to Pétain, that Pétain would have to release him or back him.

After some time, Admiral Fenard asked me to go down to town and send a telegram from Admiral Darlan to Marshal Pétain. The officer of our underground guard around the villa said I could take a telegram, but only "in clear," (i. e., not in code). I was handed a sealed envelope and de Saint Hardouin and I started back to town. I asked de Saint Hardouin to open the envelope and read the telegram to me as I drove, but he waited until we reached 26, Rue Michelet and then had one of our experts steam it open. We read the telegram which ran more or less as follows: "Late at night, I received a telephone call to come to General Juin's house, where I found myself in the presence of M. Murphy. He told me that the American fleet was off the North African coast in force. I told him I had given my word to you, the Chief of State that I would defend the Empire with our fullest force against anyone infringing upon it. (Signed) Darlan."

Needless to say, the telegram was not sent. I can't believe Darlan ever thought it would be.

At this point, President Roosevelt's broadcast announcing the landings had been heard both in Morocco and Algiers. It came a little prematurely in Morocco, as our landings were scheduled for several hours later there and it apparently gave the Vichy forces too much warning. In Algiers, things were already well under way.

I drove back to Juin's villa, this time alone, and asked Murphy if he had read the telegram from Darlan. He said: "No." I told him what it contained, and he said that he didn't care, at this point, what Darlan said to Pétain. Then he asked me if there were any word from the American landings. It was now between 3:30 and 4:00 in the morning, and there was no word yet from our forces. Rumor had it that they had landed near Cape Matifou, but the guides we had sent to the appointed beaches had not yet seen any landing parties. Later, we were told that the transports had missed the landing spots near Algiers and hit some 25 to 30 kilometers away. No motorized transport had been provided, because the Americans were supposed to land immediately outside the city. By the time the troops hiked into Algiers on foot, it was six in the morning.

I have always suspected—though I have absolutely no proof of this —that the "mistake" was deliberate. The British and American Navies do not generally drift that far off their course. I suspect that both the British and American authorities at home were far from confident about our collaborators, and that they simply did not trust them not to betray the exact point of the landings. The military authorities were, also, of course, trying to conceal the fact that the British were taking part in the invasion—a fact that would have increased antagonism in North Africa if it had been known at the time. It is significant that a pre-landing date with us and our underground was never kept. Secret wires from Gibraltar promised to deliver by boat small arms to our resistance groups several days before the landing. Picked young men went down night after night to the beaches mentioned in these wires, but the boats never arrived.

When I talked to Murphy, we did not know for certain that the troops had landed. As we stood in the gravel driveway, Admiral Fenard came out of the house again and handed me a second telegram from Darlan to the Marshal. He asked me if the first one had gone, and I replied, evasively I fear, that I had given it to be sent. He urged me to speed the second one on its way. As I backed the car away from the villa, Murphy ran after me and told me to be sure to get in touch with the fleet by radio as soon as I got back to Algiers, and urge them to get troops into Algiers at once, to back his arguments with Darlan with something more than moral suasion. I asked him to dictate the message, and copied it carefully in my small black notebook: "Western Task Force Commander from Murphy. It is urgently necessary that some Allied troops arrive in the city of Algiers as quickly as possible. Situation well in hand but unwise to let this endure too long." I said, "Allied? You mean American, don't you?" He repeated firmly, "Allied." This was the first knowledge I had that the British were actually landing with us.

As I swung the car around to leave, troops of the Vichy *Garde Mobile* suddenly burst through the gates to the villa and surrounded us, seized our little civilian guard from around the house and took them, Mr. Murphy and myself into the porter's lodge by the gates to the villa. Serious as the whole business was, it had an *opéra bouffe* quality, and reminded me irresistibly of the "Pirates of Penzance." I knew, however, that both sides in North Africa had itching trigger fingers and few scruples, and I had an authentic chill up my spine as they lined us up in front of the fireplace and told us to keep our hands up. We were thoroughly searched and stripped of our papers. One soldier said a few words in German to us, and I was so tired by this time that I thought wildly that they might be German troops in French uniforms. All of us, however, behaved with great dignity, I thought. Mr. Murphy was extremely pale, and he assured me that I was. He told me later that as he had been taken into the porter's lodge after me he had heard the order given to take us both out and shoot us. Luckily, this item had escaped me or I couldn't have answered for my dignity.

In a moment, the Commandant d'Orange, Juin's aide, rushed into the room, dressed oddly in a civilian brown tweed suit, wildly waving a huge revolver and crying: "What have you done? What have you done?" Some of the soldiers tried to arrest him, and he turned on them in a fury, crying: "I am the Commandant d'Orange, and you are under my orders." Then he turned back to Murphy and me, and said: "You know my sentiments; what made you do this idiotic thing?" Neither of us said anything: the man was so excited that he wouldn't give us time to answer, and wouldn't have listened if we had. In the midst of this Gallic scene, Juin, Fenard and Crétien appeared at the door, and said that Murphy must be brought back to the villa at once. Murphy and d'Orange asked them to include me, and Juin agreed. "I regret having to do this," he added formally to Murphy, "but your action in making me a prisoner in my own house necessitates it."

As we came out of the porter's lodge, Fenard remembered the telegram to Pétain and said it was imperative that it get off at once. I said everything had been removed from my pockets when I was searched. There was another frenzy while troops and officers searched the lodge for my things: no telegram. I looked in my pockets: the *Garde Mobile* had characteristically taken everything *but* the telegram, which was still there. Surrounded by three *Garde Mobile* soldiers with submachine guns, I climbed into Murphy's car and started for the Admiralty. As we drove down the hill, one soldier said happily to another: "*Enfin*, we are getting out of this filthy situation we have been in for two years. Now, we shall fight the Boches." "I hope you are going to," I said, in French. The soldier looked surprised, and said a few words in German. I explained to him that I could understand English or French better. "What are you anyway?" he said startled. Realizing at last why they had looked so bloodthirsty and spoken German to us in the porter's lodge at the villa, I said: "American." They looked at each other in amazement. "What are we doing here?" one said. "What indeed," I said unhappily.

At the Admiralty, I insisted on delivering the wire to Admiral Leclerc in person, to whom it was addressed. Calm and dignified, he opened it very deliberately, read it and said: "What proof have I that this is Admiral Darlan's signature?" "You have only my word," I said, "but I will be delighted to take anyone you suggest to Admiral Darlan to confirm it." "I will do that," he said, "but you will remain here."

He called in a young officer to guard me, and left the office saying that he must now, in view of the situation, take command of operations. For an hour and a half, the officer and I sat smoking and talking. Outside, we could hear the Admiralty guns as they fired, intermittently, on a British commando ship which had forced an entrance into the port with some American troops on board. It was grim to sit there, inside the Vichy citadel, knowing that it was firing on Americans. I learned later that sixty men from a Minnesota regiment were killed. As we waited, we talked politics, and I remembered the mingled feeling of relief and sadness with which I at last was able to speak freely, to tell this Vichy officer of all we felt and believed. My remarks about Pétain were long and pointed.

About six A. M., Admiral Leclerc came back into the room and told me I was free to leave. "I regret that I am not able to offer you breakfast," he added, "but we are excessively busy at this moment. I hope," he added with a gesture over my head, "that you have not spent too painful a time under the shadow of our esteemed Marshal." I turned and saw that I had been sitting the entire time under a magnificent, larger-than-life bust of Pétain.

Outside, I started for 26, Rue Michelet to report, and then realized I was in Murphy's car which was too well known in Algiers and might reveal our secret headquarters. I stopped in the street back of Rue Michelet behind Cole's car. I asked his chauffeur, an Arab named Sikki, where Mr. Cole was. He didn't know, so I tried 26, Rue Michelet. When I knocked on the dark door of Aboulker's apartment I was startled to have it opened by an enormously tall soldier in full battle dress. I hadn't seen our uniform before, and for a moment I thought it was a German. Then I heard a pleasant midwestern drawl, as the soldier asked "Are you an American?" I assured him I was. He continued: "They tell me I'm the first American soldier in Algiers. They're keeping me here until they're sure how these nervous French are going to take to us, so I'm standing guard on a drunk in here." I went into the apartment and found that the drunk was one of our control officers, a recent pre-landing acquisition, out colder than almost any-one I have ever seen. I remembered that he had seemed a little pale at the meeting the night before. He was shipped home soon after this unheroic performance on D-Day. The soldier and the drunk were the only two humans left in what a few hours before had been a teeming headquarters.

I returned to Mr. Cole's chauffeur, Sikki, and asked him to come with me and help me find Mr. Cole. We went around to Rue Michelet and started up the hill toward the Consulate at No. 119. Halfway there, I was arrested again. Another troop of the *Garde Mobile* surrounded me, and, when they found out who I was, put an armed guard in Murphy's car with me and sent me off to the barracks of the Fifth Regiment of the *Chasseurs d'Afrique*, the faithful Sikki follow-ing.

When I got there, I explained to the Colonel that I had already been thoroughly arrested and investigated and that I wanted to get back to Juin's villa. He went to check up, leaving me with a junior officer in the officers' common room. Morning had come: it was almost seven A. M. and light outside. We drank coffee and I tried to relax. Around us, the barracks were humming with activity. Tanks rumbled by; ambulances drove in, manned and ready. A few airplanes roared overhead, and there was the sound of ack-ack fire. A French woman I knew came in with one of the ambulances and spoke to me. In a way that symbolized all the confusion of that day, she told me, as I sat there in custody, of how happy she was at our landing, of what a glorious day this was for France. A moment later, an officer came up to tell me that Juin had ordered my release. "I am delighted to give you your liberty," he said, "and hope this is only the first of many acts of service I may render the Americans."

Cautiously getting a pass this time from the Colonel, I drove up to Cole's house to wash and shave. I broke the good news to the Polish waitress and the Austrian cook, who wept with joy. Then I went next door to the little English church by the villa to offer what I hoped would not be a premature thanksgiving. Frustrating as so many things that day, the church was closed.

Outside, the streets were not crowded, but I met a good many ex-cited and rather mystified passers-by, all streaming toward the harbor.

It was a lovely, clear cool morning.

Harry Woodruff came in to Cole's villa as I dressed, to pick up some clothes and shaving things for Murphy, who was still at Juin's villa and not allowed to leave. We packed a small bag, snatched a bottle of Scotch and drove over to Murphy who was waiting for us, tired and white after a night of arguing with Darlan. It was now only too evident that Giraud, though he was admired by all the secret pro-Allied forces in North Africa, which included most of the Army, was not going to be able to take the heads of that Army into our camp with him. We would have to have Juin and the others, and to get them, we would have to have Darlan. With true French logic, everything had to follow legitimate succession. Darlan was holding off to see how strong our forces were going to prove to be.

After Murphy had had a shave and we had all had a drink, we went downstairs under the disapproving eye of Madame Juin, an Algerian heiress with a reputation of adhering to the strictest neutrality. Downstairs, Crétien, Fenard and another officer waited for us. Juin, himself, was at *Fort l'Empereur*. As we lunched, Murphy left the table from time to time to confer with people. We could see a great fire burning down near the port, and hear a constant sound of firing. Three American dive bombers swooped down over the port and the Admiralty as we ate. In the midst of our first bombing, Fenard said, over and over again, as we stepped outside on the terrace and watched the intermittent fire of the Vichy forces, "This must be stopped. This is absolutely ridiculous. We must stop the firing." He was only voicing what everyone thought.

Darlan was finally convinced that the Americans were coming in force. He intimated that he was ready to talk business as soon as he could have his trusted Admiral Battet at his side. Battet had been taken prisoner some time during the night by our local resistance forces.

Fenard asked me to drive down and get Battet. This time, I asked Commandant d'Orange, who reappeared at the villa, to give me a pass. I was tired of being arrested. D'Orange had recovered from his hysteria of the night before. Calm and suave in an immaculate new uniform, he, too, was convinced that the Americans were there to stay, and was as affable as if we were lunching together at one of the nearby Black Market restaurants. He took me down to *Fort l'Empereur* to get a pass. In the big conference room there, I waited and listened to the officers carrying on telephone conversations from all over North Africa. It was a grim moment, in Juin's headquarters, to see French generals and colonels receiving news of French resistance all along the coast. I remember hearing Sevez answer a call from Oran, with the news that things were going badly for the French at Arzew, outside Oran, but that everything was going well for the Vichyites in the town proper. A bulletin from Morocco said that the Americans had tried to land at Safi but had been repulsed, and that there was very severe fighting going on at Port Lyautey and near Casablanca. At that moment, d'Orange came back with my pass and urged me to find the American commanding general to talk terms at once. I knew from this that Juin wanted an armistice, as d'Orange never took responsibility except under Juin's orders.

I had no idea where to find Battet, whom our side was keeping in custody much as their side kept Murphy. The streets were full of French soldiers, and the *Garde Mobile* seemed to be besieging the Post Office, which, of course, was held by our men.

Not knowing where to go, I went on over to the Police Station on Boulevard Boudin. I knew the police were friendly to us. Inside, a seething mass of civilians, soldiers and police were milling around the blood-stained body of a tall French colonel. D'Astier and Abbé Cordier were the only controlled people present. They told me Battet had been released several hours before. It was then 3:30 P. M.

Since no one seemed to know where Battet could be, I decided to try to locate the American commanding general for d'Orange and Juin. This time, I tried the Villa Sinetti where our secret radio station was hidden. Cole and Boyd were there, and told me the Allies were at Sidi Farruch. We got into our cars, and they guided me until I was safely on the back road to our beaches. It was a big moment to see the little harbor off Cheragas filled with what seemed to be hundreds of grey ships, the roads filled with companies of Americans marching to Algiers. (Paradoxically the Allies were landing in almost the same spot where a hundred years before the French had landed.) In every little crossroad town, Arabs and French had lined the roadside to watch them. The Arabs were particularly fascinated by the commandos with their black faces: they thought they were a new, and interesting, type of native.

At his temporary headquarters, behind a roadside hedge under a tree, I found our commanding General Ryder, a very tall, thin, stooped and handsome man, with great personal charm. General Mast and, surprisingly, Captain Randolph Churchill, son of the Prime Minister, were with him. He gave me his terms: easy ones if the French surrendered at once, tough if they didn't, and a postscript that Murphy must be present at all negotiations. I started back to Algiers. Near Juin's villa, I met Murphy on his way to find Ryder, too. We turned back together, got Ryder, turned again, and met d'Orange just leaving El Biar to surrender *Fort l'Empereur* to us on behalf of the French.

The surrender was wonderfully French, like a historical painting in some European museum. D'Orange stood before six French soldiers, lined up in arrow shape, and handed the sword of surrender by the blade, hilt extended, to General Ryder, announcing that, with this sword he surrendered the *Fort l'Empereur*, and the city of Algiers, to the American General.

As we drove down to the Fort, Colonel O'Daniel's artillery were firing tracer bullets over our cars, ready to open fire in earnest. Just then, the "cease fire" signal for the French was sounded by trumpets, with great bravura, from the windows of General Juin's two American-made limousines. Happily, the cease fire reached the American artillery just in time. Inside the Fort, we sat in a big room while Ryder, Juin, Darlan, and Murphy negotiated in an inside office. French officers, looking solemn, stood along the opposite wall. The American officers asked me to urge the Frenchmen to sit down. They didn't do this, but remained standing still in a silence that I realized (since I knew many of them personally) came from a genuine shyness of defeat rather than from unfriendliness. Their complex, and, to the American public, inexplicable psychology became plainer to me weeks later when I visited a hospital in Morocco, full of soldiers who had lost arms or legs in the battles during the landing. There was no resentment or bitterness in their hearts. They were thrilled to see an American visitor and were smiling, friendly and amazingly pro-American. They had fought as soldiers, in a tradition of great discipline, and were delighted to have lost.

Between 5:30 and 6 P. M., Algiers was finally officially surrendered. Then, I chauffeured Colonel (now General) O'Daniel around the city while he sent American soldiers back to their temporary barracks, and told isolated groups of French soldiers and aviators that it was all over. In one place, a rather ardent looking soldier worried me by pointing his gun at us in much too business-like a way. I stopped the car quickly and O'Daniel walked calmly up to him and told him what had happened. Afterwards, I said to O'Daniel, "You are remarkably calm when people wave guns at you." He replied negligently, "Oh, they always shoot at the driver when they want to stop a car." I felt distinctly more nervous the rest of the trip.

Finally, O'Daniel, a tough Irishman with disarmingly good manners in dealing with the French, cleaned up the last outpost, and we headed back to town. As darkness settled over Algiers, the shooting was over. Allied ships were already heading into the big harbor. Algiers was once more on our side in the war. It was the end of a long road for us. Yet though the city seemed calm, it was a false calm. With the military phase successfully finished, we were heading into much stormier political waters.

CHAPTER XI

Webs of Intrigue

ON THE surface, after our landings, everything was serene in Algiers, except for the outraged cries of the great landowners whose villas were promptly requisitioned. American troops poured ashore and were met with wild enthusiasm. The harbor was full of Allied shipping. Restaurants and the newly established inter-Allied club were packed with French, British and Americans fraternizing. The town had an almost holiday air as the Army prepared itself for the big push to the east in Tunisia. We even, in those early days, thought this victory would be a quick one.

But underneath this reassuring surface, Algeria was seething with political intrigue. Too long, the Vichy government had kept that most political people, the French, in a sort of hermetically sealed vacuum. When we opened the door, every political wind rushed in with us and, eventually, blew us off our diplomatic feet.

Two things must be remembered, to explain if not excuse the rather ignoble record of some Frenchmen in North Africa both before and after our landings. One was the tragic fact that France was in German hands, and that their own actions could involve many friends and relatives on the mainland. They were like men trying to fight an underworld which held hostages from their own families. The second thing was that legalism and the chain of command meant everything to French Army and Navy men. Mast, Béthouart, Giraud himself, were not, in the eyes of the generals and admirals in North Africa, patriots fighting on the right side. They were professionals who had betrayed the military tradition, "generals in dissidence," almost traitors, because they had dealt with a foreign power—even a friendly one—instead of implicitly obeying the head of their own state. It is hard for Americans, especially civilian Americans, to understand this extraordinary point of view, but it was an absolutely sincere one. Obedience to the legal head of the state was ingrained in every French military and naval mind as a part of his own honor, both as a man and as a patriot. It was a rare man who could break this tradition.

These two facts, plus the abiding French fear that we wouldn't arrive in enough strength to keep the German permanently out of North Africa, accounted for a lot of our disappointments and disillusionments immediately after the landings, as we tried to get the North African French into line. Their record from the eighth to the twelfth of November was not an attractive one.

Darlan, smooth faced and imperturbable, was in full command, living in the Fenard's villa but having his GHQ down in the town. Giraud remained at Lemaigre Dubreuil's villa, with a guard of our own underground to prevent "incidents." General Clark arrived the evening of the ninth and installed his headquarters at the Hotel St. George. He and Darlan set to work on the negotiations that grew into the Clark-Darlan Agreements, which were the scaffolding of our whole effort in North Africa.* Controlling all this first negotiating was the urgent order from London and Washington: "Get the French fleet at any price." Poor General Mast, who had acted for us and for Giraud, was swept aside by French officialdom. He was, like Giraud, *un général en dissidence*. Darlan was negotiating with us purely, he said, as the legal representative of Vichy.

Morocco went on resisting until November eleventh. Pétain, so Darlan and Noguès claimed, had finally removed Darlan, thinking him a prisoner of the Americans, and put Noguès in charge of all North Africa. Poor Béthouart, instead of capturing Noguès, had been captured by that shrewd and experienced operator. When Noguès finally surrendered, on the eleventh, he claimed that he had had a second secret message from Vichy announcing that because Pétain had learned Darlan was not a prisoner but a free agent, Darlan was in charge again. This mysterious message coincided nicely with the fact that the American Army and Navy were within two minutes of starting a mammoth bombardment of Casablanca.

The evening of the tenth, when Darlan announced that Pétain had removed him, he asked to be put in custody to show that his further

---

* Under the agreements, as finally signed, we had full charge, but promised an eventual complete restoration of French sovereignty, while Darlan in return promised complete coöperation.

coöperation with us was a forced one. In the meantime, the Germans moved into Unoccupied France, a violation of the Armistice terms which Darlan, Juin and Noguès finally decided released them from all moral obligations to Vichy and to their oaths of surrender.

Darlan soon produced both successes and failures for us. He was able eventually to bring Dakar and all West Africa into line, a very helpful thing, as we were still operating on a military shoestring and a good deal of our tough talk was sheer bluff. Darlan failed, on the other hand, in his effort to get Tunis to resist the Germans, and his cable urging the fleet at Toulon to come over was answered classically (and vulgarly) by Admiral de la Borde or one of his officers in the single, untranslatable word: "*Merde.*"

General Clark set to work to bring Giraud back into the picture. We needed Darlan politically—that was obvious to everyone who saw the reaction of the French on the scene—but we still wanted Giraud to work with us in the coming campaigns. I took several messages to Giraud, a tall, dignified figure out at Lemaigre Dubreuil's, where he still waited under guard, for his assignment. The evening of the tenth, Giraud conferred with Juin, Clark and some subordinate military figures. He realized then that the chief men in North Africa had not and were not, for the moment, going to follow his leadership. This was a bitter disappointment to him as well as to us, but he took it like a man. He begged us to enlist Darlan or anyone else who could win over the Army and Navy officials.

Giraud was a disarming, rather touching figure. I have never seen a man with a greater flame of patriotism, or a more transparent, almost childlike honesty. This childlike quality was fatal in the end, politically speaking. To Giraud, any Frenchman, especially any Frenchman in uniform was evidently and obviously a fine fellow. He judged others by himself, as so many honest men do, loathed politics, and had an abiding faith that Frenchmen could put their differences aside and march together to win the war. He simply never grasped the fact that other Frenchmen insisted on making, or at least trying to make the postwar pattern for France right then and there. De Gaulle, to him, was a general, a Frenchman and anti-German; Darlan was equally an admiral, a Frenchman and anti-German.

On the November 11th, Darlan, however, suddenly and without

telling us, revoked his orders sending up soldiers to Tunisia against the Germans and picked the cards up generally from the table. The French generals were deeply resentful over Giraud's appointment, and wanted to hold everything in suspense until Noguès arrived from Morocco. He was coming over, after his surrender, by plane. In extenuation of the French stalling at this point, it must be remembered that they were all suffering from an acute inferiority complex, feeling put upon and pushed around. First, the Germans had taken their pride away; now, the Americans wanted to dictate to them, too. They sulked and grew shifty, as people will when their pride is hurt.

Noguès finally reached Algiers the evening of the eleventh and came directly to headquarters at the Hotel St. George. I was there, waiting to act as interpreter. Most of the top-ranking French officers were waiting there, too—among them, Juin and Giraud. It was painful to anyone who loved France to see that meeting. Noguès came into the room, tense, tired and strained. He nodded and spoke to all the officers but Giraud. Someone said: "But you know General Giraud." Giraud stepped forward with his hand out, only to have Noguès turn on his heel saying: "I do not know a general in dissidence." Feeling as embarrassed as an outsider at a family quarrel, I left the room and waited outside in the corridor, filled with French and American guards. In a few minutes, all the French officers came out, and Juin, before everyone, stepped up to Noguès and said: "*Assez de votre sale politique, Noguès. Now we are going to fight the Germans.*"

I went on into Clark's office to interpret. Noguès had brought Commandant Bataille with him as his interpreter. The interview was an unpleasant one. Noguès had no intention of bringing Morocco into the war on our side. He proposed merely to give us "the right of passage": exactly the amount of coöperation in other words, that Vichy gave the Germans on the Syrian airports. Noguès seemed really afraid for French, and for his own, sovereignty in Morocco. His tenseness and unhappiness went far beyond that of the other Vichy leaders in North Africa at this time. He kept saying that he would have to send Bataille by plane to see Pétain and get some personal word from him. He felt it vitally important to try to discover the Marshal's secret thoughts.

I admired Clark enormously throughout that interview. He was completely calm and pleasant, but he knew that, with the Germans actually in Vichy, it would be fantastic to let an emissary fly there. He said to me: "Will you please impress it upon General Noguès, once and for all, that there can be no question of communicating with Vichy. We have broken relations with that government. In our eyes it no longer exists. We are not even interested in learning its views."

Finally, after long talks with all the French leaders, Clark insisted that Giraud be called in to hear the American ultimatum in their presence. If they didn't coöperate fully, he said, and if they didn't accept Giraud, he would simply take full military control and proceed as if in an enemy country. As usual, in North Africa, toughness worked where reason failed: we had no trouble with the Vichy military leaders from then on. Diplomatically, we might well have learned a lesson from this successful strong talk on the part of General Clark.

I remember riding out to the airport with Murphy the day he flew to Gibraltar to discuss the Darlan deal with Eisenhower and secure his agreement. There was no question but that Murphy was well aware of the criticism that would surely arise from any American coöperation with Darlan, but he was fortunately equally aware that at that point with the Allies far from established in North Africa, Darlan was an absolutely essential military expedient. In the handling of this whole affair Murphy was at his very best.

Eisenhower flew in on the thirteenth, and made us proud to have such a compatriot. He had left his Grosvenor Square headquarters in London (always known as Eisenhower Platz) for Gibraltar some time before; now, he could swing the North African campaign into high. Lunching with us in the dining room end of the Moorish style living room in Cole's villa, he left us all struck by his incisive energy and the way in which he reëstablished our sense of proportion, which always warps easily in North Africa. He knew every tree in that political and military wood, but he also saw the forest with unwavering vision. I had thought Clark one of the most clear-headed, energetic men I had ever met, but Eisenhower dwarfed him. He was a living dynamo of energy, good humor, amazing memory for details and amazing courage for the future. All the tired North African air seemed stirred up and left full of mental ozone after this, his first visit to Algiers.

We learned later that the moment of the North African landings was the one that caused Eisenhower the most worry during his European war experiences. I thought that possibly we had exaggerated our difficulties before the landings in Algiers; it was interesting to find the Supreme Commander had shared our qualms. He knew, more accurately than we did, just how tentatively Allied force was established in North Africa during those first days.

Our military effort, as everyone knows, went well at first. The French immediately produced an Army of 110,000 men (under Giraud this increased by several thousands) which guarded our lines of supply so well that there was never a single act of sabotage during the battle of North Africa. Seventy thousand of these men fought so bravely in the front lines—ill equipped as they were—that they lost 11,000 dead and 5,000 wounded. This army that had constantly been watched, inspected, and demoralized by the German and Italian Armistice Commissions for two and a half years had managed not only to hide arms and supplies from the prying eye of the enemy, but had also concealed the exact number of its soldiers. Under the terms of the German Armistice the French were permitted to maintain only an army of 100,000 men in all North Africa. Many thousands more soldiers appeared the moment this army resumed its fight against the Germans.

I shall never forget the sight of Giraud's soldiers when American equipment arrived later for the French Army. As they looked at the mile long rows of modern tanks, guns and jeeps drawn up for them, there were actual tears of joy in their eyes.

In the meantime, however, all sorts of slimy and unpleasant things were happening back of the scene in Algiers.

A particularly shocking episode occurred soon after the landing. Some scores of Germans and Italians were being loaded into trucks and taken off to a prison camp. A crowd immediately collected around them and began booing, hissing, throwing things and even spitting at them. It wasn't the hatred in their faces that shocked me; I shared that hatred. It was the fact that in the screaming crowd I saw many respectable North African citizens who, only a few weeks before, had been far from hostile to these same Germans and Italians at the Hotel Aletti. It seemed to me that the resisting French in the homeland, who had always frozen the Germans with contempt, had more right to hiss and spit at them later.

A much more shocking episode was a kind of bastard gestapo that was immediately set up in the former Italian Institute, just off the main street in Algiers, directed by one of our own underground men, André Achiary. Achiary had been *chef de la brigade de surveillance du Territoire*, a kind of political police force, until the German Armistice Commission realized that he was concentrating too much against them, and he was put in *residénce forcée*—a sort of semi-imprisonment. (We managed to get him out just a few days before the landing.) Unfortunately, he used his renewed power to proceed, illegally and even sadistically, against personal enemies as well as former collaborators. His third degree methods were worthy of the Nazis, and it was doubly horrifying that they didn't seem to worry his former resistance colleagues in the least. In fact, he boasted openly of his actions to everyone. "You ought to see what we've got going on down at the Italian Institute," he said to me one day, smiling broadly. When he went into a few details my hair rose, I thought, almost visibly; but I controlled myself long enough to check with some other people and find out that he was not only not exaggerating, but that the building was being protected by American soldiers. I told Rigault, who now occupied a position roughly like Minister of the Interior. When this gestapo was brought to the attention of the American authorities they cracked down at once, and the Achiary group took to underground plotting instead. We ran across their trail later.

I had a chance to see Morocco again soon after the landing. Mr. Murphy and General Clark asked me to go there to find out what had happened to the letter President Roosevelt had sent to the Sultan of Morocco on D-Day explaining our intentions in Morocco and generally saluting the Sultan as the head of a friendly state. The President had never received an answer. Communications between Algiers and Morocco were chaotic at this time, and it was actually easier to send a messenger than to telephone or write. I left by plane with a copy of the original letter in my pocket.

When I got to Casablanca, I went to see General Patton, commander of our western forces, in his elaborate modern offices at the Shell Oil Company building. I showed him a copy of the letter, which was couched in simple terms, pointing out that we were landing to guard the sovereignty of Morocco and save it from the Axis, and that we hoped the Moroccans would receive us in a friendly spirit. (This was the letter I had given Vice Consul Mayer before the landings, to be given to Noguès just before zero hour on D-Day. Noguès had refused to see Mayer, and, therefore, the document had been given to a Residency official to be passed on to Noguès and by him to the Sultan. This, Noguès had not done.)

I explained my errand and waited as Patton read the letter through, scowling, and said: "I don't like it, do you?" I answered that I thought it was an excellent letter. "There's not enough mention of the French in it," Patton said. "You see, General," I explained, "this letter originally was accompanied by a letter for General Noguès and the request that he hand this one on to the Sultan. There was no need to mention the French, for we were asking their own Resident General to deliver the letter." Patton leaned back and said: "Read it to me." I read it aloud while he listened. When I was through, he said again: "No, I don't like it." He took the letter and began to insert additions of his own.

Then, he asked me if I didn't think he had improved it. I muttered something about not feeling that any of us had the right to edit a President's letter without his knowledge. "God damn it," said Patton, banging the desk. "I'll take full responsibility for this letter." "Very well, sir, I shall tell Mr. Murphy when we telephone tonight," I said. Patton looked up glowering, "God damn it," said Patton, "I won't have you or any other God damn fool talking about this letter on the phone. Don't you know the wires are tapped?" "Yes, sir, I do," I replied. "They've been tapped for the last year and a half."

Our conversation grew more amicable, and I dared to ask some questions about the general situation in Morocco and the fate of General Béthouart and the other officers who had failed so miserably in their mission on D-Day, but had, nevertheless, risked their lives for us. Noguès had even tried to send them by airplane for trial at Vichy. He was only prevented from doing this by the intervention of some ardent French patriots. General Patton said: "General Noguès and I have a perfect understanding, and I have left all these problems of personnel up to him. Morocco is an extremely difficult country to manage. Now, the Jewish problem. . . ." Noguès had obviously used one of his favorite devices, the false issue, to distract General Patton from the fate of our brave friends.

Murphy telephoned me that night that there had been another cable from Washington about the Sultan's letter. He said I was to see Patton again the next day, and ask him to find out immediately if the original letter had ever been delivered. With my courage firmly in both hands, I did so. When I explained why I was there again, his rage was magnificent. "I told you I didn't want this discussed on the phone," he bellowed, and with a few more "God-damn its," assured me he would take full responsibility in the matter of the letter. "Then communicate with my superior, Ambassador Murphy," I said, "and tell him as much." Patton suddenly and unexpectedly reversed field. "You know, Pendar, my bark is worse than my bite," he said, with a charming smile, and buzzed for an aide.

When he did solve the great letter mystery, it turned out, of course, that it had never been delivered. The "mislaid" letter was soon delivered by the Residency to the Sultan. By that time, I was on my way to Marrakech for a twenty-four hour visit in the company of General J. W. Anderson, Patton's infantry man, a cool, modest, friendly officer. It was amusing to see the new respect with which French generals suddenly treated me at Marrakech, now that I was in the presence of our own military leaders.

During my short stay in Morocco, I learned of the way in which General Noguès had covered the flight of the German Armistice Commission to Spanish Morocco. These were men I had sincerely hoped we would capture. Unfortunately, only a few of them were taken prisoner at Fedala near Casablanca. I also learned how furious the Germans had been during their flight when they saw the movements of vast numbers of Moroccan troops, with machine guns, and other arms, all of which had been successfully hidden from the Armistice Commission.

The whole Moroccan situation had an Alice in Wonderland quality after the landings. Noguès, having finally decided to coöperate with us, was being utterly charming to the American generals, and had won their hearts with dazzling displays of French military style and gold braid, Arab horsemanship, French cooking and general colonial razzle-dazzle. French and American officers began to mingle happily at marvelous parties given by Patton's political adviser, Vice Consul Culbert, in his magnificently modern apartment in Casablanca. There was a great deal of gaiety, which seemed incongruous with men fighting in Tunisia, and yet, was right and even necessary if the French and Americans were to get to know and trust each other. At the top, strode Patton, rattling his great pistols and thoroughly enjoying his own rages. Later, I was to learn that the Vichyites, to the population's amazement, were in favor at the moment, and that they had more or less discredited our true friends to the recently arrived American soldiers. One Frenchman who had been most loyal and useful to us in the pre-landing days appeared very depressed and upset when I met him. "I seem to have been on the wrong side before the landing," he said. "Everyone agrees that the former collaborationists are the only people your military men get on with or apparently like to see." Certainly, political direction was lacking in Morocco from our point of view.

Back in Algiers, I found more serious political storms brewing. They were so melodramatic, so fantastic, that even now, they seem incredible.

At midnight, the night of November seventh, Churchill had told de Gaulle that we were landing in North Africa at that moment. At this point, obviously, the British did not trust the de Gaullist group enough to let him know our plans ahead of time. They were treating him as they did in the Madagascar affair, when they merely announced their action to him as a *fait accompli*. I do not know what de Gaulle said to Churchill, but I can guess because I do know what André Philip, an ardent and highly placed disciple of de Gaulle then in the United States, said to Henri de Kerillis, at that time a de Gaullist, who was trying to rejoice with him on the success of our landing. "*Ces salauds!*" said Philip. "*Ils ont fait ça sans nous. Ils vont le payer, et payer cher.*" ("The so-and-sos. They did that without us. They will pay for it—and dearly.")

Our own agreement with the French on the spot had been logical, and so necessary, that everyone was completely taken aback by the storm that now reached Algiers from America and England. Mr. Roosevelt, feeling the winds, issued his famous statement that our agreement with Darlan was a military necessity, and not, by implication, a permanent thing. (Darlan said bitterly: "I see they are going to treat me like an orange, to be sucked and then thrown away.") In London, we were told later, Eden finally agreed to the arrangements only on condition that de Gaulle should have some representatives in North Africa at once. We had reassured the French in North Africa by having made the landings without any de Gaullists, so this might be embarrassing. Many pro-Allied Frenchmen had been rightly afraid that the Army and the fleet would react violently, because of Mers-el-Kébir and Dakar, if de Gaulle took any part.

At this point, de Gaulle was already broadcasting from London to France that he had had, and would have, nothing to do with all that was going on around Darlan and Giraud in North Africa. This was extremely confusing to the French in Occupied France, we learned when French people escaping from France began to arrive in Algiers. It was one of de Gaulle's most overt attempts to discredit America's policy with France, and the Germans used it to make anti-Allied propaganda within France.

Already, obviously, our original American policy of keeping French politics out of the war was in danger. Our sound and simple idea of preserving France intact, so to speak, until elections could be held, of keeping any one group from using our military strength as a political advantage, was bogging down in a morass of American, British and French dissension. At this point, we would have done well to issue a public statement on our policy, and to make it plain that Darlan, Giraud, and de Gaulle, if he ever came to Africa, were to govern simply as a military, pro tem expedient (a sort of trusteeship), until the liberation of France.

As it was, we were still unaware of the basic importance of these political storms. We were so concentrated on the Tunisian campaign that there was hardly a ripple of excitement when de Gaulle's General d'Astier de la Vigerie, a brother of the one who had worked with us before the landings, arrived from London without warning or official permission. A man of bad reputation, in Morocco anyway, he established himself for some days, in December, at the Hotel Aletti, and began a series of curious meetings with various Algerian groups. He was in constant touch with the men who were arrested shortly after Darlan's assassination. Soon, some $35,000 in American bills turned up in the hands of former members of our underground who were by now passionate de Gaullists. But North Africa is always full of money passing secretly and rapidly from hand to hand, and this was only one more episode. René Capitant (later the French Minister of Education) who had produced a band of two hundred energetic young resisters for us at the time of the landing, emerged as a leading de Gaullist. His followers now announced that they had thought all along that de Gaulle was to lead the landings, an inexplicable statement in view of the fact that everyone who met the night of the landings was openly discussing Giraud's arrival. This began the well-organized and expert publicizing of de Gaullism in North Africa. Poor Giraud, politically innocent as a child, never fired an answering gun.

Behind, and simultaneous with, the de Gaullist drive, still another and more secret plot began to take form. It led directly to the assassination of Darlan.

This plot centered around the shopworn figure of the Comte de Paris, who was now whisked over secretly, by car, from Larache in Spanish Morocco, and installed in the villa of a prominent local royalist. Royalist feeling is still alive in France, and some authorities may have hoped that the French could ultimately resolve their differences around the Comte de Paris. (The reader will remember the earlier British flirtation with the "Pretender.") Many of our own pre-landing agents, like d'Astier and the Abbé Cordier, were devout royalists; Giraud, as a military man, was credited with royalist leanings and de Gaulle's own family had always been ardent members of the pre-war ghost courts in quasi-royal houses at Neuilly. In any case, the possibilities were good enough to produce an attempted *coup d'état*. After Darlan's assassination, I saw copies of the telephone recordings, police reports, manifestoes and newspapers which had actually been printed ahead of time, and held in readiness: they announced that, upon Admiral Darlan's death, the Comte de Paris had assumed control of French destinies and the French Empire.

These papers are perhaps our best clue to the still officially unsolved mystery surrounding Darlan's death. The young assassin, caught pistol in hand, made an immediate sworn statement that he had shot Darlan on December 24, of his own volition, without help or backing from anyone, and that he took full responsibility for the act. But the fact is that the fanatic, and perhaps half-crazed assassin, Bonnier de la Chapelle was, apparently, a victim of sinister dishonesty. This I learned from Rigault, then in charge of police work in Algiers. He had received a call from the two guards stationed outside of de la Chapelle's cell. They had reason to feel that the youth had been made the dupe in some underhanded intrigue.

These guards, Lieutenant Schilling and Captain Gaulard, reported that a police officer had come to the boy's cell during the night and promised him his life if he would reveal his accomplices; that de la Chapelle hesitated, broke down and told the whole story, which this police officer (who still shall be nameless for obvious reasons) pocketed. Since this document was never produced, the officer obviously intended to use it for blackmailing purposes of his own. Only the first confession was used at de la Chapelle's trial. The rest of the guards' story was a horrible one of the boy's last night, as he clung to the bars, wept, and frantically asked the guards where the messenger was who would have to come soon to bring him the pardon he had been twice promised. He told the guards that he had made his original confession only because his backers had promised that they could save him from justice. But neither the first promise nor the signed full confession saved him. He was taken out the next day and shot at dawn, a fanatic and pathetic tool of others.

From the things the guards heard, plus the usual tapped wires, plus the signed statement of another young man, Rigault pieced together a story which probably has at least a rough accuracy. De la Chapelle was a member of the *Chantier de la Jeunesse*. A group of them in a camp near Algiers had decided, under guidance well hidden by political screens, that Darlan must go, to "purify" France. Like the Suicides' Club, they drew straws for the gory honor of serving as executioner. The first young man refused. De la Chapelle accepted. He was driven to Darlan's office that day in a Citroën widely recognized as belonging to his organization, and waited in the crowded hallway, tense and drawn, to fire the shot.

In the light of this knowledge, the action of General Bergeret (who temporarily took over after the murder of Darlan) in throwing so many of our own former underground into jail after the assassination, is a little more understandable. (This action was popularly and falsely, credited to Rigault, as Minister of Interior.) At the time, most observers in Algiers thought it an unforgivable act of treachery; yet it was obviously impossible to release the whole story. Rigault's best friend was d'Astier. Rigault went to him at once, and d'Astier swore he had nothing to do with the plot. Justice, which the French as well as ourselves demanded, took its course. Dr. Aboulker and his son, José, Alexandre, Achiary, and others with pro-Allied reputations were put under *résidence forcée* in southern Algeria while the investigations proceeded, but were released shortly. D'Astier and Cordier were put in prison in Algiers where they stayed for months, and were only released when de Gaulle took over. To Americans on the scene but not on the inside, it all looked political. It was political, but not in quite the way they thought.

I would have found the inside story incredible myself, if I had not sat in the *Restaurant de Paris* only a few weeks before, and heard some of our leading pre-landing collaborators blandly discussing past acts of violence of incredible and gruesome ferocity. It is hard, but important, for Americans to realize that the spirit of violence that lies deep in human beings, the spirit that broke out in our own Ku Klux Klan, has been released on a really enormous scale in modern Europe. That release was, perhaps, the worst of Hitler's crimes. We saw it face to face in Algiers.

After Darlan's assassination, Giraud took over the political as well as military power in North Africa. Our old friend, Rigault became his Minister of Interior, our other old friend, the industrialist, Lemaigre Dubreuil, served as his political adviser. They were hardly outstanding French leaders or, in any way representative ones, though they both gave Giraud good advice which he was too politically inept to use; and Rigault, at least, remained utterly loyal to America to the end. We had used these men at first, because we had to. They were available, and no one else was. Later, we went on using them because we were committed to them. It was then that we made our first major mistake. If Murphy was too deeply committed to them morally, he should have been replaced, for his own sake, with a man of higher rank and no involvements. As it was, we followed a policy of inertia rather than our original policy of "hands-off-French-politics." There are times when taking no action is more drastic than action itself.

This was one of them.

We let Giraud go his way, with Rigault and Lemaigre Dubreuil trying vainly to steer him. And his way was one that inevitably threw North Africa into the hands of the politically-minded de Gaullists. Honest and inept, Giraud quite sincerely thought that he could keep the home front in a state of suspense while he fought the war in Tunisia. He was far too slow in restoring Vichy-crushed civil liberties, in bringing back the Crémieux Law giving Jews civil rights, and in getting rid of the whole shopworn Vichy gang in North Africa. It was not that he believed in Vichy's ideas; it was simply that he thought everyone and everything could wait until the war was won and France was free to speak her own mind. While his armies were covering themselves with glory he drifted politically; and he drifted straight into disaster. And with every military and political card in the pack firmly in our hands, we drifted with him.

CHAPTER XII

A Footnote to History

History laid a finger, briefly, on the lovely villa La Saadia where I lived in Marrakech. While I was back in Morocco from Algeria, during the Casablanca Conference, Prime Minister Churchill and President Roosevelt, together with many British and American military leaders, stayed at La Saadia. I was fortunate enough to act as host, and to get an unforgettable glimpse of great men at work.

The decisions taken at Casablanca have been canvassed by many political writers. I won't attempt to add my own opinion to theirs. I did, however, have an amazing piece of luck in seeing a part of the Conference from an informal, almost intimate, point of view. It was absorbing to see what an international gathering looks like from the inside, when the top hats are off and the photographers have gone home, and statesmen sit around the dinner table together. It was absorbing, too, to observe the enormous amount of detailed planning, the hundreds of people it takes to bring together the President of the United States and the Prime Minister of Great Britain, house them, guard them, and feed them. My domestic view, so to speak, of the Conference may be an interesting sub-footnote to the history of those crucial days.

Before the Conference I had found myself back in the perpetually intriguing, gossiping Moroccan world. I had chosen to go back to Morocco on the understanding that General Noguès was on his way out, and that I could work in the newly opened Rabat Consulate in a more friendly political atmosphere than our pre-landing one. Unfortunately, by the time I reached Morocco, our civilian and military policies were already running afoul of each other as they were later to do on the mainland of Europe. While our diplomats tried to get Noguès replaced with a more coöperative, less Vichyite character, General Patton, as I noted before, succumbed completely to the military dramatics Noguès could always produce. So did many of his top officers. I remember early discussions with some of these men which proved that they saw the Vichyite group in Morocco in its true colors. These same men, after a dinner at the Residency, where they were received with a fanfare of Moroccan trumpeters and given a welcoming escort of Spahi guards, would come away dazed and dazzled, with an entirely different point of view about Noguès and his subordinate officials. Part of this, perhaps, was due to the *esprit de corps* that seems to exist between all professional armies, friendly or enemy, and that later caused trouble in Germany. Part of it, however, was, I think, simply the curious love of pomp, ceremony and imperial glitter that beguiles so many Americans abroad.

The result was that an unhealthy state of non-coöperation continued to exist among the French bureaucracy in Morocco even after the landings. The years under Vichy had allowed a sort of political poison to permeate all those colonial officers. They were used to a hidden, adroit resistance to Germany, but had a difficult time making the transition to open warfare. It was, unquestionably, a delicate psychological problem, this business of weaning Vichyites from their timid habits, but we pulled the operation out too long. We never got the coöperation from them that I feel sure could have been achieved by a more positive and even aggressive policy.

We also suffered from our perennial American inability to get different departments to work together abroad. The State Department's representatives in North Africa as a matter of fact made every attempt to coöperate with the Army and to give them the benefit of a fairly extensive experience on the spot. In Algiers, under General Eisenhower's marvelously understanding and capable direction, the two services worked together smoothly. In Morocco, the Army showed an inclination to run the show single-handed.

When I went back to Marrakech, intending to close the villa and move to Rabat, I found a great deal going on in the sleepy Arab town. Marrakech had become the most important airport in North Africa. Its climatic conditions were so perfect that "Forts" and C-47s flew there direct from America. It was swarming with Americans, and there were endless difficulties of language and understanding that called for help from an old consular hand, as I now felt myself to be. We had some pleasant, frivolous interludes in the midst of the serious business of war work and the higher drama of the Casablanca Conference. La Saadia became a sort of inter-Allied club to which the aviators brought new swing records and American magazines which were, incredibly, only a few days old. We even gave two dances at Christmas and New Years which included every French official's daughter for miles around. After years away from home, it was heart-warming to see the pleasant, human, American quality of our men in uniform, and the unfailing politeness with which they thanked me and sent thanks to the owner of La Saadia each time they came there.

As a final sidelight on the strange and wonderful Arab mind I learned to love in Morocco, I might mention the party-to-end-all-parties given for Josephine Baker, the Negro entertainer who was such a toast in Paris for years. The party was given by Si Mohamed Menebhi and Moulay Larbi el Alaoui, a cousin of the Sultan; Josephine Baker was living in one of Si Mohamed's houses in Marrakech. Practically every American in North Africa, including most of the generals, received printed, gilt-edged invitations to dine "to meet Miss Baker." Late in the afternoon of the party day, I returned from Casablanca to find the two hosts waiting for me at the villa. They were in despair. They had no idea how many people were coming or what they should do with them when they came. I asked them for their list, but they couldn't even remember whom they had asked. I sat down to try to think of everyone in town I knew who *might* be coming and then asked them to try to remember who had told them they *might* come. With this skeleton list, I went around to the Menebhi palace, and started arranging the tables.

Within a few hours, at least a hundred guests began arriving. I stayed at the door, trying desperately to write down the names on place cards as the guests thronged in. Then, magically, numerous tables were pulled out of back hallways, and amidst a magnificent oriental confusion, jazzed up a bit for the occasion by Josephine Baker, with calla lilies and jungle-like decorations, Berber and Arab dancers, singers, American Negro Red Cross workers, white officers, civilians, women war correspondents, and Moors ranging from pure white through to chocolate brown—all had a magnificent time. It would have done some American politicians a great deal of good to see how free, how gay, natural and simple an atmosphere was created amidst this fusion of races. From the roof tops, as always, the white-clad veiled Arab women looked down into the courtyard to watch the party. It was certainly the binding cement of Islam that made this racial fusion, not only possible, but delightful. And, the fusion of races was nothing to the fusion of oriental music and jazz, and the babel of languages— everyone, from Vincent Sheean, Archie Roosevelt, and Inez Robb to obscure Arab palace politicians conversing in a jumble of English, French and faltering Arabic.

It was a far cry from this unreal, moonlit scene to the great political world which suddenly reached out to touch the little oasis city of Marrakech.

On January 2, 1943, I was ordered to Casablanca to see General Hyde of the Air Transport Command, who was flying in from near Dakar. I arrived at Casa only to be met by General Alfred Grunther, General Clark's brilliant and delightful Chief of Staff, and an English friend of mine, Colonel William Sterling, who told me to go right back to Marrakech with them. I explained I had been called to Casa by General Hyde, but they told me their request took priority. We flew back together, and lunched at the villa. Before and after lunch, the two officers inspected the villa, keeping up a cryptic conversation in which Grunther kept mentioning, "Our No. 1 man" and, turning to Sterling, "Your No. 1 man." I was thoroughly mystified, but had learned after my years in Africa to take mystery for granted. "How many people can be put up in the villa?" they asked finally, and seemed disappointed that there were only six master bedrooms and six baths. I mentioned the fact that there were a good many servants' rooms, as the lady who owned the villa was a woman of great elegance who had always traveled before the war in her own yacht and brought a large staff of her own servants with her. They inspected each room with ex- clamations of delight, and with a care that left me more mystified than ever. Finally, they took me back into the drawing room, and broke the great news.

"We are about to let you in on a secret which only a handful of people in the whole world know," they said. "In about ten days' time, there is to be a meeting of the American and British heads of state, and it is not yet decided whether it will be in Casablanca or right here in this villa. You see," they added, "while we prefer Casa for the Conference, it is within bombing range of German planes based in the south of France. In case of raids, we have to be ready to move the entire Conference here; otherwise, it will take place at Anfa-Superior." Anfa was a little settlement of snowy white glistening villas huddled around a rather streamlined, modern hotel, where the German Armistice Commission had operated until only a few weeks before. From its green, grass-covered heights, Anfa overlooked the sea on one side and the city of Casa on the other. It was an easy target for bombers.

"Even if there isn't a raid," said Colonel Sterling, "we may have the Conference here if the Prime Minister decides he prefers it to Casa. The Prime Minister would like this place; he has always been fond of Marrakech anyway. In any case, even if the main part of the Conference is held at Anfa, A-1 and B-1 will come down here at the end to be together and away from all the others." (A-1 was the code name for Mr. Roosevelt, and B-1 for Mr. Churchill.)

After fine-combing La Saadia, I took the two men around the town to show them other possible villas and the Hotel Mamounia, for billeting purposes. Then the General and Colonel left, warning me to be ready to commandeer the entire hotel at a few hours' notice, and to find quarters for any French people remaining at the Mamounia. American officers there would be moved to the airport. The Army would supply transportation. I was to be ready to have a barbed wire fence put around the entire hotel and vicinity by Army personnel on short notice. All my plans had to be made in the greatest secrecy.

A few days later, some security men appeared, eagle-eyed and serious, under Mr. Reilly of the White House security staff. This time the villa was looked over in minute detail, not only by him but by electricians searching for traces of dictaphones and the like. Everyone approved of La Saadia because the entire place of three or four acres was surrounded by a high, rose-colored wall, and there was only one entrance. The security experts decided to set up their precautions entirely on the inside so that nothing would be visible from the outside to excite local curiosity. I had to make a plan of the entire property, with the location of all neighboring houses. Then, I had to find out the name of each person, including the Arab servants, who lived in these houses. After this was done, an investigation had to be made of each of these people. It all seemed far-fetched until I reminded myself that the two arch-enemies of the Axis were moving into a country and a city where for two and a half years there had been an enemy Armistice Commission at work on both the French and native population. Then security seemed of capital importance.

Mr. Reilly decided to put the President in an inside bedroom with only one window looking out onto a courtyard. The Prime Minister was given the one next to it after less thought because the British make much less fuss about security than we do.

Then began incredibly complicated preparations. Guards had to be arranged for, and housed in the garage. American mechanics went to work on the villa's cars which had not run since 1939, and on an enormous auto bus the villa's owner had used to transport luggage, guests, and servants from her yacht. Anti-aircraft guns went into place outside the house. Extra transformers were arranged to give additional power for electric lights. (Part of the lighting system went bad during General Marshall's and Admiral King's visit, leaving those two distinguished visitors to bathe, shave, and dress by candle light.) Endless telephones went in next with bright red boxes called "scramblers" to safeguard telephone conversations, a switchboard in a little porter's room at the right of the entrance, and our own exchange on the Army system, "Atlas." There were telephones in every bedroom, on the terrace, in the *salon*, at the door, at the entrance gate, at different places in the garden, so that the secret service men could check the guards. I understood the shortage in the United States as I counted them.

The first visitors were to be the military command. I was told my own staff could run the house when General Marshall, Admiral King and their parties came to visit. When the President came, it was necessary for soldiers to take over everything, and my staff had to leave the premises. Luckily, a very efficient housekeeper and overseer employed by the owner went with the place. My chauffeur was a husky looking Moroccan Jew who liked to talk tough, hated to work, and was quite unmanageable except by me. He held me in awe. (I was much more frightened of him.) The chef, Ali, was an Arab character with a flowing mustache, who seemed to spend most of his time outside the kitchen door with the two kitchen boys, the *fatimas* who did the laundry and cleaning and my nervous but efficient Arab house boy who was always resplendent in white with a scarlet fez. This Arab was known as "Kouskous," and was the son of one of the head *fatimas* who worked in the house. I also had a French house boy named Georges, a most excitable character who, like the rest of the staff, kept going only because of the fabulous Louis, my *maître d'hôtel*. This numerous staff sounds opulent in America, but North Africa is over-populated and since the natives don't care much for work, they are paid very low wages by American standards.

Louis was in his element during all the excitement. He loved anything to do with the Army and was the greatest military snob I have ever known. He was polite to everyone, but almost burst with pride if he could wait on a four-star general or an admiral. Mr. Roosevelt and Mr. Churchill were demi-gods to him, and he walked on the clouds all the time they were there.

Finally, amid intense excitement in the kitchen courtyard, General Marshall arrived with a party which included Field Marshal Sir John Dill and Brigadier Dykes, who was killed in an airplane crash at Gibraltar on his way home from the Conference. Dykes was a delightful man who loved America deeply and sincerely. He was in high good humor during his visit, and later told a mutual friend that he felt as if he were in the Arabian Nights. "I wanted to wear a turban and those big oriental trousers there," he said. "I felt like an Esquire cartoon."

I was struck at once with the thoughtfulness and simplicity of General Marshall. Seldom have I met anyone who so completely fitted that hackneyed phrase "the perfect gentleman." The first thing he said to me, before I even showed him to his room, was: "Would you be so kind as to show me the room you have assigned to Field Marshal Dill? You know he is my guest, and I want to make sure that he is comfortable."

We had tea on the terrace in the sun where Louis, beaming, had prepared a magnificent display of fruit juices, tea, whiskey and soda, sandwiches and cakes. More men in uniform arrived and were beginning to help themselves under Louis' guidance when I noticed an older man, sitting entirely by himself, with no one near him and nothing to eat or drink. He was obviously a high-ranking admiral, and although I had never seen a picture of Admiral King, I suspected it must be he. I went over to play the host and found him definitely and gruffly uninterested in eating or drinking. Finally, I drew up a chair, thinking the least I could do was to engage him in polite conversation. He was in no mood for that, either, and didn't even want to see his room. I didn't give up, however, thinking it would be impolite. Finally, he must have felt it was a losing battle, for he took some tea, and then began to talk delightfully. I saw that we were being eyed with some amazement by the others, but I knew nothing then of his hair-raising reputation for temper. I suppose they were waiting for me to be consumed in the King fires.

Everyone was fascinated by the house and the garden. They all climbed the tower. Then, General Arnold and General Somervell and the lesser fry, like any tourists, wanted to go and buy souvenirs and sight-see in Marrakech. I went along myself to act as guide, partly because I had been told that wild rumors were already flying around the town. I told the generals of my misgivings about "security," and General Arnold told me to handle things myself, and that they would follow me. Field Marshal Dill and General Marshall stayed at the villa, and talked together on the tower, while Admiral King rested before dinner.

I had the cars stop some distance from the Place Djemaa El Fna, and we proceeded on foot, but just what I feared began to happen. The Arabs, who knew nothing of American insignia of rank, guessed at once that the men with me were not just ordinary officers but something special. The more we circulated around the Place, the more the excitement grew. The generals wanted to explore the *souks* where they hoped to buy souvenirs, but, knowing what the Arabs were saying, I led them to the top of a hotel from which they could get a safe, bird's-eye view of the whole market. I then took them by a back route to the cars, and although nothing whatever happened, I was greatly relieved when I got them safely back to the villa. General Arnold was especially full of enthusiasm and curiosity for everything he saw, and would have been a most delightful person to take on long sight-seeing expeditions. The next day, the German radio announced that the entire American High Command were at that very moment staying at the villa of Mr. Pendar, the American vice consul at Marrakech. The Arab-Axis underground was as efficient as our own had been before the landings.

I shall always remember dinner that night. The whole atmosphere was set by the dignity, sincerity and good humor of Field Marshal Dill, a great friend of the United States, whose death was a real blow to Anglo-American relations. Everyone, in fact, was in a good mood. Admiral King, and General Marshall were in splendid humor. Everyone seemed delighted with the success of the North African landing. I was amused to note that after dinner, the great men went off to bed early, while the lesser fry sat around in the drawing room telling yarns. I shall never forget the sort of glow of pride that came over me that night as I saw English and American characters again. Their intelligence, energy and good humor were like a shot in the arm for an American too long exposed to foreign personalities and I felt a million times repaid for the long black pre-landing period. I was especially drawn to Admiral King, because he was so grudgingly good-humored and so wonderfully tough. I could picture him barking out orders from his flag ship, and having the oceans themselves change position.

The next morning, the party was called while it was still dark to be ready to leave the Marrakech airfield at 8:00 A. M. As we collected in front of the villa, I offered a lift to the airport in my tiny yellow Renault to anyone who wanted it. In the half light, I heard someone say: "Would you have room for me?" I said, "Certainly, come along," and then looked around and saw it was General Marshall, himself. It was arranged for trucks to go ahead with anti-aircraft guns, and others to follow the procession of cars from the villa to the airport. General Marshall and I started ahead of the heavily armed *cortège*, as there had been no provision for my car to be part of it. All along the road about a mile and a half long, were countless Arabs on mule-back and on foot. They seemed more curious than ever as we went by. On the way, General Marshall told me that he never would forget one week-end when he had planned to go to Virginia for a day's shooting on his first holiday since the war began. Everything was set, and his wife, who wanted him to take a rest, was particularly anxious he should go. He came home only to tell her that the trip had to be called off, because he couldn't get away. His wife told him that he always thought everything was so important that he would never take a rest. "Actually," he said, "this was the time Mr. Murphy came to Washington, and all the final plans were made, the date and hour definitely set, and the whole strategy minutely planned, for the North African landing."

After the military left, I was told to stand by for a possible stop-over by the Prime Minister or the President. To our intense disappointment, the weather at Casablanca was clear, and both of their planes flew straight through. At Casablanca, the top men used a new, large airfield at a small village, about nine or ten miles back from the coast. They were driven to town in closed cars that had the windows deliberately spattered with mud so no one could see who was inside. This technique became routine during the Casablanca Conference. Around the airport, you often saw soldiers working up mud, like nursery children, and slinging it with infinite satisfaction at a clean, polished sedan or limousine.

My next orders were to be ready to receive Mr. Roosevelt and Mr. Churchill, and to arrange the taking over of the Hotel Mamounia on a few hours' notice. By now, the rumors flying around Morocco were frenzied. I was told on the best authority that the King of England and Pétain were in Marrakech, that Stalin had been seen walking in my garden, and that Mussolini was observed admiring the view from the tower of the villa. Even the Pope had been seen.

All this, while Louis was happily training the G.I.'s who had been put on the villa detail in European etiquette. I shall never forget one day when I kept hearing the strangest noises in the dining room. I looked in. There was Louis in charge of what looked to me like scores of soldiers. Fourteen chairs were drawn up to the table with a bemused Yank in each one of them. Before the carefully set table stood Louis, himself immaculate in his short white coat, with another detail of half a dozen G.I.'s. Each of the standing soldiers had a huge platter, and Louis instructed them as they proceeded solemnly and hesitatingly around the table, to serve the ranking guests first. I nearly broke his heart by telling him to stop weaving in and out and just pass the food to each person in turn. Louis felt I was letting the whole tone of the house down.

Occasionally, some of the people at the Conference would take a few hours off to fly down to lunch and sight-see in Marrakech. Field Marshal Sir Harold Alexander turned up, and one day we had the pleasure of entertaining Lord Louis Mountbatten and some members of his staff. Mountbatten had a buoyancy and gaiety that I have rarely seen. He had the sort of easy assurance that less gifted people often interpret as a lack of seriousness. One of the finest men I have ever met, Air Chief Marshal Sir Arthur Tedder also visited, and, like Prime Minister Churchill, made sketches of the views from La Saadia.

I used to go to Anfa for the day quite often, especially when Robert Murphy was there, to discuss the French situation. One day photographers were called in to take the famous picture of Generals de Gaulle and Giraud standing in front of the President and Mr. Churchill, awkwardly shaking hands. People from London to San Francisco sighed with relief and said: "At last, the French are united and we can get on with the war." Unfortunately, this was not the case. American and British diplomats at Casablanca knew the difficulties that had to be overcome even to get the picture taken. In the picture itself the handshake of these two French leaders gave not the slightest illusion of friendship.

In the photograph were all the elements of the ensuing drama— Prime Minister Churchill with his creation, General de Gaulle; and President Roosevelt with the man we were backing to lead the French armies, General Giraud. Both Mr. Roosevelt and Mr. Churchill were concentrated on the potentiality of France's military effort. They fully realized that before anything could be done, some unity had to be established between the two existing French factions. With this aim in view, the President had asked General Giraud to come on from Algiers to discuss the future military role of the French. Mr. Churchill had sent a similar invitation to General de Gaulle in London. General Giraud responded at once and arrived at Casablanca. General de Gaulle, however, did not even reply to his invitation. He had to be reminded by the British that his Free French movement depended financially on the goodwill of the British Government and the Prime Minister. Even then, two or three telegrams, each less polite than the last, had to be dispatched to de Gaulle before he finally arrived in Casablanca. It was at this meeting that General Giraud formally asked General de Gaulle to join him at once in the Tunisian war against the Germans. This de Gaulle refused to do.

After the President's and the Prime Minister's painful attempt to bring de Gaulle and Giraud if not together, at least into their first official contact with each other, Murphy had a long interview with de Gaulle. He officially invited de Gaulle, at this time, to take charge of North Africa. It is most important to remember, in judging our French policy, that de Gaulle not only declined this invitation but told Murphy, in so many words, that he, de Gaulle, did not have enough influence to do this. He estimated at this time, he said, that only 10% of the North African French would support him. Later, many sincere de Gaullists claimed that North Africa was pro-de Gaulle and that "reactionaries" in the State Department were keeping him from assuming his rightful place there. The fact of the matter, as de Gaulle himself realized, was quite different.

A small but significant clue to de Gaulle's intense nationalism also appeared during the Conference. When Mr. Murphy went to see de Gaulle in the villa which had been requisitioned for his use, he learned that de Gaulle had only agreed to enter the villa after he learned that it was not owned by a Frenchman but by a foreigner. Otherwise, he felt, the use of the villa for Conference purposes was an infringement on French sovereignty. This was the first indication we had of the attitude de Gaulle later took toward the Clark-Darlan Agreements. One of his basic objections to them was that they gave the American forces the right of requisition to help fight the North African campaign. (Actually, we never used this right except at Anfa. All other requisitioning was done by the French for us, and on the whole, done well.)

The Casablanca-Anfa Conference was the first time, incidentally, that American diplomats, on the spot, realized the full force of the storm that had blown up at home over the North African political situation. Averell Harriman, who was Lend-Lease Administrator in London at this time, came to see Murphy and told him frankly of the violent criticisms in the English press. At the same time, American newspaper clippings and magazine articles began to arrive in droves, almost all acid, suspicious, and anti-Murphy. This came as a distinct shock to Murphy and to all of us. We realized for the first time what a magnificent propaganda job was being done by the de Gaullist forces, for their party line was evident in many articles, and how completely it had already affected British and American opinion. Looking back on it, I believe this propaganda was, next to our own hesitancy in using a vigorous hand, the biggest single factor in our diplomatic defeat. It put enormous difficulties in the way of holding to our original French policy of keeping politics in abeyance until after the war. Both Mr. Roosevelt and Mr. Churchill eventually had to respond to this home front pressure.

In spite of this growing body of de Gaullist opinion at home, the Prime Minister was at this time supposed to be completely in sympathy with American policy. In fact, our policy had been greatly influenced by Mr. Churchill's expressed opinion of de Gaulle, and Mr. Churchill, himself, was believed to have gradually admitted the definite advantages to be gained by the American relations with Vichy. Casablanca was the culmination of the American-French policy as guided and shaped by President Roosevelt.

There is no question about the fact that, at Casablanca, the President was deeply preoccupied with the future of France. I heard this repeatedly from people who talked to him, and saw it myself in our brief contact. He was convinced of the importance of a revived, rejuvenated France in Europe. He was worried, like the French themselves, by the way in which French manpower was rotting in German prison camps and factories, the way in which the French birth rate was falling while the death rate was increasing. It was with this in mind that Mr. Roosevelt and Mr. Churchill drew up the Anfa agreements for rearming the French Army. This remained the keystone of our French policy until de Gaulle, and his backers in the British Foreign Office, threw us off center. This rearmament, this attempt to bring France back into the Great Power class, was important not only for the sake of France herself, but for Allied military reasons.

Under the President's plan, the new French Army was to be made up of Frenchmen in North Africa and all over the world, and also from the great masses of native Moroccans, Algerians and Senegalese on whom France has traditionally relied for superb troops. It was to number at least 500,000 men, with the possibility of growing to a million, all armed and equipped by us. Though it would have taken time to train this Army to use our latest weapons, our leaders at Anfa felt that it could be done in time to have Frenchmen play a real part in the liberation of France, and in time to release many American troops for the Japanese war.

All these hopes were destroyed by de Gaulle's unwillingness to coöperate. Though he finally signed an innocuous document establishing the principle of agreement with Giraud, in practice, as will be seen later, he refused to take any part in an over-all, non-partisan attempt to create a really national French Army.

The psychological reasons for this have often been discussed. De Gaulle's temperament is public knowledge today. His interview with the President at Anfa, at which he first demonstrated his curious egoism to Mr. Roosevelt, has been described, but I think not completely accurately. I was told by high authority at the time that it went something like this:

President Roosevelt told de Gaulle that France was in such dire military straits that she needed a general of Napoleonic caliber. "*Mais, je suis cet homme,*" said de Gaulle. She was, went on the President, in such a bad financial state that she also needed a Colbert. "*Mais,*" said de Gaulle simply, "*je suis cet homme.*" Finally, said the President, controlling his amazement, she was so devitalized politically that she needed a Clemenceau. De Gaulle drew himself up with dignity and said: "*Mais, je suis cet homme.*" It was this interview that made the President realize the full extent of the psychological problem de Gaulle presented.

Before the President and the Prime Minister came to Marrakech, the President went to Rabat to review American troops. This was the first time that Moroccans could confirm the rumor that the President was there. One Frenchman never forgot the episode. The troops were living in tents outside Rabat in the Aguedal forest of pine trees, on high ground overlooking Rabat to the sea. Every day the local baker came out from Rabat with the bread he had baked for the Army. He was there this particular day, chatting casually with the soldiers when the order to come to attention was given. No one could leave the encampment ground. The baker, forced to stay, was on the side of the road when the jeep bearing Mr. Roosevelt drove up. During the ceremonies, the President noticed this civilian and asked who he was. On being told it was the local baker, he characteristically spoke to him in French and shook him by the hand. When the baker returned to Rabat, he told everybody he had shaken hands with President Roosevelt. Everyone thought he had quite literally gone mad, but a few days later, when the pictures of the review appeared in the local papers, he became a sort of hero, and his shop was crowded all day long by French and Arabs anxious to touch the hand that had touched Mr. Roosevelt's.

The President, also, went to the Royal Palace for a *diffa* (banquet) with the Sultan. I was not at this dinner, but the President told me about it afterwards. It had made a great impression on him. The French Resident General was present, as he always is in any contact the Sultan may have with foreigners, to insulate the Moors from any foreign influence. Yet, during this dinner, the President and the Sultan had a long talk together out of earshot of the Resident General, an episode extremely irritating to local French officialdom. It was, I believe, the first time in the history of Morocco that the Sultan had met the head of any other foreign state than France. While the French fumed, however, the Sultan and the very politically-minded Moors were overjoyed. They didn't, to my surprise, jump to the conclusion that we were going to take over the Protectorate, but they did see themselves being treated, at last, as a sovereign state. They considered this a proof of our sincerity in the Atlantic Charter. It was amusing later to find that almost every Arab in Morocco thought he knew the whole story of this *diffa* and everything that was said, just as if he had been there. I'm sure every detail of King Farouk's, Haile Selassie's and Ibn Saud's visits to the President at Cairo were known to their subjects in the same way.

When I was finally told that the President and Prime Minister were coming down to stay at La Saadia on Sunday, January, 24, I had another call from the White House security people, arranging every minute detail of the visit. More ramps for Mr. Roosevelt's wheel-chair had to be made, and the ones already made put in place so that he could be wheeled anywhere in the house and garden and at the same time walk (with railings) in case he wanted to. They had to be placed carefully and inconspicuously so they wouldn't be constant reminders to him and to everyone else of his infirmity.

Then came the big day. All the staff including Louis were told to leave the house, but Louis later got a special dispensation when the Lieutenant put in charge of the household detail had a nervous break-down over his responsibilities, and had to be locked up in his room with the liquor he too obviously enjoyed.

Just before lunch on Sunday, an airplane load of luggage, some security men, and the Prime Minister's and President's personal servants arrived. Prettyman, the President's colored valet, slept on a couch in the library, so as to be in a room connecting with the President's. Sawyers, the Prime Minister's servant, was a character. When I showed him his master's room which was a show piece in Morocco, I said: "Well, Sawyers, I hope your master will be comfortable here." Sawyers looked sadly around the room, and said in a dull, flat voice: "Oh, it isn't too bad, I think it will do." Much amused, I turned to leave, saying: "Why, damn it, Sawyers, you are now in the finest bedroom in all of North Africa, if not on the whole bloody continent." With this, Sawyers came running after me, and said: "It is lovely, sir. Thank you, sir. Very good, sir." I went in to see how Prettyman was making out, and I found him smiling from ear to ear as he installed the President's things, his dark, friendly face looking incongruous in that atmosphere of ornate carvings and sunken marble bath tubs.

I had been told that the President's and the Prime Minister's parties would leave Anfa by motor just before lunch, and that they were taking a picnic lunch with them to eat on the way. I sat with some of the officers of the guard in the big *salon* to wait. Every half hour, we would get a bulletin by telephone. "They are now passing through Settat, going at about 35 miles an hour," then again, "They have stopped to lunch by the roadside." It was like listening to a radio description of the Grand National. Suddenly, came the final call: "The party is now turning toward the villa and should arrive in ten minutes."

In a few minutes, a huge Daimler limousine, painted olive drab, rolled up. In the back seat, serenely chatting, were the President and the Prime Minister. Plain-clothes-men jumped from the front of the car and the one behind it and ran straight for me. "Who are you?" they asked. I explained that I lived in this house and had been instructed to act as host.

With this, Mr. Churchill alighted, came up and shook me warmly by the hand. On the other side of the car, I saw men busying themselves with a wheel-chair, and assisting Mr. Roosevelt out of the car. He was, as prearranged, to be wheeled around through the garden to the terrace and from there could more easily enter the house without having to go up the six or seven steps to the front door. I entered the house with the Prime Minister and showed him to his room, and then went out through the drawing room to the terrace to meet the President and show him to his room, in turn. Both men were in overcoats because, out of the sun, the Moroccan air had a cool edge to it.

Shortly, everyone came out onto the terrace again where Louis had set up a tea service that looked like an Oriental potentate's. As Mr. Churchill came into the *salon*, he said: "Well, Pendar, I must say your soldiers get the beauty prize. In my whole life, I have never seen such a magnificent lot of men as those American soldiers who lined the road on our way down here." Guards had been posted the entire one hundred and fifty miles from Casa to Marrakech. We all sat on the terrace in the warming sun, overlooking the emerald green pool and the garden. Opposite the terrace, above the garden wall, hung a large piece of green canvas between two cedar trees, to blot out a window in a nearby house from which the terrace of La Saadia could be seen.

Both Mr. Roosevelt and Mr. Churchill seemed to be in high spirits, and spoke with admiration of the superb view of the Atlas Mountains they had seen for the last fifty miles or so of their journey. This was the President's first trip to Morocco, but the Prime Minister had been in Marrakech before, and had even gone up into the Atlas to the *casbah* of the Glaoui at Telouet. As we drank our tea, Robert Hopkins, Harry Hopkins' son, made movies of the occasion.

Soon, as invariably happened at La Saadia, people began to speak of the beauties of the house and garden. I saw Mr. Churchill gazing up at the house and tower and, finally, he came up to me and asked if I would be kind enough to show him the tower. As we climbed up, I saw his shrewd eyes taking in everything. From the open terrace, he told me how much he loved Marrakech and how much he had enjoyed sketching here before the war, during his last visit. Finally, he said, "Don't you believe, Pendar, that it can be arranged for the President to be brought up here? I am so fond of this superb view that it has been my dream to see it with him. All during the Conference I have looked forward to coming down here to this beautiful spot."

We went down to ask the President and, on the way, Mr. Churchill carefully counted the steps. On the terrace again, he turned to Mr. Roosevelt and said, "Mr. President, both Mr. Pendar and I are most anxious for you to see the view from the tower. It is unique. Do you think you could be persuaded to make the trip?" We had already spoken with the President's attendants who would have to do the carrying as the staircase was too narrow for a chair. The President replied: "I have every intention of going up there if these good men can take me."

Two men carried the President up with his arms around their shoulders, while another went ahead to open doors, and the rest of the entire party followed. The Prime Minister suggested that someone bring along a wicker chair so the President could rest if he wanted to *en route*. The Prime Minister and I brought up the rear of the party. He was in high spirits, and kept humming and singing to himself a little tune with the words: "Oh, there ain't no war, there ain't no war." The President didn't rest *en route*, but amidst much laughing on his part and sympathizing with his carriers went straight up to the open terrace, some sixty steps above. There, the chair was arranged for him close to the parapet where he could command the entire view of the Great Atlas range.

We all looked out for a quarter of an hour or so at this most superb view. Never have I seen the sun set on those snow capped peaks with such magnificence. There had evidently been snow storms recently in the mountains, for they were white almost to their base, and looked more wild and rugged than ever, their sheer walls rising some 12,000 feet before us. The range runs more or less to east and west, and the setting sun over the palm oasis to our right shed a pink light on the snowy flank of the mountains. With the clear air, and the snow on the range, it looked near enough to touch its magnificence. As the sun went down, the air grew chilly, and the Prime Minister seeing the President had shed his coat at tea on the sunny terrace, sent someone down for it and, himself, put it over the President's shoulders. From where we sat, we could see the whole town of Marrakech below us, its walls a deeper rose than usual, its mosque towers rising high in the rosy light.

The whole town is dominated by the famous Koutoubiya tower and the President asked me about it. I told him how it had been built by Arab invaders at the end of the Twelfth Century, and that it was designed by the same architect who had built the more famous Giralda tower in Seville, and the unfinished tower of Hassan in Rabat, as well as the magnificent ruined tower in Tclemcen in Algeria.

Just as the sun set (we were all silent) the electric light on the top of every mosque tower in Marrakech flashed on to indicate to the faithful the hour of prayer. There was a feeling of suppressed drama in the landscape at this moment, heightened by the beauty of the mountains and the thickening light. The points of electric light on all the mosque towers was like a gong announcing the end of the day. From where we were, we could see the going and coming of the in-numerable Arabs on camel and mule back, as they made their way in and out of the city gate of Bab Khemis. Both Mr. Roosevelt and Mr. Churchill were spellbound by the view, but it became perceptibly colder, and the whole party started down again. (Marrakech is too hot in the sun, even in winter, but at night, the water in the fountains sometimes freezes.)

The great men went to their rooms to rest and dress before dinner, while the younger fry had drinks in the *salon*. The gaily painted shutters and the great doors leading out onto the terrace had been closed, the central heating had been turned on, and lights turned up that showed off the beauties of the ceiling decoration.

Cocktails were at eight o'clock, and dinner at eight fifteen. There were thirty people staying in the house, but the main dining room could only hold fourteen, so the others ate in the servants' dining room. When I reached the *salon* at eight, the President had left his wheel-chair, and was alone, stretched out on one of the couches at the far end of the *salon* near the dining room door. As I came up to him, he put out his hand to me, and said with an engaging smile: "I am the Pasha, you may kiss my hand." Then the others arrived, the Prime Minister in what has been called his "siren suit," heavy blue flannel, made like a union suit with a belt that buckled over his well-rounded figure, and wearing black velvet slippers, like pumps, with "W. C." embroidered on them. The President had an "old fashioned," and the others one of Louis' magnificent concoctions, a sort of cross between a "side-car" and a "martini." Louis always carefully made one cocktail for each guest and no more: seconds could be had only if someone refused the first round.

When dinner was announced, the President was wheeled up to his place and then transferred into one of the mammoth dining room chairs. I had the honor of sitting between the Prime Minister and the President, with Averell Harriman and Harry Hopkins beyond.

Louis outdid himself, with Army help, on the dinner, which included lobster, *filet mignon*, salad with *pâté*, and a peculiarly magnificent dessert, which arrived after an agonizing pause (for the host), and was a complete surprise to me. It was a *profiterolle*, a *pièce montée* as Louis proudly called it—at least three feet high, a reproduction in nougat of the Koutoubiya tower with a candle inside to make the effect still more dazzling, and a sort of substructure of spun sugar, perhaps representing the Atlas.

The Prime Minister turned to me and said: "I see the pastry cooks have been busy for days and days, preparing for our secret visit." Then, he looked incredulously at the platter and said: "How on earth does one attack a thing like that? That's easy," he added, and looking up at the soldier passing it, said with a smile, "My man, you should pass that to the President first." The soldier stepped around to the President, who said: "Why that's easy, Winston, this is the way you do it," and he took the top off the Koutoubiya tower, and laid it on his plate.

My first conversation at dinner was with the President. He told me about his talk with the Sultan and the extraordinary interest he found the Sultan took in America and everything American. We then talked at length about Morocco and the Arab problem. To my amazement and delight, I found that the President had an extraordinary and profound grasp of Arab problems, of the conflict of Koranic law with our type of modern life and its influence on Mohammedans, and of the Arab character with its combination of materialism and highly developed intuition. He even had all the facts of our unique diplomatic position in Morocco at his finger tips, down to the names of the treaties and the dates. (I must have become over-enthusiastic in this conversation with the President for, some six months later, when I was in London talking with Averell Harriman, he began to laugh and said: "I will never forget your conversation with the President. I enjoyed hearing you explain to him, in no uncertain terms, that the New Deal simply wouldn't work in Morocco.")

I told the President that his letter to the Sultan had caused much excitement among the Arabs, and that they had been flattered to be treated, for once, with the respect they felt due their sovereignty. The President said that the Sultan's answer to his letter was not of the quality or tone he would expect from the man he dined with the other night. He seemed much interested in the Moroccan gossip that there were actually two answers to his letter, one written by the Sultan, himself, and the other by his Grand Vizier.

My next conversation was with the Prime Minister. I asked him about de Gaulle; he looked annoyed and replied with a typical Churchillian phrase: "Oh, let's don't speak of him. We call him Jeanne d'Arc and we're looking for some bishops to burn him." After this, our conversation grew into a three-cornered, half-joking one with Mr. Hopkins, who began teasing both the Prime Minister and the President about how little work they had done at Anfa. He said, "You seem to think you've accomplished a lot of work at Casablanca, but Murphy really did the work, and you know it." The Prime Minister said: "Now, Harry, when you get back, urge on everyone the importance of getting arms over here as quickly as possible. It's the only way to build up the French." A moment later, he added: "You know, Harry, you missed your vocation. You would have been a great strategical general."

When I turned to the President again, I told him I had just had word from England that a very dear friend of mine, Lady Berkeley, had lost her husband. I knew this would interest Mr. Roosevelt because Lady Berkeley was a close friend and cousin of his. He was distressed to hear the news, and later I learned that he wrote her a long letter. It was Lord Berkeley, he said, who had taught him to swim when he was a little boy at Homburg, where he had gone with his mother who was taking the cure. "And," he added in the letter, "you know, Molly, what swimming has meant to me in my life."

In the course of dinner, I heard the President express his deep admiration for the French and French civilization, and his deep concern for France's future. There was much talk about the French Army and the wisdom in building it up to the greatest possible size in order to give back to France not only her self-respect but her great-power status, so necessary to the democratic Atlantic world.

Once dinner was finished, the President proposed a toast "To the King." Everyone, except the President, rose to his feet, then the Prime

Minister proposed a toast "To the President."

I was struck by the fact that, though Mr. Churchill spoke much more amusingly than the President, it was Mr. Roosevelt who dominated any room they were in, not merely because he was President of the United States, but because he had more spiritual quality than Mr. Churchill, and, I could not help but feel, a more profound understanding of human beings. I was very much surprised by this because, having seen Mr. Churchill often in the pre-war days, I had felt sure that no one could eclipse his personality.

About midnight, we left the dining room, and found a table laid out with drinks and a mighty display of sandwiches and other tidbits. Louis had outdone himself again. After a nibble or two, the two great men set to work. The problem was to arrange a temporary sort of writing table for them and adequate light: the *salon* at La Saadia was not meant for work. We finally perched a lamp up high on two tables, so as to give adequate light, and arranged two chairs on either side. Then, Mr. Hopkins and Mr. Harriman sat down to work with them. They were composing a summary of the Anfa Conference and messages to General Chiang Kai Shek and Marshal Stalin. The Prime Minister's two secretaries, Mr. Rowan and Mr. Martin, were established in the library, typing and drafting these documents. Mr. Hopkins and Mr. Harriman would take parts of them to their separate rooms and work on them and then come back into the *salon* and show them to the Big Two. The rest of us went outside into the courtyard, and some of the party went to bed. From time to time, work would stop for a moment, and we would all be called in for a drink or a sandwich, and a joke or two. At one point, the President was wheeled into his room so that he could work alone at a dressing table which he used as a desk.

Finally, about 3:30 A. M., the documents were composed and in final order. Both men seemed much relieved and very pleased. The whole atmosphere of the evening was that of the end of a long period of work, successfully accomplished. Both men had a catching quality of optimism, but with the President, I kept feeling that it was tinged with a deep realization of far distant and over-all problems. The Prime Minister seemed much more in the present and more of an extrovert. The President, on the other hand, often sat gazing into space as he worked. That night, he had a look that was not exactly sad, yet it was the look of someone who comprehended sadness.

During the working period, I heard strange noises in the back court. I went out to investigate, and found Sawyers had misjudged the strength of Moroccan wine but was still full of cockney dignity. Louis assured me that the Prime Minister's hot water bottle was already in place, and that Sawyers wouldn't be missed.

As the party collected in the *salon* for a final night-cap, the Prime Minister moved over and relaxed on the sofa where the President had sat before dinner. The President turned to him and said: "Now, Winston, don't you get up in the morning to see me off. I'll be wheeled into your room to kiss you goodbye." "Not at all, Mr. President," said Mr. Churchill, "I can get into my rompers in two twos, and I'll be on hand to see you off." His "siren suit" did indeed look like blue-grey rompers as he sat relaxed on the sofa with his round figure and his gay pink and white face.

I think that only once did I hear the Prime Minister call the President "Franklin," and I am not wholly sure of that. He invariably called him Mr. President. The President, on the other hand, almost always called Mr. Churchill "Winston."

The President's departure was scheduled for 7:30 A. M. from the villa, and the airplane was to leave at 8:00. Prompt as royalty, the President was wheeled out to the front steps at 7:30. He had breakfasted in his room. Only the Prime Minister and I went to the airport to see him off. All the Americans left with the President except Averell Harriman, who took a plane later in the morning to Gibraltar and London. (It was this plane that crashed at Gibraltar, killing Brigadier Dykes, but only shaking up Mr. Harriman.) I gave him, as I did everyone who went to England, great baskets of oranges, lemons and grapefruit, forgotten wonders in England, to take with him to London.

The Prime Minister and the President rode together. When we reached the airport, there was a cordon of guards all around the field, almost invisible in the early morning mist that hung over the field. Above this mist, one could see the clearly outlined and sunlit peaks of the Great Atlas range. Lying at their feet like a great bird was the magnificent airplane to take the President back home, a wooden ramp up its side. As soon as we arrived, Mr. Churchill jumped out and ran up the ramp to see where the President was going to sit. This time, the Prime Minister had on the weirdest outfit I have ever seen. The base was his "siren suit." He also wore his black velvet slippers with W.C. on them, an Air Marshal's blue cap, and, over his suit, a dressing gown with a black velvet collar and cuffs, made out of what looked like a patchwork quilt. With all this, he had the inevitable huge cigar.

On his way down the ramp the cameramen started to take a picture of the Prime Minister in this very original costume. He stopped, took the cigar out of his mouth, and using it as a pointer, shook it at them with a smile on his face and said "You simply can not do this to me." They all laughed and lowered their cameras. Mr. Churchill said goodbye to the President at the foot of the ramp, then, turning to me, said: "Come, Pendar, let's go home. I don't like to see them take off."

We climbed into the limousine, and I looked out of the back window to see the plane start up. By then, the engines were roaring, the sun was breaking through the mist with a magnified brilliance, and the outlines of the mountains and the palm oasis around us became more distinct. The field and the surrounding country were so flat that the airport seemed the biggest in the world. Although the plane was enormous, it looked tiny in all that space. Mr. Churchill said: "Don't tell me when they take off. It makes me far too nervous." Then, putting his hand on my arm, he went on: "If anything happened to that man, I couldn't stand it. He is the truest friend; he has the farthest vision; he is the greatest man I've ever known." With this, we lapsed into silence. A little later, he asked, "Pendar, don't you think your countrymen will be thrilled when they hear that their President has flown here with the courage of an eagle, and has seen and reviewed the troops in the theatre of battle? Don't you think they will be universally thrilled by this, and that it will catch their imagination?" I could only agree, adding that we are, however, a very unpredictable people. Mr. Churchill's comment made me realize, however, that the President must have thought very long before making the decision to come to Morocco, a decision which, apparently, Mr. Churchill had encouraged.

Just as we approached the villa, a French officer friend of mine rode by on his horse. Almost snarling, the Prime Minister said: "Look at that little yellow Frenchman. Why isn't he fighting?" I said, "I don't think you can say that about that particular man. He's a friend of mine, and I know how desperately anxious he is to fight." At this point, a couple of Arabs went by on mule back, and the Prime Minister was distracted. He quickly held up two fingers in the V sign for victory. They stared at us in amazement and delight.

Back at the villa, we went in to breakfast and found the rest of the party at table. Sir Charles Wilson (now Lord Moran) the Prime Minister's doctor, who was always vainly trying to cut down the Prime Minister's smoking, sat opposite. Mr. Churchill looked at him jauntily and said, rolling his cigar around in his mouth: "There is one nice thing, Sir Charles, about getting up early in the morning. You can get in an extra cigar." After some coffee, Mr. Churchill retired to bed again, and an hour or two later, Field Marshal Sir Alan Brooke, the head of the Imperial Staff, arrived with other officers.

Soon, there was a terrific commotion outside the Prime Minister's room, and I was told he was in a vile humor storming around the blue-green-and-silver bed like a furious cherub. Finally, there were loud shouts of "Sawyers, my painting things. Please put them out on the tower." A sigh of relief went through the British officers. This, I learned, meant the humor had changed to a good one. I sent in word that luncheon would be at one o'clock on the terrace. About eleven o'clock, the Prime Minister emerged in a smock and an enormous hat, and went up to the tower where he began painting the view we had admired the night before. He worked under an umbrella, and the silhouette of the Prime Minister and the umbrella could be seen all over Marrakech, verifying all the rumors that were flying around. This picture, incidentally, turned out very well, and was sent to the President as a souvenir of the visit.*

The Prime Minister was in towering good spirits at luncheon. By this time, even the American guards had left the property, and had been replaced by British Marine guards, beautifully trained and very military. As we sat at table, we could see the guard across the garden marching up and down with magnificent precision on the path next to the wall. Right beside us on the terrace, walking up and down around the corner of the villa outside the Prime Minister's bedroom,

* It is now in the Roosevelt Memorial Library at Hyde Park.

was another Marine guard in battle dress, with gun and tin hat jauntily cocked over one eye. Each time he made his turns, as he arrived at the terrace where we were, then walked away and made a half-turn to go on toward the front door, the turn was a work of art. Never have I seen anything so precise or so deliberate. During the whole meal, this fascinated the Prime Minister, and twice he got up from his seat and ran down to the corner of the house to watch the guard turn by the front door. He came back each time saying: "Isn't he wonderful, that guard? Have you ever seen such perfection?"

It was a beautiful day, and the sunlight dappled the white flower-embroidered tablecloth through the leaves of the olive tree that shaded us. As Louis brought on *hors-d'oeuvres*, then a kidney pie, and finally, *tournedos*, the Prime Minister, smacking his lips, and sunk down in his chair, shaded by his big hat, said: "Two meat courses in one meal! Don't tell Lord Woolton" (the British Minister of Supply). During the meal, the Prime Minister spoke of the fusion and closer Anglo-American coöperation that must exist for the future world. In speaking of an eventual common currency for the two countries, he picked up a pencil and on the back of a scrap of paper drew the L-shaped symbol of the pound sterling with a dollar sign superimposed on it, saying, "This is as I see it—the money of the future, the dollar sterling."

As the conversation went on, he turned to me and said: "Pendar, what a wonderful country, this Morocco, all this sunlight, this wonderful air, these flowers. We English have always needed a place like this to come to for sunshine." Then, straightening up in his chair, and making a gesture toward me, he said mockingly: "Now, Pendar, why don't you give us Morocco, and we shall give you India. We shall even give you Ghandi, and he's awfully cheap to keep, now that he's on a hunger strike."

Captain Randolph Churchill, all during luncheon, had been arguing with his father, leading him on in a discussion about the much-discussed Beveridge Plan for Social Security in England. During this conversation, the Prime Minister repeated: "Yes, that's all very well, but some arrangement will have to be made whereby the careful savings made in insurance companies by good earnest widows and poor people aren't just scrapped."

Then the subject shifted again and the Prime Minister described in detail the financial and other problems he had had to deal with in Cyprus when years before he had been in the Colonial Office. Finally, he turned to India. He said, largely for my benefit, I felt: "There are always earnest spinsters in Pennsylvania, Utah, Edinburgh, or Dublin, persistently writing letters and signing petitions and ardently giving their advice to the British Government, urging that India be given back to the Indians and South Africa back to the Zulus or Boers, but," he continued, "as long as I am called by His Majesty the King to be his First Minister, I shall not assist at the dismemberment of the British Empire." Churchill, in conversation, constantly uses phrases from his speeches, and as he talks, appears to be inspired to coin phrases, brilliant ones, and seems mentally to note them down for future use. "And," he continued, at this time, looking across at the Marine guard by the garden wall, "just as I am sure that, if at this moment someone came over the garden wall to attack us while we are lunching here that Marine guard would willingly give his life to protect us; so I shall, with the last drop of energy I have in me, defend His Majesty's Empire; and I hope I can do as good a job as I am certain that Marine would."

After luncheon, he went up again into the tower to finish his picture, and came down about tea time, and sat around the drawing room in a state of vocal indecision as to whether to leave at once or to stay through the night. He couldn't make up his mind whether he should go directly back to England to answer the questions that would come up in the House of Commons as soon as news of the Casablanca Conference was released, or if he should go on east to Cairo and the Turkish frontier where he planned to meet President Ismet Inonu of Turkey, to try to stop up the last hole through which there still was a threat of German aggression. He discussed this all quite openly with everyone, asking their advice. Finally, he left at 6:30 that night for Cairo, by his small plane. Sir Charles Wilson and Commander Thompson asked me to have a supper prepared for them to take in the plane, and gave me the official luncheon basket.

At the airport, Mr. Churchill, unlike the President, would not quietly board his plane and leave, as the guards wanted him to do, but insisted on talking to everyone he saw around, thanking them for their courtesy and attention, and discussing with them any problem that came into his head. I was told that the security people had a terrible time with him wherever he went. Before he left the villa, he handed out some signed photographs to those of the American soldier household staff who had had courage enough to ask him for one. Just as he was leaving, he said to me: "Now, Pendar, I would like to send you a copy of one of my books. Which would you like, 'The Life of Marlborough' or 'The World Crisis'?" I hesitated, and he added: "Oh, we're not out of the world crisis yet. I'll send you 'The Life of Marlborough.' That's over."

The next morning, a steady stream of sightseers, reporters, and soldiers came to ask to see the villa and the gardens where the President and the Prime Minister had stayed. I had several fantastic offers to buy the bed in which the President had slept.

The news of the Casablanca Conference and the Marrakech visit were released on the following Tuesday, just before the President's arrival back in Washington. Shortly after, I flew back to Algiers to report to Murphy, and had the thrill of traveling for the first time in a "Flying Fortress" from which I could see, through the glass nose of the ship, the whole of Morocco and Algeria spread out before me, a mighty sweep of the North Africa I had learned to love so well.

The Conference was over. A short time later, I had the following note from the President:

"That very wonderful collection of prints has come and will always be a reminder to me of my visit to Marrakech. I think that if I had ever done water colors, I would have stayed over with Mr. Churchill.

"What an amazing house you live in! All of our party was struck by the beauty of the house and the gardens, and I think we envied you your post.

"It seemed, and still seems, difficult to realize in those peaceful surroundings that French North Africa has become such a political football. Marrakech seemed far from wars and rumors of wars."

CHAPTER XIII

The Fine Art of Politics

AFTER the Casablanca Conference, de Gaulle for a time seemed much more friendly to both England and America. The British, who had been worried by his flirtations with Moscow, were reassured by his apparent return into the western world, and new efforts were made by their representatives and ours to try to bring all Frenchmen into one fair, carefully planned, provisional government. Giraud took part in this without enthusiasm, he wished to concentrate on the war in Tunisia.

An intense political period now began in Algiers, full of events even more turgid than our pre-landing intrigue or the machinations leading to Darlan's assassination. These post-Conference manoeuvers were what finally made me realize the full dangers of de Gaullism, and turned me from what my French friends called "the most de Gaullist of the American Vice Consuls" into the state of mind that must, by this time, be obvious to the reader. All the doubts and qualms I had had about de Gaulle before, from reading his books, from his speeches, from his intransigeance with us and with other French groups, had been only premonitory twinges, a suspicion that the man I had hoped would restore France to national health might, like many other great men, have feet of clay. By the summer of 1943, I knew that the situation wasn't as simple as that: that de Gaulle, who really is a great man in the Carlyle sense, is great in all the wrong ways, in ways that are ominous for the peace and happiness of France and of Europe. I won't pretend that this was a brilliant discovery of my own: plenty of others knew it then too. But by that time public opinion as a whole had been well mobilized behind de Gaulle.

Well-meaning, honest Giraud undoubtedly helped as much as anyone to bring about the triumph of de Gaulle in North Africa, which meant his political domination later in liberated France. Mr. Murphy tried to steer Giraud, particularly in the matter of cleaning out officials;

tinged with anti-Allied feeling, but Murphy's piloting was never vigorous enough. Rigault pleaded with Giraud during January and February, urging him to make a speech announcing the wiping out of all the restrictive Vichy legislation. Giraud finally did make this speech on the 14th of March, but by that time it was too late. His character had been established by the foreign press and the de Gaullists as a reactionary, Vichy-minded general. He was accused of being anti-Semitic, a manifestly untrue charge. For the Committee of French Liberation, which Giraud later formed with de Gaulle, it was Giraud who nominated two Jewish members, René Mayer, in charge of Communications, and Jules Abadie, in charge of Justice, Education and Health. Rigault, like Murphy, urged Giraud to get rid of the worst of the Vichyites in North Africa, the Yves Chatels and Noguèses who gave fuel to every fire of criticism in England and America. But to all these arguments, that winter of 1942–43, the old soldier merely replied that he was busy with the war, that politics must wait, and that it was no moment to try to find out, in the North African political mists, which men of all ranks had been collaborationists, which loyal, in a misguided but not vicious way, to Pétain.

The criticism around Giraud grew even worse when Marcel Peyrouton was called in to succeed Yves Chatel who was finally ousted as Governor of Algeria. Peyrouton had been Resident General in Tunisia at one time, but was Vichy's Ambassador to the Argentine before he came to Algiers. He was known as a tough and able administrator, with a knowledge of Arabs and of the whole North African world—something we very much needed at the moment. We had reason, as a matter of fact, to think that he was far from being a collaborationist: he had personally arrested Laval at the time of his purge in late 1940. His appointment produced a tornado of understandable criticism in the Anglo-American press. The M. Chevereux who tried to get Noguès on our side before the landings was Murphy's second choice. He too, had held office under Vichy, however, so he might have been equally unpopular with the public.

As Giraud concentrated on the war and ignored all political rumblings, and as we allowed him to do this, still with the idea that we were keeping hands off French affairs, American prestige began to fall in North Africa. The representatives of the OWI (Office of War Information), OSS (Office of Strategic Services) and other Washington agencies who came to North Africa were at loggerheads with the State Department policy. The heads of all the agencies coöperated, but their subordinates left the French feeling that we, as Americans, had no clear policy or ideology of any kind. Newspaper writers as well as radio commentators, like William Collingwood and Edward Murrow, were often passionately critical of our entire North African policy. We were badly divided among ourselves on the whole French question, and there was too little integration from the very top in Washington. Absolutely contradictory directives arrived from different departments or from men presumed to be "close to the White House."

This sort of spotty and confusing policy was too reminiscent of the France of the Thirties. Our whole official line should have been thoroughly canvassed at home, both officially in Washington and fully and freely in the press. The policy finally decided upon should have been explained frankly and clearly to the world. Once it was decided, and backed by the American people, we representatives in the field, from State, OWI, OSS and the rest, should have either coöperated or gone home. As it was, the State Department sulked in wounded dignity in its tent while it was so widely misunderstood, and the British-American press was thoroughly indoctrinated by the extremely articulate de Gaullist forces. By the time official interpretation came, it was too late. Demaree Bess' articles, Kenneth Crawford's book on North Africa, Robert Sherwood's inspection trip, during which he came to agree with the State Department, all came after the harm had been done. By that time, we had so thoroughly washed our own dirty linen in public that we stood out as fumbling and confused amateurs in the international diplomatic scene. Everything that happened in North Africa that annoyed anyone, from food problems to the delay in restoring civil rights to the Jews, was thenceforth blamed on America and her inexperienced and divided cohorts on the scene.

At this point it seems obvious the State Department should have put their entire negotiations in North Africa into fresh hands. Mr. Murphy was too tired and overworked to take vigorous action. Above all a fresh point of view was needed, and an envoy of Cabinet rank if United States' prestige was to be saved.

Our amateurishness stood out in sharp contrast to the smooth professional functioning of our British colleagues. They had two representatives in Africa who far outranked Mr. Murphy in the official scale. In Accra, they had Viscount Swinton, a man of Cabinet caliber. In Algiers, the British Minister was Harold MacMillan, who had been in Britain's War Cabinet, a man of wide background and distinction, and Roger Makins, a younger, brilliant Foreign Office official. None of them had any commitments to any particular person or group in North Africa—a fact which from the start gave them a better bargaining position than Murphy, who was still morally obligated to all our useful but unreliable pre-landing underground.

After our landings, de Gaulle had not only ignored Giraud and the North African Army but had allowed his organization in their broadcasts to France to deny any connection with the Frenchmen in North Africa then fighting the Germans at our side. This had effectively put out of the question any negotiations between Giraud and de Gaulle until they had been almost forcibly brought together at Casablanca. After the Conference, the British-American matchmakers set painfully to work again to try to prevent French disunity from hampering the war effort.

The first move was the flying trip made by John McCloy, Assistant Secretary of War and that Department's political man, in February, 1943. He came to try to achieve better collaboration between the military and political forces in North Africa, and he also discussed with Mr. Murphy the forthcoming arrival of a new figure in the African drama and a close friend of Mr. McCloy's: Jean Monnet.

Prime Minister Churchill had already suggested to Giraud, at the Casablanca Conference, that he send for Monnet, a pro-British Frenchman who had been in the United States for several years, and who was a friend of such varied Washington figures as Justice Felix Frankfurter and our ex-Ambassador to France, William Bullitt. Among his refugee backers was André Meyer, a Frenchman in New York and a Lazard Bank partner. Giraud finally accepted Monnet as his technical adviser after McCloy's visit and shortly Monnet himself arrived in Algiers.

On the surface, Monnet seemed just what was needed in the disturbing Anglo-American scene. He had ties with everybody. A wealthy cognac manufacturer and banker, he had first appeared on the international stage at Geneva, where he worked in the secretariat of the League of Nations. He left Geneva to become a partner in Blair and Company, international bankers, and was also closely associated with Lazard Bank and other international banking organizations. Just before the war he was in this country placing orders for armaments. During the first stage of the war, he had been in England and then on the French Purchasing Commission in the United States. After France fell, he moved over onto the British Purchasing Commission, to merge the remaining French contracts with theirs. He knew everyone, everywhere, and already had the reputation in London and in Washington of being a Frenchman the Anglo-Saxon "could do business with."

Although Monnet supposedly came to Algiers as a technician to expedite American arming of the North African Army, he soon became a key political man. This was considered hopeful in Algiers. He was reputed to be a top negotiator, a mediator, a man who could bring the two poles together into a happy equator. In a situation that desperately needed a solvent, it was hoped he might be the colorless liquid that would resolve all our difficulties. It was also believed that he would be able to do this as a skilled business negotiator operates, and in full sympathy with the American official policy of keeping any one faction from dominating the French political scene.

Seldom have hopes been more disappointed. Monnet (who now heads the French financial mission in the United States) ended up by simply handing North Africa to de Gaulle, and helping him to ease other Frenchmen out of the picture with the adroitness of a party chairman at a presidential convention. He did this without the knowledge of all his old American friends and supporters and in violation of many statements of his own in Washington. Others, like André Meyer, knew he had gone to Algiers for this purpose.

Monnet arrived in North Africa as an experienced traveler, a sophisticated man of the world, might arrive in a provincial capital. He seemed so rich, spoke in such big figures, was apparently so familiar with power in all its material forms, knew the answers to all questions, had lived so long in so many more important capitals, appeared to be so intimate with the great and near great of every country, that he dazzled the North African colonials as well as a good many Americans. In spite of warnings to the contrary, Mr. Murphy rapidly became con-

vinced that Monnet was not only a brilliant but a reliable implementer
of the American policy of keeping French politics out of the war. His
point of view was reinforced by Monnet's backers in Washington. The
English, however, knew him well and were always inclined to watch
and direct him carefully. We didn't because we were unaware.

Some political observers who watched Monnet work in Algiers in
the spring of 1943 suspected that he was hoping to see de Gaulle and
Giraud consume each other like the calico cat and the china dog. They
seemed equally matched politically at that time, our backing of Giraud
balancing de Gaulle's superior public relations and his Foreign Office
connections. With the Generals out of the way, Monnet may easily
have hoped to emerge as a key political figure in postwar France. For a
time, the British were worried about his strategy, of which our diplomats at first were unaware. For the British certainly believed from the
start that Monnet was completely behind their political line, just as
Americans in Washington and Algiers were convinced that he believed in keeping French political factions out of war.

Monnet's conversation, which was widely repeated in Algerian social circles seemed to confirm British fears. He was as contradictory
with different groups here as he had been in London and Washington.
He told North Africans generally, for instance, that he was heartily
in sympathy with the American policy there. Yet he equally insisted
to an anti-de Gaulle Frenchman I knew, that he, Monnet, believed
that de Gaulle should take over. He may, of course, have been simply
feeling his way, trying, in the manner of the *entrepreneur*, to sense
the strength of the political forces.

Giraud, who longed for more material for the French forces, was
given to understand that Monnet was the only man who could get him
all the guns and tanks he needed. Monnet moved in not only as Giraud's technical but political adviser, too, and for a brief moment we
even proposed to give him a desk in our own Civil Affairs offices, where
he would have seen all official American correspondence. Luckily, more
cynical counsels prevailed, and he moved into French headquarters.

Though Monnet had been sent over from Washington as someone
in total sympathy with our hands-off-politics views, he soon showed
that he not only did not intend to represent a Franco-American point
of view but did not even share our ideas. He gave Giraud to under-

stand in April, 1943, for instance, that Washington would withhold further military supplies to the French unless the de Gaullist and Giraudist forces were merged. This was totally untrue: our policy then, as always, was to arm anti-Nazi Frenchmen regardless of their shades of political feeling. If Monnet had been really anxious for a fusion between the Armies he should have firmly urged Giraud to invite de Gaulle again to come and take his place as a soldier in the fighting in Tunisia. Monnet never gave Giraud this advice. Instead de Gaulle was allowed to build himself up as the martyred war leader, snubbed by his North African countrymen and their American Allies.

Such military unity would have done much to produce political unity, and to assuage the anti-de Gaullists' feeling that de Gaulle did more talking than fighting during the war. In the light of Monnet's subsequent manoeuvers, however, it became obvious to Americans on the scene that the clue to his actions could be found in his close relations with the Foreign Office. Though he came via Washington, he had long been associated with British interests, and his policies, during the formation of the French Committee of Liberation, became more and more those of the Foreign Office and of de Gaulle. Monnet was to prove a great disillusionment to his Washington backers.

By that time, the American Army was in North Africa in force and we could have successfully sponsored de Gaulle as a military figure though not as a political one. This would have demonstrated that neither the Giraud group or ourselves had any personal prejudice against him and that we were only seeking to submerge politics and produce military unity.

Monnet did finally manage to get an exchange of letters started between Giraud and de Gaulle in the spring of 1943. On his side, Giraud stressed the Constitution of 1875, and urged that any temporary French Government remain within that Constitution and reiterate its determination to restore French rights intact after her liberation. He dwelt on the Treveneuc Law of 1872 as the procedure for this restoration. De Gaulle heartily agreed: he himself had cited the Treveneuc Law as one of his basic principles in his Brazzaville Declaration. He added: "I strongly oppose the building up of personal power by any individual or group, or the introduction of totalitarian methods." We soon heard more and more talk of de Gaulle's coming to North Africa, and of the formation of a Committee as a sort of provisional government, holding France's sovereignty in trust until the liberation. Early that spring, de Gaulle sent as his ambassador to Giraud, General Catroux. Catroux had been in command of the region of Marrakech at one time, and knew North Africa well. He had been out in Indo-China in 1940, managed to get through to Singapore and finally to London, where he joined de Gaulle. Polished and adroit, like Noguès, he had had a long colonial experience and even thought and acted, the Algierians said, more like an Arab than a Frenchman.

As Monnet talked to Catroux and both listened to the Foreign Office and watched our own incredible fumbling and confusion, they obviously realized that the dynamic de Gaullist forces already had a dramatic lead over Giraud, and that the official American policy of keeping any one political group from getting control of postwar France was doomed to fail. Monnet's conversation became more and more overtly de Gaullist, and I was told on high authority that he even suggested to one American de Gaullist from another agency that things might be "arranged" to recall Murphy and have him take Murphy's place.

Though when he arrived he had been looked upon as a mediator, Monnet was already distinctly on one side rather than in the middle. By this time Monnet's position had become so inflated by Algerian gossip of his high connections and his letters supposedly direct from the White House that he eclipsed Mr. Murphy who actually held the title of Personal Representative of the President at Algiers. Murphy, his new assistant, Samuel Reber, and Giraud, however, still felt sure that Monnet would manage to do the necessary conciliatory job, in spite of warnings from within the Civil Affairs office and even from Washington. The State Department, in fact, was, by this time thoroughly alarmed at the reports of Monnet's activities, and at the dominance he had assumed over our own strategy. Warnings were sent, but Monnet's Algiers and Washington backers continued to reassure Mr. Murphy.

In the midst of all this intrigue, on February 14, North Africa was suddenly brought to its war senses by the Allied reverses inflicted by the enemy. If the advance of Rommel's *Afrika Korps* at the Kesserine Pass in Tunisia had not been stopped the very safety of Algiers itself was threatened. With the danger passed, however, once more the Tunisian battlefields seemed far away to the politicians at Algiers.

I was still stationed in Morocco at this time, but I saw the Algiers situation crystallizing on my frequent extended trips there. Although no workable agreement had yet been reached between de Gaulle and Giraud, de Gaullist officers and agents from London began to trickle down to North Africa in considerable numbers. The British sent them in and this helped very much to trouble further the African picture. In Morocco, following a definite plan, they circulated with lists of key officers and men they were to see. Many of the officers approached by these de Gaullists came to see me in great consternation. The thing that horrified them the most was the anti-American attitude of the de Gaullists. Sometimes this was shown, I was told, by subtle implication in attacking Giraud and sometimes quite openly in attacking us. I was even approached by some and clearly sensed the depth of their factionalism.

One of the things that began to worry our men in Algiers more and more was the direct recruiting the de Gaullists were now doing in the very barracks of the Giraud forces. De Gaullist agents set up shop near the troops' barracks, and in a way that was really reckless in the midst of a dangerous campaign against the Germans, persuaded men and officers alike to desert to de Gaulle with offers of better pay and more rank. During the following months desertions rose into the thousands, and there was a large, secret, deserters' camp near Algiers.

Giraud became alarmed. He felt that the French military performance in Tunisia was vital to prove France's courage to the world and restore her self-respect. By the late spring of 1943, several officers, whom I shall have occasion to mention later, had come to Algiers to help Giraud in his effort to rebuild France's military strength. One of them was General Robert Odic, once head of North African air forces for Weygand, and who had recently been in the United States. Another was Admiral Muselier, a former de Gaullist who joined Giraud from London and who was put in charge of the military security of Algiers and the environs. Both were honest and capable officers although neither had very recent contact with France. Giraud was never able to bring out from France the able men he should have had in North Africa. One reason was our diplomats did not realize the need for them and another was because there was a Foreign Office-de Gaullist control over liaison with the French underground. Only those passed by London could be brought out from France.

When I was living in Algiers in May, I often consulted Muselier when friends of French soldiers in Tunisia came to me in consternation about the desertions going on, and the persuasion being used to make them desert. In July a report on this whole subject was sent to President Roosevelt and Mr. Churchill by the French High Command.[12] Most soldiers, of course, remained loyal and stayed at the front in their regiments. By late spring, best estimates were that the de Gaullists under arms still numbered less than 15,000, including forces outside North Africa, while the Giraud Army still numbered some 125,000 men.

In April I saw de Gaullist recruiting methods in Marrakech, too. A steady stream of French aviators, soldiers and sailors escaped from France and made their way through Spain to Lisbon and thence to North Africa. (A French and an American agent—Colonel Malaise and Colonel Stevens—conned them through Spain; this was one reason why we were fairly gentle with Franco.) In North Africa, they were taken in groups to Marrakech and kept in barracks while experts went over them carefully and weeded out any Fifth Columnists. Marrakech was now the center of an air network reaching Dakar, the United States and London, and so many people were flying hastily around the world that spies might easily have slipped through on forged papers.

My doctor in Marrakech surprised me, that spring, by borrowing typewriters, typewriter paper and numerous other office supplies from my house. I couldn't imagine why he needed them until I began to talk to some of the young men, fresh from France, in the barracks. Then I discovered that organized de Gaullist recruitment was going on there, and that my doctor wanted to use these supplies for recording enlistments. The de Gaullist agents told these confused young refugees, eager to fight the Germans, that America would never arm the Giraud forces. Purely because I was the only American available, several hundred of them came individually and in small groups and talked to me. I told them, of course, that we did intend to arm the North African Army. I particularly remember two young men I had known well in France, who were in a state of despair as they realized the profound political differences that already existed between Frenchmen. They were asked if they wanted to join the de Gaulle Army or the Giraud Army. "We should never have left France," they said. "There, at least we were united." They went back to their barracks to think about what they should do. When I next saw them, I asked them how they had finally decided to fill in their enlistment papers. "We simply drew a line through every question," they said, "and wrote 'We want to fight for France.'"

At the same time, in the United States, similar methods were being used that came under the censure of our highest military authorities. Several French warships, including the great battleship *Richelieu*, had come to United States ports. De Gaullist agents in this country began causing so many desertions amongst their crews that, in a press interview in Washington on March 13, 1943, Secretary of the Navy, Knox said; "As a result of various circumstances, there have been numerous desertions amongst the crews of these ships, and if this continues, the vessels will be left so under-staffed, they will be virtually immobilized." Efforts were made to stop desertions, but they continued to such a degree that Secretary Knox was obliged to comment again, in a press conference on March 19. One French ship, he pointed out, had recently sailed minus forty per cent of her crew, which, as he mildly put it, "added to the perils of her voyage." Another French merchant ship lost eight or ten of her gun crew through desertions, and was later sunk with her American war cargo. Such French factionalism so retarded the Allied war effort that American authorities began to take a very gloomy view of the desirability of continuing to arm the French.

In April, I moved back to Algiers, where I shared a villa with a Britisher, Major, the Viscount Duncannon, who was my opposite number on Mr. MacMillan's staff. I found Giraud still reposing perfect faith in Monnet, and Murphy, like the British representative, Harold MacMillan, still urging Giraud to lean heavily on Monnet's advice and counsel. Monnet's friends in Washington were also still plugging for him, I learned. The State Department itself as noted before, had come to feel differently. The Department's warnings, for some reason, did not seem to worry Murphy. He was apparently not worried, either, by the widespread gossip about Monnet's activities in

Algiers. He had faith in the fact that both the President and Mr. Churchill knew de Gaulle and were awake to the dangers of de Gaullism, and he must have still hoped that Monnet could aid in forming a Provisional Government of compromise political coloring for France.

The whole atmosphere in Algiers was intensely political by this time, and the "Battle of the Villas," as it was called, was in full swing. The Allied military situation was firmly in the capable hands of General Eisenhower. He allowed none of the miasma of political jealousies and rivalries to penetrate his headquarters at the Hotel St. George. In fact, he had done a great deal to clarify the whole atmosphere of Algiers by strictest disciplinary measures against any bickering between the British and Americans. General Marshall later said of Eisenhower, "The degree of unity attained . . . was the greatest single Allied achievement of the war." We saw this well on the way to fulfillment in North Africa. He certainly fused the British and Americans into working allies. Unfortunately in the diplomatic and political field there was no General Eisenhower. The strange influence of Africa had upset any real unity even between the different American agencies, and the centuries-old atmosphere of intriguing Algiers was far too much for the French. While the Armies fought our battles in Tunisia and Giraud wanted only to hand over his political powers to a non-partisan Committee and get on with the war, a series of groups with an axe to grind used the press and pulled wires to get their way.

De Gaullist agents among the French, Britishers trying to achieve French unity under British leadership, Americans in OWI and OSS who were sincerely (if, I think, misguidedly) de Gaullist, all took part in this manoeuvering. It is hard to understand the de Gaullist *coup* in North Africa, unless one realizes the atmosphere of dissension and misunderstanding there, the fact that Murphy was very much overworked, that our military battles were desperate and absorbing, and that many people simply didn't realize the importance of the political issues being settled—or even that they were likely to be settled soon.

As Giraud and de Gaulle discussed and debated between Algiers and London through M. Monnet and General Catroux, the British enormously strengthened de Gaulle's hand by putting Madagascar under his control, but above all, by deciding to channel their contact with the French military underground through his headquarters. I shall discuss this development more fully in Chapter XV. De Gaulle's closer connection with the underground was one of his strongest cards in the 1943 negotiations in Algiers.

All during this formative period, there is good evidence that the British, above all their Foreign Office, had a spare policy they were nursing from time to time in case we failed in our initial efforts. This was not Machiavellian on their part, as propagandists often try to make out, but merely good diplomacy. No foreign power can ultimately control the decision of the people of another power so the possibility of reserve foreign policies must always be left open. In North Africa we did not use these subtle shades so necessary in an active diplomacy. Instead, when later it was evident that our policy was not getting under way, we improvised as we went along, trying to repair damages as they occurred, without much plan covering any alternate choice.

Early in 1943 I began to realize there were several reasons behind the Foreign Office-de Gaulle policy. First, in those days I thought there was an idealistic motive due to still sincere belief in de Gaulle as a man. Second, I knew there was a realistic motive: the Foreign Office wanted to build up impaired British prestige in France not only because she is England's nearest neighbor but because she represented for England the only possible post war force in western Europe to be used to balance Russia's growing importance. (This was to appear more clearly after the Teheran Conference.) The pattern of British Foreign Office reasons I was to see more clearly as our French dilemma drew out. On the spot in North Africa there was too much going on for deep analytical thinking.

I shall never forget the victory parade of May 10 in Tunis. A bitter battle, the first in the liberation of France, had ended. Giraud's soldiers wore the smiles of men who had restored their own self-respect. They had wiped out the bitter memories of 1940 with their blood. Ill equipped, even ill fed, they had fought as respected allies beside the British and Americans. May 10 should have been a day of great happiness and unity for Frenchmen. Instead it was utterly spoiled for thousands of them by the fact that the de Gaullist forces, under General Leclerc refused to march beside their shabby North African comrades. They withdrew themselves to a separate part of the victory parade and marched with the British. It was tragically symbolic to see the big group of North African regiments, the small group of de Gaullists, marching apart from each other, all brave men, and hopelessly divided.

Finally, in May, after many false rumors, we learned that de Gaulle was definitely coming to Algiers to meet with Giraud and form a French Committee of National Liberation. All the previous months cables had been flying hot and heavy between Algiers and London. All of them passed through the Anglo-American Civil Affairs Offices. I was amused by one reply from the de Gaullist agents in Algiers to their London office early in the year. The London office had cabled to settle the details of the General's arrival. They discussed ceremonial honors, and wanted to know if suitable transportation would be at the airport for the General himself—an open car—something in which the Algerians could see him at his best. The Algiers de Gaullist men cabled back "Suggest armored car."

On May 27th, in order to reassure the de Gaullists who said they were afraid one man or group might use the French political situation for personal advancement, Giraud issued a decree forbidding the use of pictures of any Frenchman on posters, and also forbidding the use of any political symbol. The idea was to strip North Africa clean of political atmosphere and to give the coming Committee a chance to start fresh and unprejudiced.

Like so many acts of compromise with de Gaulle, this turned out to be a purely unilateral gesture. The great man arrived by air on May 30 and went temporarily to the Germaine Villa to live. His first act was to go down to the *Monument des Morts* for a special service. While the General made an impressive and dramatic arrival, his agents handed out pictures of de Gaulle and pins in the shape of the *Croix de Lorraine,* among the crowd. In a few minutes, Algiers was well covered with political symbols again. While he spoke the crowd roared *"Un seul chef, de Gaulle"* in much the way that other crowds had roared for a single *fuehrer* ten years before. "Such a chief is distant. . . . Below him there are murmurings. . . . (But) when the crisis arises, it is he who is followed." *

De Gaulle stood sternly making the sign of victory with his arms

* Quotation from de Gaulle's book "Le Fil de l'Epée," published in 1932.

to the crowd. It was a symbol of more than one kind of victory.

North Africa is a fatally emotional and dramatic place. The de Gaullist minority—which they themselves had estimated at about 20% of the electorate a few weeks before—seemed to grow before our very eyes that day. You could almost hear the thunder of feet running for the bandwagon, the shiny, nationalistic bandwagon, so different from Giraud's classic and traditional vehicle, as unpretentious and French as a Paris taxicab. Going back to the villa, the de Gaulle car was surrounded by motorcycles while the General rode erect within.

Back at his villa, de Gaulle gave a large press conference, in which he talked darkly of the "sovereignty" of France, which he felt had been infringed upon by the Clark-Darlan agreements, and even more darkly of "purges." He seemed to feel some drastic purges were needed. He followed this up two days later with a magnificent dinner to the press, including such North African rarities as lobster and turkey. It was a visible symbol of the way in which de Gaullists shrewdly, and rightly, kept their publicity going. No other French group had any discernible press relations at all; and the State Department, representing our own North African policy, never seemed able to explain its own actions or counteract the de Gaullist line without seeming to criticize many utterly sincere and liberal Frenchmen, Englishmen and Americans. After de Gaulle's arrival the de Gaullist public relations section kept things humming in the British, United States and South American press,* with active support from the Communists who had now attached themselves to de Gaullism.

On the morning of May 31st, the French Committee of National Liberation met for the first time in Algiers. Six members had been previously agreed upon by an exchange of letters. Giraud and de Gaulle were to serve as co-chairmen; two men—Monnet and General Georges, a friend of Churchill's, were to represent the Giraud point of view on the Committee; two others represented de Gaulle's, Catroux, and René Massigli, a Foreign Officer official who had been the Vichy representative in Turkey and who was now de Gaulle's Commissioner for Foreign Affairs. On the surface, everything looked promising for a genuine coalition, non-partisan trusteeship for France.

* *France Nouvelle*, published in Buenos Aires.

But at this point Monnet finally and fully confirmed the fears of the State Department and many highly placed men in Washington and baffled the sincere Americans who still backed him, by throwing his weight against our policies and interests. Murphy and Reber, like many others, thought that he was genuinely interested, like ourselves, in forming a merger, or keeping a balance of powers, between the various French factions, or at least keeping any one man from using the political impotence of France to assume supreme power. He proved that he had become a de Gaullist at once. At the very first meeting of the Committee, de Gaulle announced that instead of a balanced Committee of two men from each side, plus two chairmen (as had been previously arranged by letter), he wanted three men on his side. André Philip, his contact with the French Resistance Forces would have to be put on the Committee. Monnet unexpectedly voted with de Gaulle on this, and Philip joined the Committee which at that moment became to all intents and purposes a de Gaullist group, with only Giraud and Georges left to balance de Gaulle, Philip, Catroux, Massigli and the supple M. Monnet.

This sudden transformation of the Committee from impartial trustee to factional political group rocked Algiers. The first thought of Americans there was for the future of the French Army. General Eisenhower made it abundantly clear that the Supreme Command would brook no tampering with the French military command. Giraud was to keep this in his hands. (Less than a year later, poor Giraud was to be ousted from this post, too, by the de Gaullists.)

I shall never forget the incredulity and dismay with which Monnet's action was received by the American diplomatic authorities in Algiers. They felt the way Eisenhower would have if Giraud had suddenly decided to fight a separate campaign. From then on, Monnet had to be accounted an out-and-out de Gaullist. Slamming the barn door shut after this particular horse, some old notes full of misgivings about Monnet's intentions were made up into a report and sent back to Washington.

In spite of this crisis, the Committee proceeded with its work. It announced at once that it would return French sovereignty immediately after the liberation, and that it acted only in trusteeship. Then it settled down to a series of inner manoeuvers and jockeyings from which de Gaulle was to emerge the complete master of North Africa and in which American influence, and even a feeling of friendship for us, vanished from sight. Not only at the time but upon looking back on our failure with France, it seems more obvious than ever that Murphy's and others' misplaced faith in Monnet, at Algiers, was one of our major mistakes.

CHAPTER XIV

De Gaulle Captures North Africa

THE next operation of the French Committee of Liberation began with a typically stormy incident.

It had been agreed between Giraud and de Gaulle that Peyrouton, then Governor General of Algeria, should resign and let General Catroux, the de Gaullist, take his place. Peyrouton tried to resign to Giraud a few days before the Committee of Liberation first convened, but Giraud refused his resignation. It would be more proper, he said, for Peyrouton to resign to the Committee as a whole, to take the whole affair out of personal politics.

As the Committee met for the first time in a converted camouflaged school building, high over the teeming city of Algiers, Peyrouton dutifully sent duplicate letters of resignation to both de Gaulle and to Giraud. For reasons never explained, the Giraud letter was never delivered. To Giraud's amazement, Gaston Palevsky, head of de Gaulle's personal cabinet, then announced, on June 2nd, that Peyrouton had resigned to de Gaulle and that de Gaulle had accepted his resignation. Furthermore, it was announced that Peyrouton would immediately join the de Gaulle army in Syria with the rank of captain. The press congratulated de Gaulle on what seemed an outstanding act of statesmanship. Peyrouton telephoned Giraud in some bewilderment, found he had never received the duplicate letter, and asked him what to do. Giraud told him to do nothing until the misunderstanding could be cleared up; and not to resign until he could publicly and officially resign to the entire Committee. Peyrouton withdrew his resignation and waited.

This threw de Gaulle into a towering rage and he at once resigned from the nascent Committee.

This, it seems to me, was our big chance. No one who knew the whole inside story of exiled French politics at that time had much faith left in de Gaulle. Mr. Roosevelt, Mr. Churchill, the British and

American diplomats and military heads on the scene, all realized that he was at best a little unbalanced in his nationalism and egoism and a few of these realized he was possibly something much more sinister. The British point of view about him was a complicated one: he remained their best hope for a French Government friendly to Britain, and they hoped he would remain an ally, if an uncomfortable one. They were aware, too, he had already won the first rounds and established a position that might be hard to undo without ruining Franco-British friendship in the process. But they had no illusions about him. Late in the summer of 1943 I was to learn more definitely that the Foreign Office with understandable desire to rally post war western Europe into a bloc sympathetic to Britain was counting on and firmly backing de Gaulle. But by early summer these Foreign Office manoeuverings often looked as if they were directed at having British influence usurp American influence with France.

Shortly after de Gaulle came to North Africa, there was an amusing and characteristically British exchange of cables between the Prime Minister and the British Minister in Algiers. These messages became a joke in Algiers. Churchill cabled the single, cryptic phrase: "See Matthew 7, Verses 15–21." MacMillan capped the quotation with "Doing my best. See Revelations 2, Verses 2–5." (The first reference is the famous passage beginning: "Beware of false prophets which come to you in sheep's clothing, but inwardly are ravening wolves. By their fruits ye shall know them. Do men gather grapes of thorns, or figs of thistles? . . ." The second reads: "I know thy works and thy toil and patience, and that thou canst not bear evil men, and didst try them which call themselves apostles, and they are not, and didst find them false; and thou hast patience and didst bear for my name's sake, and has not grown weary. But I have this against thee, that thou didst leave thy first love.") Because of the weight of British public opinion, thoroughly under the spell of de Gaulle propaganda, the Prime Minister was to be more and more forced into the position of very grudgingly and unwillingly backing de Gaulle.

When this heaven-sent opportunity of de Gaulle's resignation dropped into our laps, however, Murphy, Reber, MacMillan and Makins were unwilling to take it. I remember going into the Civil Affairs office feeling enormously relieved that de Gaulle had at last proved to the outside world something the diplomatic world already knew: that he insisted on being supreme, solitary and responsible to no one but himself. Here, I thought, was our real chance to use our still enormous strength in North Africa to insist upon the formation of a French Provisional Government that would be genuinely provisional, representative, and jealous of the political and personal liberties of Frenchmen until they were in a position to vote for themselves. Inside the office, I was amazed to find that another opinion was held. Giraud was told not, under any circumstances, to accept de Gaulle's resignation. When I revealed my dismay, I was shown a message to reassure me. In essence, it said that Mr. Churchill and the British would always prefer American friendship to French and President Roosevelt's to that of de Gaulle if there were any conflict between the two. This seemed so obvious that it did not impress me. I felt my superior was misinterpreting its significance and I told him so. The top men, I was assured, understood de Gaulle thoroughly and wouldn't let him become a menace to the freedoms of France or the peace of the world. The Committee, I was told, hadn't really formed yet. It would be much better to let de Gaulle prove his ruthlessness and will to power by allowing him to resign after the Committee was really functioning. And, the argument concluded, he was sure to do just that: he could never control himself long enough to work on a committee of any kind. Though I knew it was out of line for anyone as junior as myself to show it, I felt, and expressed, utter discouragement with this idea. About a week later, as a matter of fact, de Gaulle boiled over again and resigned a second time, but again it was felt the time was not ripe and Giraud was urged to smooth him down. If our trust in Monnet was our first diplomatic mistake, this was certainly to prove to be our second.

While the Committee of Liberation had its prolonged and painful birth, I tried to meet all the de Gaulle officials I could. I was genuinely curious to know what sort of men de Gaulle had around him and also to learn what I could of the cryptic and towering General himself.

The first thing I ran into was the *mystique* that had already risen around de Gaulle, the almost hushed reverence with which he was surrounded. A tiny but significant anecdote illustrates this. I went to pay a formal call, in the correct diplomatic way, at his villa soon after his arrival. In the big, plaster hall of the villa I saw one of those huge chests which are often kept near the front door for coats, hats, sticks and those little silver plates of calling cards. Automatically, I dropped my hat and gloves on it, and was nearly knocked down in a concerted rush by two French Majors who snatched my belongings off the chest and handed them back to me with the glare of policemen who have caught some one desecrating a national shrine. "That chest," they said, "is for The General." I looked, and sure enough, there was the slim bamboo swagger stick, the military hat with the two stars, reverently disposed, as on an altar, in the middle of that mammoth chest. That same night, Gaston Palevsky, the suave, social chief of de Gaulle's personal staff since 1940 in London, was asked to dinner at our villa by my English colleague. Mlle. Nicole de Brignac, the same gallant ambulance driver who had kept our secret documents for us during the landings, was there. Palevsky said to her: "This is a great moment for me, so long an exile from France, to meet at last a real French woman, a *Parisienne*. And tell me, Mademoiselle, what do you think of us de Gaullists? Do you look upon us as outsiders, as revolutionaries?"

She answered: "No, not at all; although I must in all candor tell you that for me, as for most of the forty million French who didn't leave France or couldn't, there can be only one flag, the Tricolor, and we don't want to see any cross, Hitler's or de Gaulle's, superimposed upon it. But do tell me," she added, "something about the man you call 'your general.' "

Palevsky is a very sophisticated, cynical, very adroit, Frenchman, with a long and well-known background in political and international intrigue. It was hard for us to believe our ears when he said, with a mystical, faraway look: "For me, he is the greatest man I have ever known. Long before the war, when I was with Reynaud in the government, we saw in General de Gaulle the man of France's future. He has a strange power of reflecting in himself every thought, every feeling of every Frenchman. If you want to know what the humblest peasant in the most remote province of France is thinking, you have only to ask my General. He has a sort of magic contact with them. In fact, there is always beside him—even when he sleeps—a little casket filled with the soil of Lorraine. From this martyred soil of France, a sort of emanation flows into his veins and gives him a mystic unity with the beating heart of France." Coming from a different sort of man, this would have been rather moving, if eerie; coming from Palevsky, it produced a complete silence in which someone changed the subject. We all wondered why de Gaullism always dealt in this rather Wagnerian mysticism, instead of in Gallic realism with true French clarity.

I think the thing that instinctively frightened me about this *mystique* was the obvious fact that this sort of easy nationalist emotion and hero-worship is almost always associated with totalitarian ideas and ways. It was too close, both to the old Norse god nonsense of Hitler and the more traditional, but still dangerous, mystical nationalism of Pétain. The Pétainist motto—*Soyez Francais, agissez Francais, pensez Francais*—was being taken over bodily by the de Gaullists. The feeling of "purification," the dedication to a leader, were there, too. De Gaullism even took over Pétain's (and Hitler's) interest in a "youth movement." Youth was malleable and could be stamped with the proper pattern. Youth was vigorous and could act. Several young de Gaullist officers in criticizing Giraud's sixty odd years told me that people over fifty were utterly useless in the world after the war.

De Gaulle's anti-British and anti-American feeling, which are now common knowledge, were obvious in Algiers at once. His close associates shared these feelings intensely. I remember Commandant Mangin, son of the great General, at lunch in Algiers one day. "France would never support an Anglo-Saxon occupation," he said to me, as we speculated about the final campaigns in Europe. "But when we invade Europe," I said, "it would be as allies of France." "Are you our allies or aren't you?" he asked. I said I thought our early military support of de Gaulle and our attitude in North Africa proved that we were. "Not at all," he said, very politely, "you come as occupants and nothing else."

M. Clauzon, André Philip's assistant, said much the same thing to me. The French, he said, were so disgusted with the German occupation that they could never, for a minute, support the presence of an American or an Englishman in France. They had had enough of occupation, and had no need of us. "Let's be practical," I said, "and admit that France needs us very badly just as we very much need France in Europe." He told me with rising emotion that the French had no need of any Anglo-Saxons as they had their strong allies, the Russians. As he left, he told a mutual friend that he would never forget or forgive a phrase I had used—"let's be practical."

It was easy to understand why many de Gaullists, deeply humiliated by 1940 and by Vichy, should have such a dangerous and touchy brand of nationalism. Some of them, of course, remained remarkably free from it, but they were not in evidence at political headquarters. The General himself showed the most violent anti-American feeling of all. From Morocco came word that he had told his cousins, the Maillots of Rabat, for instance, that he could have nothing to do with us or with Giraud because we had conspired together to give the United States the ports, railroads and mines of Morocco on a 99-year lease. This attractive story spread throughout Morocco where it caused a lot of unnecessary trouble for us. The North African atmosphere was perfect for whispering campaigns. They began with a fury and were almost all aimed directly or indirectly against the Americans. De Gaulle's own paper in London, *La Marseillaise*, was increasingly and virulently anti-American, so much so that the British Government finally, on June 27, 1943, had to suppress the paper. The New York de Gaullist newspaper, *Pour La Victoire*, on January 16, 1943, had already refused to republish any more of its material.

De Gaulle's totalitarian methods also became evident very soon in Algeria. When Catroux succeeded Peyrouton as Governor General, one of his first acts was to deport Jean Rigault, who had given good, if unavailing, advice to Giraud and was still one of his close advisers. Rigault was given no reason for this action; secret police simply appeared at his house one night, and without even giving him time to get in touch with the authorities or with his own friends, forced him into a car and drove him to Morocco. Murphy and the Americans generally were given no explanations, either, though it was well and widely known that Rigault was one of our pre-landing agents and our good friend. After a few days Murphy protested mildly a few times, to no avail, and there the matter ended. We considered this an affair among Frenchmen and took no firm steps. We already had a reputation all over North Africa for not standing by our friends (we had allowed Béthouart, Magnan, and other friends to be attacked in Morocco) and this confirmed it.

I would have thought Rigault's expulsion had more moral fervor back of it if de Gaulle had not tolerated so many people of equally or even more spotty backgrounds. His only criterion, really, was total and complete obedience to de Gaulle. Colonel "Passy," the chief of his secret police, whose real name was de Wavrin, had a Cagoulard record, longer and far blacker than Rigault's, and de Gaulle was equally receptive to the very Communist leaders who had done their best to undermine France's defense in 1940. It was ironic that Rigault, left to his fate by us, remained loyal to the end to the United States, as did Lemaigre Dubreuil, also a reputed Cagoulard, who was forced out of Giraud's entourage in March 1943. (Both men were finally, after several arrests, released from prison in Paris in May 1945, as the only charge that could be brought against them was that they had been negotiating with a foreign power.)

A final twist on the Rigault affair was given me when I had a discussion with a British colleague about the de Gaulle official who had been mainly responsible for Rigault's being expelled from Algiers. "General X. seems to me to use utterly totalitarian methods," I said. "Oh, you're quite wrong about him," the Englishman replied seriously. "He's all right. I know, because we have a secret agreement with him." "Secret?" I asked, "from whom?" "Oh, well, we pay him. He's a good man." It was symptomatic of the utter confusion in Algiers at this point that my colleague, a man of integrity, could have thought a man's honesty was proven by the fact that he was operating as a French Government official while being paid by a foreign power. The episode left me wondering how many de Gaullists had this ambiguous color.

A previous episode that illustrated de Gaulle's totalitarian methods was the dismissal of Brunot, Governor of the Cameroons, who was ousted in a most high-handed manner after he had played a vital role in bringing the colony to the de Gaullist side. A French parliamentary group which had been formed in London studied this case, decided it had dangerous implications, and wrote to de Gaullist headquarters for an explanation. The only answer they got was from de Gaulle's Commissioner for the Colonies, René Pleven, who answered simply:

"No one has the right to criticize, or to have information, when it is a decision of the Leader."

This hair-raising point of view was evident, too, in the later de Gaullist treatment of the press. If I had not suspected before that he had essentially fascist tendencies, I would have known it from the typically fascist way in which the de Gaullists at once began to handle the Algerian newspapers. There had been such a long German control through Vichy of the North African newspapers that everyone was avid for news. Yet when this Vichy control stopped, these newspapers seemed to remain paralyzed for a while. The Giraud forces did not correct this as quickly or as energetically as they should, the de Gaullists, however, showed more speed with increasing success for their side.

Monsieur Fouchet, for instance, a respected publisher who had been widely known, before our landings, for his pro-Allied, anti-German sentiments, published a paper called *La Revue Fontaine* in Algiers. Early in the summer of 1943, he received a visit from de Gaulle's press representative, M. Schumann (the radio voice of Free France from London). Schumann simply told Fouchet that in the future he "would come under de Gaullist direction." Fouchet told Schumann that he had never been, and never would be, under anyone's direction, that he would continue to function as an independent journalist. "Ah," said M. Schumann, "in that case, you will receive no paper. It is extremely difficult to publish a review with no paper." This was only the beginning; by the spring of 1944, the entire press was under this sort of open and severe political censorship.

Long before this final dim-out of democracy in the colonies, de Gaulle's refusal to allow his own, special army to be merged with the bigger Giraud forces in North Africa—a decision he made at the first meeting of the Committee of Liberation—also sent a premonitory chill through many observers. Democratic leaders have no need of special, separate armies. They use the Army of their country, not an elite corps of their own.

During all these hot June days in Algiers those of us deeply interested in the attempts being made to bring about French unity discussed nothing else. I remember one of many conversations I had with a British colleague.

"These de Gaullists you have had with you all these years in London certainly dislike my country," I said.

"Yes, they seem to," he admitted, "but it is because they don't know you. That will change."

"I'm not so sure. In spite of all your kindness to them, they haven't been too generous in their coöperation with you."

"But that is because their country was defeated and they're touchy," he explained.

"I know, yet traditionally the French people like the United States better than England for the very simple reason that our interests have never conflicted. Why don't we both use this sympathy to build up a strong French-British-American friendship? We'll never let you down because our democratic interests lie together," I said.

"All you say is true, but you must consider our position," he replied. "France is only a few miles across the channel from us, and what guarantee have we that once the war is over your country won't become isolationist again?" It was just such conversations that showed me British fears during the trying period of the Committee's formation.

After its dark beginnings, the ill-starred French Committee of National Liberation went on its tortuous and politics-ridden way. De Gaulle, having won his initial stranglehold, was quiet and subdued; his followers were vociferous. Officially, the Committee from its beginning made several good moves. Noguès was finally removed on June 4th—an act that was long overdue. (He is said to be living in obscurity in Portugal today.) The Committee declared war on Japan. As noted before, early statements emphasized the fact that France would be returned to her own duly constituted government as soon as liberation permitted. De Gaulle paid tribute to the action of the British and Americans in promoting French unity, and said it would help realize the greatness of France. He also spoke often of the "laws of the Republic."

But during this same time, de Gaullist propaganda split the French beyond hope of unity. It would be hard to convey the extent and ruthlessness of this propaganda to an American reader, used to a free press and unused to a coolly and deliberately planned campaign of lies and half-truths. Some of the propaganda, like the widely printed accusation that Giraud was actually pro-German, and that his escape from Koenigstein prison in Germany was a German-planned plot, reached this country and was repeated by de Gaullists here. Some of it was so out of line that even the American de Gaullist press, as noted before, began to stop printing it. But nothing was too virulent to be used, and believed, not only in North Africa but in England and the United States. Some of the men the de Gaullists wildly accused of being pro-German later died fighting those Germans in Italy. The whole totalitarian smear campaign geared into an equally totalitarian campaign of extolling de Gaulle in terms that sometimes became ludicrous. In the midst of it, de Gaulle would sweep dramatically through the streets of Algiers, his car preceded by flying squads of motorcycles and secret service men, his face stern and elevated. His drama, his showmanship, his appeal to one-man leadership delighted the Arabs and struck fire from the tired, confused North African French. Their hurt national pride revived magically in this dangerous and aggressive but none the less glittering atmosphere.

Some people realize from the start that the situation was potentially dangerous. An official who had watched Monnet climbing to the exaggerated position of posing as the spokesman for the United States at the time of the formation of the Committee in Algiers told the State Department on his return that men of more weight and authority were badly needed to handle American interests in North Africa. Mr. Roosevelt was informed, and expressed concern; and Mr. Churchill, who was at the White House at the time, offered to stop by Algiers on his way home to look the situation over. He did this, conferring with both de Gaulle and Giraud, with the Foreign Minister, Mr. Eden, at his side.

June 7th, however, the Committee took another step in its long case history in how to achieve one-man control. It produced a new government in which de Gaulle had eight representatives. Giraud four, of whom only General Georges remained faithful to the Giraud point of view. (Giraud by this time was so increasingly tired of politics, so weary of the whole conspiracy against him and any real Provisional Government, that he eventually capped his previous political *naïvetés* by voting against himself.) Eisenhower continued to insist, however, that Giraud keep command of the Army, and de Gaulle continued to insist that de Gaullists would never march with any French soldiers who had not sworn personal allegiance to de Gaulle. I remember the bitter discussion this caused at the Inter-Allied Club in an old Moorish palace where all Algerian gossip centered. General Béthouart, the man who had tried to help us in our Moroccan landings, and the late Antoine de St. Exupéry, the famous aviator and author, were in despair over the spectacle of two rival French Armies at a time when France itself was occupied by its most ruthless enemy.

By the time I left North Africa, in July, 1943, the bitter comedy was well on the way to its climax. I returned to Washington via London, where I had a chance to fill in many mysterious gaps in the growth of de Gaullism, and to get more glimpses of the tangle of power politics and strong-arm methods by which the leaders manipulated the brave, honest men among those who followed the banner of the Free French.

CHAPTER XV

To the Heart of De Gaullism

ON THE 9th of July, 1943, I left the new airport of Ras-el-Mar next door to Fez, Morocco, for Gibraltar and London. A delay of one day made me miss a plane connection in Gibraltar on my schedule. It was the ill-fated plane taking the great Polish mediator, General Sikorsky. I did not realize how near an escape I had had until arriving in London, I read of my death in the London papers, and found the hotel room which friends had engaged for me had been canceled.

It was good to be in London, the capital of all resistance. The effect of being in a green, northern country, where English was the mother tongue, was indescribable after the exoticism of North Africa. I was anxious to make contact with England, London, and, above all, my English friends, to get their reaction to the whole French-Anglo-American drama which, by now, preoccupied me. I had left North Africa with a great many misgivings as to the future of British-French-American relations. I had been repeatedly assured that, basically, England and the United States were in complete agreement on a policy for dealing with the French, but, in spite of these assurances, I had seen far too much evidence in North Africa that, although on the highest level the over-all policy was declared to be the same, the Foreign Office was producing another policy of its own. It looked very much to me as if they were firmly and permanently committed now to de Gaulle.

In London, the basic unsoundness of de Gaullism became overwhelmingly evident. Here I gathered incontrovertible data on aspects of the de Gaullist movement and of the man's personality that illuminated much that had seemed mysterious in North Africa. I learned more of his dictatorial and anti-democratic philosophy and technique, more of the dangerous tendencies of some of the men around him, more of the adroit way in which he managed to associate himself with Anglo-America liberal thought and, in the public mind, with the

French liberals and the entire French resistance movement. And above all, I learned how the whole de Gaullist issue had become an issue in internal British politics just at the moment when our British allies and ourselves were preoccupied with more direct war issues—a fact that certainly helped de Gaullism to win out over the better judgment of Anglo-American war leaders.

Right away I got in touch with two friends who had been deeply interested in the French problem since the very beginning of the war. One, Alastair Forbes, a British subject, though American by birth, had been with General de Gaulle on the ill-fated expedition to Dakar. Since then, ill health had forced him out of the Army and he had become associated with the London *Observer*. From him, and from our Embassy, I learned of the famous Dufour case that was slated to come up shortly in London. This law suit was brought by a French exile, a former resistance worker with the British in France, against General de Gaulle himself and a group of his headquarters men. I have reproduced in the Appendix of this book a complete copy of the case as it was presented in King's Bench Court in London on August 6, 1943.[18] The case was finally dropped by the plaintiff. I learned from a high-ranking American Naval officer, in liaison with the French in London, that this had been done after Dufour had received a very large sum of money from the de Gaullist organization to withdraw the case. Many witnesses had originally offered their testimony on Dufour's side against de Gaulle and his associates, but had withdrawn these offers, I was told, after threats of reprisals against their families inside France. The whole tone of the evidence presented in this case was alarming, but no more so than many things I soon learned about the inner workings of de Gaullism in London.

What kept the English and American public back of de Gaulle was the impression of pure and patriotic fever still left from his early speeches, especially the one of June 18, 1940. Around this speech all the symbolism and mysticism of de Gaullism had been built. But underneath the patriotic surface in London, as in North Africa, were very disturbing elements.

In Algiers, I had heard Frenchmen arriving from England express many misgivings about de Gaulle's Carlton Gardens headquarters in London. They had said, "Be careful of that group. They are a gang of Cagoulards." In London, I confirmed this accusation. At the head of General de Gaulle's secret agents was the previously mentioned Colonel de Wavrin who went by the name of "Passy." (Many of these Cagoulards in London took the names of Paris subway stations. One of Passy's associates, for instance, called himself "Bienvenu Martin.") I had heard of these men in France in the middle Thirties, when this fascist Cagoulard organization was actively trying to overthrow democratic government in France, and I knew of their violence. I also knew that there had been a split within the Cagoule. Certain elements, believing that they should not weaken France by internal disputes just when a European war seemed imminent, had given up their activities. But the main section of the Cagoule had continued underground in all of its fascist fervor. One of this latter group was Deloncle, to whom Colonel Passy had served as secretary. It was far from reassuring to find these elements again in London, grouped around a man striving behind a liberal facade for the political leadership of the greatest European democracy.

I already knew about the brilliant military record of the de Gaullist Generals Koenig and Leclerc in North Africa: the heroic stand of the Fighting French troops under Koenig at Bir Hacheim was in the same tradition of greatness as de Gaulle's original resistance speech of June 18, 1940. It was in London, however, that I learned of the good work of the de Gaullist Navy. The British were enthusiastic about the coöperation they had had from the 5,000 French sailors fighting the war at their side. I learned, however, that the English attributed this coöperation, not to de Gaulle, but to the efficient services of Admiral Muselier. I knew the Admiral had broken with General de Gaulle and I was curious to know what had caused the break. This was Admiral Muselier's story:

The trouble went back to Dakar. General de Gaulle had a great deal of explaining to do to the British, in the autumn of 1940, after the failure at Dakar. That expedition had been undertaken and backed by the British on the formal assurances of General de Gaulle that Dakar would rally to the de Gaullist-English side. Not only did this not happen, but there was good evidence, as I have noted before, that the defending forces at Dakar had been forewarned of the expedition. The British returned from this expedition, not with a sense of the bad faith of General de Gaulle, but certainly with a distinct sense of the inefficiency and the amateur character of the de Gaullists as men of military action.

There was one outstanding de Gaullist who had not been in favor of the Dakar expedition, Admiral Muselier. In December, 1940, he was arrested for about a week by the English on the basis of a letter supposedly written by him to important people at Vichy, revealing military secrets. Muselier had always been extremely popular, not only with the French Navy but also with the British, because of his efficiency. At the same time he had often been in disagreement with de Gaulle, who never liked even a shade of difference or competition.

There was such a reaction against Muselier's arrest on the part of the French and British Navies and the British War Cabinet that a thorough investigation was made. The letter in question was found to be a forgery and was finally traced to the office of Colonel Passy. The man who actually did the forgery was imprisoned on the Isle of Man and Muselier was released. This forgery could not be traced directly to de Gaulle or Passy, who denied knowledge of it, but there are many reasons to believe that it was done with their knowledge. The personal and dictatorial character of the de Gaullist organization precludes the idea of a subordinate doing such a thing on his own. De Gaulle saw the letter in question, said nothing to Muselier, and transmitted it himself to the British Security people in order that they might take action. This in itself was most irregular because if he believed Muselier had committed an act of treason it was certainly the duty of General de Gaulle as commander-in-chief of the Free French to take immediate action himself.

But all of this took place in the rushed, critical time of 1940. The British naval lines had to be kept going, so Muselier got on with his naval work, and became more and more the man in the de Gaullist headquarters on whom the English Admiralty depended. This coöperation between de Gaulle and Muselier lasted until December 1941 when the affair of St. Pierre and Miquelon occurred.

Muselier set sail for Newfoundland and Canada to inspect French interests in that part of the world and to look into the question of suppressing the Vichy radio station on the Miquelon Islands. After talks with the Canadian and American authorities at Ottawa, he realized that it would be unwise to take any immediate action as there was a plan being worked out whereby the Canadians would take control of this radio station. Muselier was further confirmed in this decision by a telegram from his chief of staff, Captain Moret (or Moulec as his real name was) in London:

"Informed by Foreign Office United States President formally opposed to operation planned."

De Gaulle, on December 18, 1941, sent Muselier a telegram which became famous among the Allied authorities because it gave such a clear indication of the sort of coöperation de Gaulle was ready to give the Allies. Here is the text of the telegram:

"As requested, have consulted British and American Governments. We know from certain (?) that the Canadians intend themselves to (destroy) radio station at St. Pierre. Therefore, I order you to carry out rallying of Miquelon Islands with means at your disposal and without saying anything to the foreigners. I assume complete responsibility of this operation which has become indispensable in order to keep France's possessions for her."

At this point, Muselier was both a member of the Free French Committee at London and Commander-in-Chief of the Free French Naval Forces, which he had brought up from Gibraltar after the Armistice and turned over to the British, and which were finally incorporated into the de Gaullist forces. Soon after his return from St. Pierre and Miquelon, he resigned from the Committee of the Free French. As a French officer, he had felt forced to carry out the orders sent him by the Supreme Commander of the Free French Forces, but to show his disapproval of this order, he could—and did—resign his place as Commissioner of the Navy on the Committee.

De Gaulle promptly removed Muselier as Commander-in-Chief of the Navy. Muselier refused to accept this action, and was backed by all the French sailors in a bloc, as well as by many of the British naval authorities. He further maintained that it was only because of him that de Gaulle had any naval forces, and that de Gaulle therefore could not tamper with them.

Admiral Dickens of the British Navy made a complete investigation of the Muselier incidents, and of the methods generally used by de Gaulle with the French Navy. This report was seen by many prominent

French people, as well as the English authorities, among them Captain Moret, Muselier's chief of staff. In the report, the words "violence," "lies," and "blackmail" were used in referring to the methods employed by de Gaulle. Moret described this report before a meeting of Free French Naval personnel. De Gaulle promptly protested to the Foreign Office that the British had no right to interfere thus in French affairs. Foreign Secretary Eden replied that the Foreign office had "received no communication of this report" from the British Admiralty. This, however, did not deny its existence.

In North Africa, I had heard French officers recite, with a great deal of misgiving, the form of oath that had to be sworn before entering into the inner circles of de Gaullism. In London, I found that this same sort of oath had caused many English authorities a great deal of concern.

A leading French woman in London in June, 1940, heard of the oath de Gaulle planned to have administered to potential agents. She tried in vain to have the terms modified. General Eon, in an open letter addressed in London to General de Gaulle, gave the text of the oath as follows: "I swear to recognize General de Gaulle as sole legitimate chief of Frenchmen, and to engage myself in the work of making Frenchmen recognize him, by employing if need be, methods and ways similar to those I would have used against the Germans." The Secret Service at Algiers at the beginning of 1943, gave me the same formula, ending with the words: "I swear on my honor to obey the orders of the leaders who will be given me before, as well as after, the liberation."

Another unpleasant sidelight on de Gaullism was the Youth Movement manner in which groups of young French people met in a Free French headquarters near London to study de Gaullist principles. I read with some interest one of the key books used in these studies: *La Technique du Coup d'Etat* * by Curzio Malaparte, an Italian adventurer who was involved in almost every European revolution from 1917 on. In this book, a technical handbook rather than a theoretical study, Malaparte gives his analysis of the various techniques used in taking power.

* American edition *Coup d'Etat, the Technique of Revolution*, E. P. Dutton & Co., 1932.

That summer of 1943, London was buzzing with talk and rumor of the French underground. This underground was never a single, unified movement, as it seemed over here, except that it was united psychologically, of course, against the German invaders. It was, rather, a series of different movements which often overlapped, and which were effective in different degrees on different levels. Our Embassy in London was, naturally, deeply interested in this whole chain of undergrounds. While we had an Embassy in Vichy, it had kept in close contact with underground leaders. In those days, the main underground had been grouped around the figures of General Weygand, General Rever, and General de Lattre de Tassigny, now Commander of French Occupation Forces in Germany. General Giraud, as soon as he escaped from the German prison at Koenigstein, had established contact with these men. In fact, his escape had been arranged by their agents.

When France fell, she had almost four million men mobilized. Under her armistice terms with the German conquerors, she naturally had to demobilize this army, but a secret mobilization immediately started. Arms were hidden, and new ones made. There was a regular *état major* and command posts. The first contact of this military underground, of course, was with the British, as we were still neutral. Rather regular services were established between England and France, by submarine and airplane. There were even many air fields so hidden that, by night, British planes could land men, make contact with the underground and bring them various supplies but very few arms.

As time went on, the military underground established contact with American representatives, too, and asked us to equip them with modern arms. This would have involved such risky operations as trying to debark secret shiploads of arms on the southern coast of France, and we never were willing to undertake it. (In North Africa, in the spring of 1942, I received a copy of a detailed plan for American military aid, as requested by this French underground. A more complete list had previously been given to Mr. Murphy.) It was this military underground, with its highly organized and honest general staff, which planned and timed the sabotaging of transportation, production and everything else. It was they who sent instructors to the many cells that carried out this work. The timing and spotting of these acts of resistance had to be carefully considered so that the reprisals made by the Germans would not outweigh the value of the sabotage.

This military underground had very little faith in the de Gaullist underground movement for three reasons: first, the latter was more a propaganda organization than a military one; there was no general staff. Second, German agents were known to have infiltrated into the movement; and third, the de Gaullists did very amateur things which ruined "security." They actually, for instance, broadcast data on specific acts of sabotage, loose talk which helped the Germans make reprisals.

At the moment of our landings in North Africa, as noted before, the leaders of this military underground had been led to expect simultaneous landings in the South of France. Generals Weygand, de Lattre de Tassigny and Rever waited in France to cover these landings. Had we been able to accomplish these, it is one of those sad "might-have-beens" of history—the underground resistance of the Generals' 300,000 men would have at least allowed the French fleet to escape to North Africa. When the Germans moved into Unoccupied France, it became increasingly difficult for this underground to act. They had showed their hand too much at the moment of our African landings. Both de Lattre de Tassigny and Rever later escaped from France, and General Weygand was promptly put in Giraud's old prison at Koenigstein by the Germans.

There were two definite and rather tragic facts that resulted in the small role finally played by the original French Army of the underground. First, the French had deep-grained misgivings about the military efficiency of the British. They had a positive belief in American war potentiality, but, also, a mistrust of what they considered our inexperience, our easy attitude toward publicity, and our lack of security in the military sense. Exacerbating their doubts and inability to act was the ever-present fact of their being under German rule. They were defeated, and their enemy never let them forget it. France was isolated from our world, and completely preoccupied with her tragedy. The military underground therefore lost sight of the fundamental importance of constantly having close and serious contact with the English and Americans on the highest levels. This was a grave mistake on their part.

The other reason for this lack of confidence was certainly the fault of the Allies. We, too, had suspicions, and in the liberty and luxury of being unconquered, overemphasized, I believe, our feeling that large parts of France had somehow betrayed us. This feeling was certainly kept alive by de Gaullist propaganda against the people remaining in France, and against the leaders of the army which had been defeated. Both facts resulted in the military underground never being taken seriously enough by the British or ourselves to receive the material aid in the form of armaments and supplies they desperately needed to fulfill their potential usefulness to our common cause.

This underground began the very day of the armistice. As months and years passed, and the treachery of the Vichy Government became increasingly obvious, a staunch political underground began to take form, too. This was, alas, kept separate from the military underground because of the suspicion that always seems to exist, in the time of national tragedy, between civilian political forces and active military ones. This political underground found expression notably in the clandestine newspapers, *Combat, Liberation,* and *Franc Tireur.* Toward the end, when liberation was imminent, even Frenchmen who had never been in the original resistance movement joined the political propaganda underground, accomplishing intermittent acts of sabotage, and making up the group known as the F.F.I. (French Forces of the Interior).

When Laval began to send French workers into Germany by force in 1942, the so-called *maquis* began to form. People anxious to avoid deportation or forced labor for the Germans simply left their homes and lived in more or less organized bands in the forests or mountains or were hidden singly or in small groups by farmers in removed parts of the country. This *maquis* group served as a manpower "pool" for all three different branches of the underground resistance.

An increasingly important element in the French underground was the Communist party. When Hitler invaded Russia on June 22, 1941, they began to work with the military underground. After 1942, they became a more or less separate "resistance," directed politically by the Communist party and in touch with Russian agents, particularly in the south of France. At the time de Gaulle took over in Algiers, he made overtures to the Communists because he knew the growing political force they represented within France. The Communists, in turn, rallied to de Gaulle because particularly in the case of the Communist deputies released from prison in North Africa after our landings they needed whitewashing with the many French people who couldn't forget Communist responsibility in 1940 in the defeat of France.

It was during my stay in London that I learned these intricacies of the French underground from one of its original leaders, a contact of our former Embassy in Vichy, André Girard (known as "Carte" in the Underground). He explained the way in which the underground kept contact with the outside world. I have since confirmed his facts, which have never been published, with my own experience, our Embassy in London, our services in Washington, and British colleagues. But the real importance of Girard's story is the way in which it illustrates the conflict between American policy with France and that of the Foreign Office in the spring and summer of 1943.

Until the spring of 1943 the French underground contacts with the British were kept distinct and separate from the de Gaullist group in London. This was done on strict and repeated orders from the British authorities. They had already had so much trouble with the de Gaullists, that they preferred to work directly with the French in France. British secret radio stations communicated directly with the command posts of the underground in France. The liaison officers sent by the British military services into France acted on over-all directions from the Foreign Office. The Frenchmen who went to London were, also, in contact with the Foreign Office on political matters. None of these contacts passed through the de Gaullist headquarters in Carlton Gardens. This was one of the things that exacerbated de Gaulle's hatred of the British.

One of the heads of the French Military Intelligence Bureau connected with the underground Army at this time was the celebrated Colonel Vautrin. He had left early in 1943 and gone to London by the secret transportation route maintained throughout the war between France and England. This trip was made on British invitation to try to get more arms and closer military coöperation with them. He left behind, as his deputy, Girard. One day, Girard, received a message, over the clandestine radio from London, asking him to come to London as soon as possible. The message read, "Colonel Vautrin finds himself in a delicate situation here because of your absence and therefore asks you as a personal service to come to England." Girard arrived in England by airplane only to find Vautrin had left for Africa by plane the very night Girard arrived. Girard thought it strange the Colonel who had sent him his orders should not have waited to see him. On this African trip, Vautrin was killed "under circumstances," as Girard wrote, "that still make me wonder."

In London, Girard was in contact with the English officers whom he had worked with in the military underground. He asked them to put him in touch with the American representatives in London interested in his underground problems. He was told by these officers that there were no such Americans. It was by sheer chance that he finally established contact with men in our Embassy who were far from disinterested, and who had, as a matter of fact, been hoping and trying to get in touch with high-ranking members of the military underground with which they had worked back in the Vichy days, some months before. The Foreign Office had just decided to channel all underground contacts through de Gaulle's headquarters, believing he was their best means of strengthening Anglo-French relations. This was not American policy. Again, as so often, there was a conflict of services and of policies, well illustrated while I was in London in the case of André Girard.

When Girard had first come out of France, he had been given the job of running the secret English radio that communicated with the command posts of the underground in France. This radio station was called *Radio Patrie* and had been established by the British in the middle of September, 1942, upon Girard's request. It was used to send orders by code to all the "cells" in the military underground throughout France, and was of vital importance in the organization and synchronization of their resistance work.

On the 15th of April, 1943, Girard was suddenly told that this radio was henceforth to be run from de Gaullist headquarters. Girard not being a de Gaullist could no longer speak to France over *Radio Patrie*. As a French resistance worker he could not take de Gaullist resistance seriously, and as a Frenchman he could not be a part of their anti-Anglo-American attitude and aspirations for political supremacy in France. In England he had seen enough of the de Gaullists to have his original ideas on de Gaullism strongly reinforced. This action with *Radio Patrie,* of course, was part of the British Foreign Office's plan to back de Gaulle completely. From the planning of our African landings up until this time, the official British policy had been to encourage, in fact, to insist upon, the incorporating of the lesser forces of General de Gaulle into the greater armed forces of North Africa, and to work with the military underground. Until the victory in Tunisia, the military aspect of the whole French question took precedence with both the British and American Governments. With African victory, however, the Foreign Office began to be preoccupied again with the political future of Europe generally and their position with France and Russia in particular.

The American Embassy, which was, of course, following American policy took more interest in the more immediate military problems facing France and arranged to have Girard go to North Africa to continue his work with the French secret army through the Intelligence Bureau of the North African Army. An American officer, in London, working closely with the British secret services, heard of Girard's plans and mentioned them to his British colleagues. Here the conflict of British and American policy suddenly came into full view. Girard, having his exit visa from the Home Office, was stopped at the airfield by orders from the S.O.E. (British military secret services) the moment he was about to leave for Algiers.

This action coincided with the turbulent moment I described in Chapters XIII and XIV of the attempt at Algiers to fuse the Giraud and de Gaulle elements into The French Committee of National Liberation. André Girard was awaited impatiently by the Giraud elements in North Africa. He was their contact with the military underground that General Giraud had left behind in France. The Foreign Office, however, did not want this. Any close tie up with the French underground would be too great a political card for the rival. They were backing de Gaulle. Girard's failure to reach Algiers helped enormously to give the de Gaulle forces there the necessary time to win.

Later upon demand from the State Department Girard was given his exit visa from England by the Foreign Office after they let it be understood by word and letter how strongly they held to their principle that Girard should never be allowed to go to North Africa or speak to

France over the radio. In the meantime British agents went to France and told the clandestine radio stations that they were sent by "Carte" or André Girard. Since he could never deny this over the air there was no way for his *Radio Patrie* stations to know this was untrue. Girard, by this time, was anathema to all de Gaullists and some British (they said he represented a "reactionary, fascist-tinged army group"). In spite of this, he remains a pro-English and pro-American Frenchman who preserved (and preserves) the respect of leading Americans concerned with our French relations. One of them said to me after the liberation of France, "It is now obvious Girard was consistently right; if we had only gone on working through him our French relations would certainly now be better."

From this time on we allowed the Foreign Office and the de Gaullist services to remain in full charge of the underground lines with France. By an agreement dated July, 1943, our American services worked only through British lines. This was understandable, in view of the fact that the British had had these lines long before we were in the war, but it meant the sacrifice, again, of the original American policy of keeping any one political group from taking over the political control of France while she was helpless. It also meant that our Anglo-American contact with the underground became much more political than military due to de Gaulle's constantly greater emphasis on political questions than on military ones. (The feeble part played by the returning French Army in the early days of liberation was the result of this policy.) Moreover the channeling of our service through British-de Gaullist lines definitely meant that a powerful organ of anti-American propaganda was allowed to establish itself in pro-American France. But, as I point out later on, the real tragedy of all these manipulations was that they eventually worked against British interests, too.

In London I also learned that a year before all these events, de Gaulle had established, in the summer of 1942, another set of contacts with another French underground—the political, propaganda one. Emmanuel d'Astier de la Vigerie (brother of Henri d'Astier we worked with in North Africa) had gone to England from France that same summer, using secret routes of the military underground. A journalist and politician he at that time headed a group of about forty resistance men who ran a clandestine newspaper called *Liberation.*

In London, he made contact with General de Gaulle, and found that British were still entirely concentrated on the military underground and not much interested in a political one. It was he who convinced de Gaulle that propaganda in the clandestine French press could have great political weight. De Gaulle issued a statement, at the time, that he had had a long conference with a "great leader of the underground in France." D'Astier de la Vigerie returned to France with financial backing in the form of millions of francs from de Gaulle. From then on, de Gaullism was quickly taken up by all of the clandestine presses in France. The three leading ones, *Combat,* *Liberation,* and *Franc Tireur* published the Proclamation of General de Gaulle of June 24, 1942.[14] This proved to be one of de Gaulle's most astute moves toward his desire for political domination in France. Ironically, d'Astier de la Vigerie's paper, *Liberation,* is today one of the voices of the opposition to de Gaulle in France.

It was during this same summer of 1943 that I again saw General Odic who had first been in North Africa with Weygand and later had returned to work with Giraud. I knew Odic's anti-German, anti-collaboration reputation, and that he had left North Africa in the autumn of 1941 for the United States. But the thing that most interested me at this time about him was that though he had early made contact with de Gaulle, he had not joined the de Gaullist movement. I wondered why. He gave me the statement which follows, more or less in his own words:

"When I associated myself with the French resistance, my declaration was widely circulated by radio by the de Gaullist propaganda department. In it, I reviled the servility and expressed my horror at the feebleness of the Vichy Government in the face of the mass executions of innocent hostages. I explained the open war I had now undertaken against Germany, following the appeal of General de Gaulle.

"On my way to England, I received a personal telegram of thanks from General de Gaulle. When I landed from the bomber in which I traveled, a plane was waiting to take me directly to London.

"I arrived on December 12, 1941, and was taken at once to Carlton Gardens, where General de Gaulle was awaiting me. My reception, the embrace, the photographers in evidence, everything marked a *desire to woo* me, politically. I had already met General de Gaulle four years previously at Metz, but I did not remember him. I did, however, accord him the merit of being the symbolic representative of French resistance against the enemy. He was, to me, the ambassador and the voice of a France which was speechless. However, his first words displeased me.

" 'I give you,' he said to me at once, 'the supreme command of my land, sea and air troops in Africa, stationed at Brazzaville.'

"I was astonished by this abrupt beginning, which seemed to intimate a form of payment for my allegiance. (I learned later, of long bickerings which had preceded the appointments of other adherents, and I suppose that these may perhaps have influenced his interview with me.) My gesture had been spontaneous, without conditions, dictated by a patriotic obligation, and I wished it to have this character. Besides, having already been in command of an army during the war, and being Grand Officer of the Legion of Honor, I had not come to London to be given a title. My idea was more modest in form, and more ambitious in fact, than the ridicule of becoming a Commander without troops, in a fictitious theatre of operations.

"I reminded General de Gaulle that the reason I had come to London was to try to prevent a Franco-German alliance which Vichy seemed about to accept. De Gaulle replied in these exact words:

" 'On the contrary, France must be in the war by the side of Germany to be able to prove the guilt of the men of Vichy.'

"If I had been shocked by his first remark, I was horrified by the second. Where was I? Had I really heard correctly? Like a flash the mist cleared, and I realized that at Carlton Gardens, the war was not being fought against Germany, but against Vichy.

"I have no fondness for Vichy. As well as any Frenchman, I know those guilty there, and I take it for granted that French justice, in its good time, will decree the rightful punishment. For myself, I had fought Vichy when its policy was one of abdication to the enemy. But, I always encouraged it, each time, when I felt that it followed the will of the people to further resistance.

"To be frank, de Gaullism as such, is epitomized in the reply of its founder. His cynicism is the essence of it. Realizing this, one understands how it was born, how it evolved, and the end to which it aspires. The whole French problem, as seen by de Gaulle, is brought down to the level of opposition to any possible political rival. It involves the systematic destruction of French unity.

"Meditating on these bitter thoughts, I walked back to the hotel where I passed the four months of my stay in London. It had been decided that I should make contacts with different members of the London Committee before having my second interview with General de Gaulle.

"With the exception of the Service of Naval Affairs, the impression I received did not lessen my initial amazement. For fifteen years, I had worked in various ministries in Paris, and I could, therefore, judge how completely artificial this London organization was. It reminded one of the trappings of a theatre, in which the actors waited for the photographers and the publicity agent. At the entry, one was offered portraits of the heroes with explanatory notes.

"Too often, these heroes had forgotten to fight at the moment of battle, and had become merely oral soldiers. Too many of them found in de Gaullism a remunerative occupation which ended their enforced idleness. Some in uniform passed as heroes who had conspicuously gone into hiding during the storm. Not one name comes to my mind belonging to anyone who represented French public opinion. It was evident that people of consequence would not submit to the rules of Carlton Gardens. Decisions were taken by General de Gaulle, and countersigned by a Commissioner who might not even belong to the Department concerned. Such methods eliminated all responsibility, and permitted the development of dictatorship.

"When, three days after our first meeting, General de Gaulle asked for my opinion, I did not hide my feelings.

" 'From a French point of view, all this means nothing,' I said to him.

" 'It is not my fault if the leaders have not followed me,' he replied. I was not yet in a position to judge the value of this answer.

"During the following weeks the matter was made clear to me by independent Frenchmen in London. I soon noted that there were many of these who either kept themselves apart from the de Gaullist Movement, or were openly hostile to it. I learned that, from the beginning, it had appeared to them to be more of a political faction than a military assembly. These men had no sympathy for Vichy, and did not hide their admiration for England. One of them, who bore a well-known name in France, had given up his position there, but had not joined the de Gaullist Movement. A number of French officers who desired to continue the war against Germany, preferred renouncing their rank, and joining the English Army as lieutenants, rather than receiving higher rank plus English pay among the de Gaullist troops.

"The opinion of these Frenchmen was that, far from having tried to enlist the sympathy and allegiance of well-known Frenchmen, de Gaulle had systematically avoided them.

"I, nevertheless, gave General de Gaulle all the information I could concerning France. During a subsequent conversation with him, I broached the question of France's political future. Without ignoring the importance of the military side of the resistance, I observed that because of the dictatorship introduced by Vichy, one must consider the conditions under which the country could revert once more to Republican institutions.

" 'Do you still believe in those things?' de Gaulle asked me. I believed in them decidedly, and I shall always believe in them. It will not be sufficient for France to find military freedom unless she can, also, attain her independence, and her place in the democracies of the world.

"I had not wanted to form my opinion of de Gaullism following the first conversation which I had had with its chief, but I was progressively led to the confirmation of my original opinion. Vichy and Carlton Gardens seemed to me to be more and more alike. National Revolution and de Gaullism advertised the same methods, and voiced the same intentions; two rivals, each playing the game of chance best suited to their own advancement.

"During the whole month of January, 1942, I did not once go back to Carlton Gardens. My mind was made up, but I wanted to compare my conclusions with those formed by others who had been eighteen months in London. I met the English, the French, and the de Gaullists. Among these last, a few became confidential. They confessed to having made a mistake, and asked what they should do. To all those in uniform who were doing useful work, either as combatants, or in training combatants, I said: 'Close your eyes, and go on with your work.' Thanks to them, France continued to figure in the war.

"It was, however, necessary for the leaders to take a position, and I had decided not to remain under de Gaullism. At first, I thought it better not to reveal the facts related above. But, I realized that France would gain nothing by identifying herself with a movement whose mistakes and defects were already known in well informed circles.

" 'It seems to me to be unbelievable,' I said to de Gaulle, finally, 'that anyone should try to cultivate the hatred of French against French. There are not many who are guilty, and they must be punished, but that must not constitute a system. French political life is based on something else. I know the feelings of the authorities in North Africa. They are not collaborationists, or, in any case, they are not so today. It is essential to get in contact with them, and without compromising them, prepare them for their eventual reunion with us. If the bridge which separates us is widened, time will increase the breach, instead of healing it.'

" '*As this is the way you think,' said de Gaulle, 'you had better go back to North Africa, and I shall fight you.*'

"I informed the British Government that honor forbade my becoming associated with the movement which I had unmasked, in the same manner in which it had prevented my remaining with the Government of Vichy. Not only had I met people in London who confirmed my impressions, but I was the witness of events which reinforced them.

"The words spoken by de Gaulle are not without importance, because they attest to the personal responsibility he has for acts one attributes to his entourage. The acts, themselves, are, however, of more importance because they cannot be denied."

This 1941–1942 experience of General Odic's tragically confirmed the suspicions I had already had in Africa of the good intentions of General de Gaulle. I felt more and more that President Roosevelt's firm stand against de Gaulle's political ambitions was well grounded. It had always been the declared American policy to aid in every way those people who wished to take up arms and fight our common enemy, but this could not be stretched to mean that we would aid in every way factions who definitely wished to take over political power with no mandate under democratic forms. Our first objective, in our French policy, was military victory, and I realized beyond a doubt that the President was right in keeping it our first objective. The second objective was that of trusteeship—of guarding the sovereignty of France for the French people.

Early in the summer of 1943, President Roosevelt and Prime Minister Churchill seemed agreed on the danger of de Gaulle's political ambitions, both to our military ventures and to our relations with France. At that time, Mr. Churchill sent a report to the American Government, a summary of which Ernest Lindley published in the American press.[15] It is of such importance in an understanding of British-American relations with France that I reprint the essence of this article:

"The hypothesis that it is American influence that is being brought to bear to persuade the British government to modify its attitude toward General de Gaulle is destroyed by the high points of a statement of British policy on this question recently sent to this country, and understood to be the views of the Prime Minister.

"1. De Gaulle can no longer be considered a reliable friend of Britain. In spite of all that he owes to British assistance and support, he has left a 'trail of Anglophobia' wherever he has been.

"2. From August, 1941 on, he has tried to play Great Britain against the United States and the United States against Britain.

"3. He has striven to create friction between the British and French in Syria.

"4. He clearly has 'Fascist and dictatorial tendencies.'

"5. In spite of these grounds for complaint, the British government has treated de Gaulle fairly and recognizes the value his name has come to have in France—chiefly through British publicity. It still hopes that he will coöperate loyally as co-President of the new French National Committee of Liberation. So far, however, he has struggled for complete mastery.

"6. Peace and order and smooth communications in the French North African territory are essential to the great military operations now being prepared. (The statement was written before the invasion of Sicily.) Likewise it is highly important to avoid throwing into turmoil the French forces which the United States is now arming."

This statement was especially important because de Gaulle's very political existence was due to the Prime Minister and the British Government. It was impossible for President Roosevelt to take unilateral action against him. If political de Gaullism was to be eliminated as a menace to France and her Allies, it was the Prime Minister who would have to act. He had made de Gaulle, and he would have to break him.

The repercussions from the Churchill report were especially serious in England.[16] De Gaullist propaganda had great weight there, and even more importantly, political opposition to Prime Minister Churchill was being born within his own party. That summer of 1943, I often heard English men and women of his own political affiliations say: "He has been a magnificent war leader, but he is not a man with whom we can make the peace." His anti-de Gaulle feelings confirmed liberal belief that he could not be trusted in foreign affairs. The Foreign Office also opposed Mr. Churchill on de Gaulle, considering, and with good reason, that their policy with de Gaulle was bearing fruit. British prestige was growing every day in North Africa, but American prestige was sinking rapidly. In France, itself, attacks were being made on American ideas and even on the personality of the President by the de Gaullist clandestine press.

The Prime Minister knew Mr. Roosevelt's strong views on the French problem and his determination to hold to them. This knowledge had unquestionably influenced his anti-de Gaulle report. Some sections of English opinion began to feel that their Prime Minister was too much under the influence of the American President just as in this country certain elements began to think the contrary was true. At the same time the fact that American prestige which had been so high in November of 1942, at the time of our landing in North Africa, could fall so rapidly, in spite of American aid to the French, presented real political issues to be handled by the British Foreign Office and the State Department. These unfortunately were grounds for friction.

In England I endeavored to inform myself on the over-all lines of Foreign Office policy in this increasing French dilemma. It must be understood to follow the rest of our defeat with de Gaulle. I had had impressions of its aims in Algiers but in England they appeared clearer. The Foreign Office's primary desire was to strengthen British relations with France. In addition to her proximity as a neighbor, France was most useful as a balance against the growing power of the Russian colossus on the continent. England's leadership in French relations was as important to her as we consider our leadership in Pan American relations. In de Gaulle, they felt at once that they had someone who would prove a "good neighbor" and who could also help balance the European scales in Britain's favor. De Gaulle had spasmodically flirted with Russia, it was true, but he was essentially, as the Foreign Office knew, conservative and inclined toward the pre-revolutionary French Catholic state. Their unpleasant experience with his temper and lack of balance actually made it tempting to the average bureaucrat, once this policy was in force, to give in to him on detail. A series of small resultant compromises then made de Gaulle's victory much easier.

Mr. Churchill was vigorously attacked in the House of Commons on July 22 for his report against de Gaulle.[17] In the attack, his opponents first seemed to think the article that had appeared in the American press was erroneous, but Mr. Churchill directly and clearly stated: "I take full responsibility for this document, the text of which was drafted personally by me. It is confidential document. I am not prepared to discuss it otherwise than in secret session, and then, only if there were a general desire from the House to have a secret session."

The Prime Minister's point of view was obviously not shared by the majority of either his cabinet or his fellow members of Parliament. The de Gaulle issue had been thrown into internal British politics. The Prime Minister had two choices—either to acquiesce before his Foreign Office and the pro-de Gaulle majority or fight for his point of view in Parliament, using all of his powers of persuasion and his great prestige. To do this, he would have had to reveal, not only to the members of Parliament but, eventually, to the British public, the large amount of evidence he had against de Gaulle and de Gaullism. (In the spring of 1943, the Prime Minister had already been asked by an important Englishman to publish a "White Book" of all the detailed relations between the British Government and de Gaulle. This Englishman feared the effects of de Gaullism on French relations as well as on Anglo-American relations if its evils continued to be hidden. Mr. Churchill thought such revelations then unwise.)

This was the summer of 1943. The war was far from won. It was not until almost a year later that we even dared to attack the coasts of

France. The British people and Government, since June, 1940, had generously and in all good faith, backed General de Gaulle and his movement. If, three years later, the Prime Minister had intended to liquidate him, there was a great deal of explaining to do. Mr. Churchill apparently decided to let de Gaulle win.

CHAPTER XVI

The Policy of Appeasement

THE history of our dealings with de Gaulle from then on is the story of people who have lost their footing on a slope and find themselves falling helplessly down hill. We had slipped in North Africa and we were never able to retrieve our errors. We had lost command of the situation.

When I got back to Washington, I found the makers of our foreign policy bitterly aware that we were fumbling our handling of the French problem. Important elements in the State Department, not yet sure where we had gone wrong but horrified by our falling prestige, wanted to recognize de Gaulle at once. They felt that to delay recognition was simply to martyrize him. Working almost frantically under a barrage of unfavorable publicity, and improvising almost from day to day, the State Department tried to reconcile this rather fatalistic feeling about de Gaulle with the President's original French policy. Mr. Roosevelt still held to this, and did his best to implement it that summer of 1943.

A final attempt to buoy up the sinking figure of General Giraud, and with it our hopes of restoring French military effectiveness, came that summer. Giraud visited the United States. The visit, unfortunately, came too late. When the General emerged from his long, careful talks with the President, he said to members of his *entourage*, "Why was I never told in Algiers how strongly the President desired to help us rebuild our armies? All would have been different had I realized that the President felt as strongly as he does."

The realization was a belated one. In August, 1943, Mr. Churchill met the President at the Quebec Conference. At that conference we were finally committed to a policy of appeasement with de Gaulle. I was told in Washington that the Prime Minister explained to the President that, because of the political situation at home, he would have to give in to the pro-de Gaullist faction in Britain. He had a majority both of the House and the Cabinet against him. The President, rightly feeling that Anglo-French policies must coincide in view of the plans for a second front, reluctantly yielded. On August 26, 1943, we gave the de Gaulle-dominated Committee partial recognition.[18]

The Committee, with its two chairmen, General de Gaulle and General Giraud, were to be the trustees of all French interests, and the authority in the liberated parts of the empire. (Russia recognized the Committee more fully as "representing the interests of the French State" on the same day). This partial recognition on the part of the United States and Great Britain was not a compromise. It was only the fulfillment of what General de Gaulle had originally demanded in the Brazzaville declaration of organic de Gaullism in 1940. From then on, however, the story of our relations with de Gaulle became one of constant appeasement on our part and of growing but helpless disillusionment in London and Washington.

By the time of Giraud's Washington visit, however, de Gaulle's political domination of the French Committee of National Liberation was already complete. Giraud still had control of the Army, but de Gaulle had no intention of letting him keep it. He used the same ruthless weapons in taking the army over that he had used in the battle for political domination of the Committee of Liberation. When Giraud returned to North Africa, he found the Army had been exposed to still more de Gaullist pressure. It was obvious, with all of this fratricidal intrigue going on in the hot oriental atmosphere of French North Africa, that American arming of French troops had to slow up—if not stop entirely. We could not afford to expose the Allied supply lines running from England and America through North Africa.

On Giraud's return from Washington he threw himself into war preparations. De Gaulle concentrated, as usual, on politics. At the end of September, 1943, after the Corsican campaign, which was the only purely French campaign from North Africa, de Gaulle and Giraud again met head on. Corsica was the first French soil to be liberated. After this had been accomplished, General Giraud, as Commander-in-Chief of the French Army, visited the scene of victory. He was hailed enthusiastically by the Corsicans with shouts of "*Vive Giraud, Vive La France,*" as he made his tour around the island. But, Giraud remembered that he was not only Commander-in-Chief of the French

Forces, but Co-Chairman of the French Committee of National Liberation. He stopped his car at once, and explained that there should be no more "*Vive Girauds.*" "*Vive La France,*" yes; but he, General Giraud, was but a colleague of General de Gaulle's. There must, also, be "*Vive de Gaulles*" if there were to be "*Vive Girauds.*"

Then, in his political role as Co-Chairman, and following the agreements that had been made with de Gaulle, Giraud invoked the Treveneuc Law of 1872 for the reconstitution of democratic processes. He appointed the General Councilors who had been disbanded when Pétain took control in 1940, empowered them to take over the administration of the island and to name the people who were to coöperate with the Committee at Algiers.

When de Gaulle heard this, he flew into one of his now notorious rages. "*Vous avez volé ma Corse,*" he cried to Giraud. "You have stolen *my* Corsica." He repudiated any idea of using the constitutional procedures he had twice promised to follow. He then had his own Algiers Committee hand-pick the local *Préfets* who were to administer Corsica.

But de Gaulle now fully realized, from Giraud's popularity in Corsica, that the old General remained an effective, if unwitting, political rival. So he began building up his Committee, to give it the appearance to the world of a full-fledged Provisional Government for France. His first act was to form, and progressively enlarge, what was known as a "Consultative Assembly" to act as an advisory body to the Committee itself. The members for this assembly were appointed, in many instances, by General de Gaulle himself, from Frenchmen all over the world. Certain French parliamentarians in exile were called to Algiers to serve on this assembly. Other places were filled by men brought out from France as "representatives of resistance groups." Among the parliamentarians used were some Communist deputies, the same Communist deputies who had been arrested at the outbreak of the war in 1939 because of their anti-war party "line." An evaluation of this assembly and its eventual work in redrafting the French Constitution is well given by E. B. Wareing in the London *Daily Telegraph.*[19]

Some parliamentarians in exile refused to serve on the Consultative Assembly because the Assembly had no power except an advisory one.

They did not wish to lend themselves to what was called a representative legislative body, when it actually was not. Of the five exiles invited from the United States, four refused to go. Their point of view is clearly expressed in an open letter written by Henri de Kerillis, whom I have mentioned before, to Félix Gouin, President of the Consultative Assembly.[20] They felt as American Congressmen might, if, while America was under Japanese occupation, some patriotic but self-appointed West Point graduate, set up an official American government in Puerto Rico.

On November 6, 1943, the Algiers Committee, using the excuse that the leader of the French Army could not also hold a political office, voted Giraud off the Committee. (Some members of the Consultative Assembly protested this vigorously) M. André Le Trocquer was made Commissioner for War and Air and from then on, Giraud was told that he was under Le Trocquer's order. Opposition to this new military setup began in the ranks of the North African army. Le Trocquer asserting his new authority confined several high-ranking officers to their quarters.

The method used in ousting Giraud was a typical one already employed several times by the de Gaullist faction, and used even more often in succeeding months. The authority cited for the action was Article 4 of a decree dated October 2, 1943, providing that should a member of the Committee assume "the effective control of the Armed Forces" he would cease functioning as a member of the Committee. The action taken against General Giraud was cited as "foreseen" in the decree of the preceding month to which, at that time, no one had paid any attention. In fact, General Giraud himself had signed the decree that was to remove him from his Co-Chairmanship of the Committee, and was then called upon to reconsider the formula by which he had ousted himself.

London and Washington were concerned over this reshuffle in Algiers because, first, they were afraid it might prevent French participation in the Allied war effort and, second, because they foresaw that it might hamper a future free choice of government by the French people. The Anglo-American attitude was summed up by Mr. Churchill in a Churchillian phrase: "The French National Committee are not the owners, but the trustees, of the title deeds of France."

During this period, General Giraud threatened several times to resign as Commander-in-Chief of the French Forces, but the Anglo-American authorities urged him not to. On this point, the American diplomats might have been firmer in advising Giraud. It would have been more effective to resign than to give in to this shameless political pressure. Although we no longer spoke with our former authority in North Africa, we still had power enough to prevent this injustice to the leader of the Armies who had fought so gallantly at our side in Tunisia.

The ever-combustible Near East next exploded in our face. When the Free French forces took over in Syria in 1941, General Catroux, speaking for General de Gaulle, told Syria and the Lebanese States that de Gaulle accepted the principle of the termination of French mandatory rights in these countries. During the war, however, it was agreed French authority would be maintained there under the leadership of the de Gaullist Committee.

In November, 1943, Nationalist elements in the Lebanese Government became restive under French domination. De Gaulle impetuously ordered the French Delegate General in the Levant, M. Jean Helleu, to arrest the protesting politicians. This action caused so much excitement throughout the whole Middle East, with demonstrations of sympathy as far away as Cairo, that all Islam seemed likely to catch fire. London and Washington both protested to the French Committee, and demanded the release of the Lebanese leaders. Catroux, with some charged words implying British connivance in the whole affair, because of the long-standing Anglo-French rivalry in the Middle East, went to Beirut to settle this incident.

The fact that we had had to intervene in this affair was a grave blow to French prestige in the Islamic world. The repercussions were felt across the whole face of Islam through North Africa to the Moroccan coast. General de Gaulle, in an effort to court favor in the Arab world, then put through a decree offering full French citizenship to "several tens of thousands" of Algerian Arabs, regardless of whether or not they gave up the rules of the Koranic law and accepted French law. The whole problem of the status of these Algerian Arabs, who live in what is legally a part of metropolitan France, must some day be reconsidered. But it was of dubious legality for a Committee which was only a trustee of French interests to grant the precious right of French citizenship to these people when the Republic itself had never been prepared to take this important step. This attempt to buy Arab friendship was considered an internal French matter, however, and we never protested though the action went far beyond the functions for which we had recognized the Committee.

De Gaulle, dissatisfied with the amount of recognition he had received from England and the United States, then reopened his flirtation with Russia. In a famous speech he spoke of *cette chère, puissante Russie*. This was hardly the tone of friendship he used with his other allies, particularly the United States. That winter, in fact, there was what seemed to be a concerted effort upon the part of the de Gaullist group in Algiers to undermine Franco-American friendship. Darlan's assassin, for instance, became almost a martyr in Algiers; the Justice Ministry of the Committee of Liberation issued a statement exonerating him, and flowers were put on his grave by de Gaullists. The whole episode was used to highlight anti-American and chauvinistic feeling. The de Gaullists also started stories—which had to be officially denied from Washington—that the United States Government intended to deal with Vichy after the liberation of France. The State Department went so far as to call the reports "inspired."

In early February of 1944, observers were shocked to see de Gaulle begin a campaign of purges. In one of the most famous cases, that of the infamous Pucheu, the accused deserved little sympathy from the democratic world because of his black collaborationist record; the illegality with which the trial was conducted, however, was repellent to both the British and American public.

An even more disquieting episode occurred in February, 1944, when André Le Trocquer, de Gaulle's Commissioner for War, wired General Montsabert in Italy to return one Maurice Carré for internment on a charge of collaboration with the Germans. General Montsabert wrote back that he could not comply with the order because Captain Carré had just been killed in action against the Germans under such heroic circumstances that he proposed forthwith to make him a Chevalier of the Legion of Honor. Carré was one of the 140 officers on the de Gaullist blacklist, many of whom died fighting the Germans before they could be brought to trial as "collaborators." Alexander E. Bogomoloff, the Russian representative in Algiers, said one day to de Gaulle:

"We had our purge, too, but we had it before, not during, the war."
Even General Juin was called back to answer certain political questions. He refused on the grounds that he considered the war against
the Germans took precedence until final victory. All these events so
disturbed the American authorities that they continued to hesitate to
send arms to the French for what they feared might turn into inter-
necine warfare.

Our relations with the French became more and more important
after Teheran, with the imminence of D-Day. Mr. Churchill, after his
illness in Cairo, came back to Marrakech and Villa La Saadia in January, 1944, to recuperate. There he had a conference with General de
Gaulle lasting some days. A friend of mine told me: "Churchill washed
de Gaulle's head in the fountain of the house where you used to live."
Whether his head was washed or not, de Gaulle returned to Algiers
confident, and full of praise for Mr. Churchill.

Teheran had decided the English once and for all to back de Gaulle
completely in the hopes of having a Western Europe to balance Russia's Eastern European power.

We were now entering the final phase before the great day of liberation, and, as this day approached, de Gaulle became even more in-
transigeant. He was trading on his discovery that Britain and America
could be made to follow a policy of appeasement. He made further decrees covering the political censorship of the French press in North
Africa. This was a complete violation of the French right of free speech,
and the entire management of *France-Afrique* News Agency in Algiers
resigned in protest. Wareing, in the London *Daily Telegraph*, wrote
an interesting exposé of this action.[19]

The most dictatorial action of all came on April 6, 1944. The Allied
world, at this time, was waiting impatiently for the opening of the
Second Front. De Gaulle, now the unquestioned political leader of the
exiled French, realized that his compatriots in France would be more
interested in the general who came in with the liberating Allied forces
than in any politician, and it also looked more and more as if the
Allies intended to deal entirely through the military on D-Day. So,
with characteristic bluntness, the de Gaulle-dominated Committee, on
April 6th, removed General Giraud from Commander-in-Chief of the
French Forces, offering him the same title of "Inspector General of the

Armed Forces," that de Gaulle had offered Muselier in London in the spring of 1942, when he wished to liquidate him. When the press called this a "resignation," General Giraud at last acted with political firmness. He made it abundantly clear that he had actually been dismissed, and that he would take no face-saving position.

By a decree of April 4, de Gaulle then became the supreme military as well as civilian authority, taking over the same complete power that five months before had been forbidden as illegal, to General Giraud. If ever the shape of a *coup d'état* was obvious, it was now. American journalists on the scene reported that the whole situation had the atmosphere of the *Brumaire*, Napoleonic *coup d'état*.

The next episode in our uncertain dealing with the now triumphant de Gaulle was a curious one. Our own policy makers in Washington seemed to be at odds. On April 7th, President Roosevelt indicated in a press conference that he felt it would be unfair to France to allow one group to take full political control before free elections could be held. "Would you," he said, "on the question of self determination, let the determination be made by people who are not in France?" Yet two days later the State Department officially expressed exactly the opposite point of view. On April 9th, Secretary of State Hull, in his speech on foreign policy, said, "We are disposed to see the French Committee of National Liberation exercise leadership to supervise law and order under the Allied Commander-in-Chief." Secretary Hull was perhaps responding to the pressure within the State Department itself, and in the American press. Hull's statement was a great victory for de Gaulle and the British Foreign Office. Yet it became obvious as time went on that President Roosevelt did not intend to give full and complete recognition to the Committee as the Provisional Government for France. Again de Gaulle moved swiftly. On May 15, 1944, he announced that his Committee *was* the Provisional Government of France, whether anyone wanted to recognize it or not.

By that time, the most critical point in the war was approaching— the Allied invasions of Normandy. On April 11, 1944, General de Gaulle appointed General Koenig as French liaison officer on Eisenhower's staff in London with the questionable Colonel Passy as Koenig's Chief of Staff. Under their orders, some 500 French officers were chosen for their knowledge of the Norman coast and of the English language, to act as liaison officers with the debarking troops. They worked closely with us during the long, hard weeks before the invasion.

On the eve of invasion, Prime Minister Churchill's airplane was sent to fetch General de Gaulle to London. He arrived, and was finally told the date of D-Day. De Gaulle insisted that the hour of the landings be communicated at once to the French Forces of the Interior within France so that they could take part in the liberation. This was obviously unwise for security reasons and Allied Headquarters refused to do it. This, added to the fact that de Gaulle was not allowed to speak to the French people on the radio before General Eisenhower made his appeal, threw him into a characteristic rage. He forbade the French liaison officers who had been working with us to embark with us on the great venture of the liberation of their homeland. General Koenig, knowing the wishes of the Supreme Command, begged General de Gaulle to relent. Finally, and grudgingly, he did allow a handful of some twenty liaison officers to land in France with the liberating forces. After all our efforts to rebuild France's greatness, to give her back a great French Army, only twenty Frenchmen took part in the great day of liberation. This was the crowning blow to our original policy with France.

On D-Day, the great day of which poor Giraud had dreamed so long, he was in Algeria, in a villa near Oran. Here in August, 1944, incidentally, he was the victim of several attempts on his life, during one of which he was badly wounded. These attempts were highly suspicious.

After D-Day, de Gaulle sat back in London, watching the liberation of France from a distance, renewing a campaign for full recognition. He made one flying visit to the Normandy beach on June 14, 1944, and then returned to London. (The same day, in the midst of the tremendous sacrifice of American blood and matériel in France, a New York *Times* reporter, Harold Callender, wrote from Algiers describing the anti-American spirit there. "Algiers," he said, "is not a pleasant place for Americans.")

During these weeks and months of Allied advances in Normandy de Gaulle's men went into France behind the lines and began to "exercise leadership to supervise law and order." They named *Préfets* and other local administrators, a power that in such circumstances only the General Councilors held temporarily under the Constitution of France and not a group of Frenchmen returning from exile. When we allowed de Gaullists to circumvent the legal processes already set up by law for reorganizing France, we legalized illegality. We acted as bad trustees for our still helpless French allies. Finally, after Paris had freed itself, on August 23, 1944, de Gaulle went to Paris with two American-equipped divisions under General Leclerc.

When de Gaulle first arrived in Paris, he went to the Hotel de Ville where the resistance leaders who had struggled so courageously throughout the occupation asked three things of him: First, that he make a declaration maintaining the Republic of France according to its Constitution; second, that he include in his Provisional Government leaders of the resistance named by the resistance forces; and third, that he convoke the General and Municipal Councilors according to the Treveneuc Law under the French Constitution. De Gaulle refused all three of these demands.

Paris was in an uproar, and the de Gaullist forces seemed unable to quiet it. "French officials pressed for a show of Allied strength in the uneasy city when the Allied commander visited Lt. General Jacques Pierre Koenig there. General Eisenhower, after reviewing the political situation, ordered the diversion of two United States divisions and they marched—the General was careful to use this word, not paraded—through the city on the way to the front east of Paris. No British troops were immediately available for this purpose." This was done to "strengthen the position of General Charles de Gaulle and help in the solution of his particular problems." * Our de Gaulle policy ended in a final irony; we had to maintain by force of arms the very man whose anti-American feelings were well known and whose assumption of supreme power we had so long opposed.

We followed this military support with the final political gesture. On October 23, 1944, de Gaulle was given full recognition for his Committee as the Provisional Government of France from both the American and British Governments. This final appeasement was no more satisfying to de Gaulle than our other gestures. When Mr. Eden and Mr. Churchill came to Paris in November, 1944, de Gaulle refused to make an Anglo-French alliance. The next moment, he turned around and made a Franco-Russian alliance. His next act was decid-

* New York *Times*, August 31, 1944.

edly anti-American.

A meeting between President Roosevelt and de Gaulle was arranged by American and French diplomats at the time of the Yalta Conference in February, 1945. To the surprise of George Bidault, the French Minister of Foreign Affairs, de Gaulle agreed to meet the President on his way back to the United States in any place in France designated by the President. The meeting was fixed for Algiers, but de Gaulle at the last minute refused to keep the appointment. This action could only be interpreted in this country as a direct snub to the head of the government that had spent the most in matériel and blood to liberate France. The French people also interpreted it the same way, and de Gaulle received severe criticism in France.

Today, General de Gaulle, who proved indifferent to Giraud's efforts to build a great French Army, is calling for just such an Army, and, characteristically, blaming the United States for not giving it to France. His just claims that France should occupy the Rhineland, the Saar, the Ruhr, and play a predominant role in the occupation of Germany, become hollow ones when France lacks sufficient military force to fulfill these obligations. If arms are lacking for the French, de Gaulle is more responsible than any other Frenchman. His demands for American economic aid are doubly ironic in view of his notorious and long-standing anti-American policies, dating back to his first emergence on the world scene. Those policies have been continued since his return to France. Certainly de Gaulle's ultimate and greatest disservice to France and, indeed, to the democratic world is the fact that he is responsible for a wave of anti-French feeling in the United States. All of France and every Frenchman is associated with all his unfriendly actions. Old ties of friendship have been strained by the attitude of a political party striving to stay in power. The results are ominous for our interest in western Europe, and for the peace of the world.

CHAPTER XVII

Problems of Our French Dilemma

FROM this story of our French dilemma some obvious points emerge. Our failure in this field is widely admitted. How did the break-down in Franco-American relations come about? There were various turning points, I believe, at which our diplomacy could have better defended American interests and preserved Franco-American friendship as well.

Perhaps the one underlying diplomatic mistake was the failure of the State Department to recall Mr. Murphy once his original mission had been ably accomplished. Mr. Murphy and his group of Economic Control officers were sent to North Africa, as it turned out, to make a revolution. Our job was to get North Africa to revolt against the questionable neutrality of the Vichy Government. People who set out to foment revolution cannot use the very elements maintaining the status quo: in this case the French Army, Navy, and Vichy officials, all under German pressure. Mr. Murphy had to dig into the North African underworld to find agents. These agents were often far from representative of the best elements in France. Yet we were left definitely in their debt.

I do not wish to impugn the patriotism of the Frenchmen who helped us, but it is true that, in many instances, they turned to us solely because of our potential strength. With success, they seemed to expect a personal reward and to have us take time to fill all their individual ambitions and aspirations. This was obviously impossible, above all in the midst of a war. The State Department should have immediately removed Mr. Murphy and every one of his assistants once the French were fighting as our allies in Tunisia. Had this been done, the diplomatic job would have been infinitely easier. This was, I believe, a necessity that should have been foreseen. Our American diplomatic policy should have been carried out, preferably, by a man of Cabinet rank, well briefed in all our pre-landing activities and allegiances, but with no personal debt to anyone. Diplomacy cannot be implemented by "provocative agents" and this is the most accurate term to describe the Murphy mission.

Even if the State Department weren't prepared to do this, there was another factor that should have been taken into consideration. Mr. Murphy and the rest of us, had been bogged down in the details of the pre-landing job too long and had lost our usefulness in the bigger picture. Fresh minds and energy were needed to accomplish this first extension of the United States into European politics with force and sureness. Contrary to all his many critics, I sincerely believe Mr. Murphy's work was excellent until the French were at war in Tunisia. His task had been enough to exhaust a much younger man. It was understandably difficult for him to see his way through the barrage of problems that came up in 1943 and to avoid the mistakes that were certainly made.

In spite of all this, our over-all policy could have been successfully implemented in North Africa if four problems had been handled differently while our military strength was at its apex. We never again had a chance to solve them successfully.

First, in regard to Jean Monnet: he was essentially a business man with international banking experience and had never been a diplomat. By his very training and experience a business man is ill fitted for diplomatic service. A banker or an industrialist if he is not satisfied with negotiations with some company can turn to any number of rival concerns to accomplish his objective. He thinks in terms of competition, which means almost infinite choice. The diplomat has no such range. A representative of the United States Government negotiating Franco-American relations has but one choice. He is obliged to deal with France. Again, unlike a business man, a diplomat must deal with intangibles. His job is to guard national human interests as well as material ones. In guarding the former the highest degree of moral integrity and personal disinterestedness is needed; in guarding the latter what is sometimes called "commercial honesty" is all that is required. Finally, the business man can wash his hands of an unprofitable enterprise, whereas, the diplomat's mistakes become history, and his country must live with them. The Monnets of this world should never be allowed to carry business methods into international affairs.

Our second mistake was in our handling of de Gaulle in the early stages. When he arrived in North Africa, he proved almost immediately his determination to carry out France's political role and not her military one. He showed his lack of balance right away by resigning in a burst of temper from the Committee. This resignation should have been accepted at once. Then as a general he had but one choice: join his compatriots on the field of battle or get out of the French picture entirely. Such a clear opportunity never presented itself again. At that moment France's political future, as has since been proved, and as President Roosevelt then realized, depended upon her military rebirth. If General Giraud and the Committee, continuing its role of political trustee of French interests, had been firmly and clearly advised at this moment to accept General de Gaulle's resignation, put French politics aside for the duration and had actively thrown their energies into building a great Army, the whole French story would have been different.

This leads me to my third point.

All through the Algiers episode, General Giraud was given advice that wrecked him politically. I do not maintain that it is the role of an American diplomat to *force* a foreign leader to take any particular advice. I do maintain it is his role to present his country's over-all policy so clearly and forcefully that a foreign leader will be *persuaded* that it is to the national interests of his own country to coöperate with that country's most useful friend. General Giraud, as I have said repeatedly, showed total political ineptitude, but he was sincere and trustworthy, striving always to see his country retake her place with her allies by having Frenchmen liberate France. American prestige was so great in 1943 in North Africa that it is a sad reflection on our diplomacy that we handled Giraud so weakly.

Foreign Office policy made all three of our mistakes more likely, but still not unavoidable. At the period of our fourth and final chance to stem de Gaulle's march toward total power our previous failures had so increased de Gaulle's influence that the Foreign Office fulfilled their ambitions for de Gaulle much more easily.

By the time we went into Europe, de Gaulle had eliminated all political competition. We had to recognize him as active trustee of French interests as well as work with his government on our military problems. But we should never had allowed the de Gaullists, when they entered France, to name *Préfets* and all sorts of local officials. The local administration of France was intact and working, not because of the Vichy Government but in spite of it.

Why did we fail at all four points?

One obvious reason is the personal failures of our men on the scene which I have already mentioned. This brings up the whole much-discussed question of how we can attract qualified men to serve in the State Department. There is no space here to go into this very complex subject but it is obvious from our North African experience that we need men with not only training but assurance in dealing with the foreign elements that too often dazzle or mislead us.

Henry James once wrote: "It is a complex fate—being an American —and one of the responsibilities it entails is fighting against a superstitious valuation of Europe." Over a hundred years ago in a situation very similar in many ways to our present French problem, the famous "XYZ Affair," John Marshall, Charles C. Pinckney, and Elbridge Gerry had to assert the rights of a newly-born United States with the powerful and wily Talleyrand. Gerry made "a superstitious valuation" of this suave European statesman, but the more able John Marshall was not deceived. Staunchly he defended our country's interests, and found his backing in the American people. We need more men with this sort of courage.

But beyond this failure of our diplomats on the scene was the failure on the highest Anglo-American policy levels. Mr. Roosevelt held firmly one point of view in which he was, in principle but not always in practice, backed by Mr. Churchill. Another and conflicting point of view was held by large sections of British and American public opinion. This weight of public opinion was shrewdly used, as we have seen, by British Foreign Office policy makers. Our State Department eventually followed their ideas. We should have realized sooner and more completely the whole trend of Foreign Office policy if we were to have a strong policy of our own.

What is the moral for Americans? We must know more, obviously. Policies must be openly thrashed out and backed by informed public opinion. This does not mean that negotiations also should be openly publicized. Often, and especially in time of war, negotiations cannot for obvious reasons be revealed. But the policy governing these negotiations can always be publicly weighed in a democracy.

At this writing, the future of Franco-American relations is dim. When de Gaulle was installed in France a French Government with an active and determined anti-American point of view came to power for the first time in modern history. Consequently American political influence there is on the wane. This is true all over the European continent as American troops return home. Alas, it looks more and more today as if our State Department in following the British Foreign Office by supporting de Gaulle had indeed misspent their energies. What is more, there is increasing evidence that he holds profoundly anti-British views as well.

The one hopeful sign in all this picture is de Gaulle's increasing unpopularity with the liberal elements among the French people. But this in itself is dangerous for Anglo-American relations with France for if de Gaulle is thrown from power, England (and the United States) will be rightly blamed for having inflicted him on France, yet if he stays, there is little evidence so far that he will look to us with sympathy.

Our moral leadership in France has passed to Great Britain. The hope of the democratic world must now be that an informed British public will realize the true situation in France, the key to western Europe, and will do everything possible to strengthen French democracy and to keep France in the Atlantic, democratic world. This important task would be unnecessary if Anglo-American policy with France had sincerely sought to restore democratic liberal principle in France. In order to have accomplished this the grave facts in the whole de Gaulle history should not have been hidden by the British and American Governments from their French allies as well as the British and American public.

The British public, like the American public, has a remarkable moral instinct. This has been constantly demonstrated throughout English history. But never in recent times was it shown more clearly than when this just political instinct of the English people was in direct conflict with their Government's foreign policy in the Abyssinian affair. The Foreign Office was only too complaisant and compromising. The British public, however, proved with what shrewdness they sensed the Fascist menace and how profoundly shocked they were by Fascist aggression. An amusing demonstration of this, on a small plane, was the fact that several Italian seed firms went bankrupt because British subjects all over the world stopped buying birdseed for their pets from these firms. But on a larger plane, the British public in the Great British Peace Ballot of 1935 showed their horror and their courage by an overwhelming vote in favor of sanctions, knowing full well sanctions meant war. At that time this was not Foreign Office policy. Then as I believe now in the French problem, the Foreign Office was out of line.

The hope for peace in the world, like the hope for better relations between all the great democracies, rests with the people themselves, so full of instinctive moral wisdom. They must never allow themselves to be by-passed by the manoeuvering of professional diplomats who are unresponsive to their desires. If both the British and American people had been fully informed, we would never have been defeated by the political ruthlessness of de Gaullism. If the peoples of our two democracies take a fuller and more informed mutual interest in the detailed workings of diplomacy, we need never fail again.

APPENDIX

1

Goods Shipped Under the Weygand-Murphy Agreements

Sent on French boats from the United States to French North Africa between March 1941 and August 1942.

Petroleum products	43,501	metric tons.
Coal	20,489	" "
Tar	1,117	" "
Coke	896	" "
Paraffin	702.23	" "
Sugar	21,498	" "
Cotton fabrics	5,198.68	" "
Cotton thread	73	" "
Tea	1,570.40	" "
Tobacco	1,537.37	" "
Condensed Milk	1,435.61	" "
Binder twine	1,113	" "
Bags	178	" "
Copper Sulfate	798	" "
Nails	350.55	" "

Also smaller amounts of medical supplies, spare parts for farm machinery, wire, etc.

Sent to the United States from French North Africa Under the Same Agreements.

Cork	8,320	" "
Tartar	993	" "

Also smaller amounts of local products.

2

The Basis for Negotiations between the Vichy Government and the British Government

(I) English View Point

(A) *Decision of the British people and Government to carry on the war until the downfall of Hitler.*

False ideas concerning the effects of the London bombings. . . .
The people are stoical, even happy, and accept the risks of the bombings. . . . Daily life pursues its course. . . . It is necessary to give up
the idea that collective fatigue may force the government to sign a
compromise peace. The most peaceful nation of the world is ready to
transform itself into a great war machine. Woman's significant role in
this mobilization of all the nation (different auxiliary services).

(B) *The Capacity of the British Government to Carry on the War.*

1. Total financial help of the U.S.A.

2. Increase of military apparatus: 10,000 airplanes for combat by
next spring, bombers with a field of action permitting them to bomb
all the Italian cities by attacking from Egypt. . . . Mastery of the air
by 1941.

(C) *Probable Duration of the War Depending Upon the Attitude of
the French Empire.*

1. With a revolt of North Africa which would permit the establishment of bases in Tunisia...............*ONE YEAR.*

2. Without bases in Tunisia, but with the possibility of stopping
the German advance in the direction of the Suez Canal and Iraq
..........*TWO OR THREE YEARS.*

3. With the loss of the Mediterranean and Egypt. . . . *TEN
YEARS.*

The attitude of the French Empire may therefore decide the length
of the war, consequently decide the material and moral fate of the
peoples of Europe. An enormous responsibility rests, therefore, on the
shoulders of the chiefs responsible for the Empire.

(D) *Great Britain's Decision Regarding France.*

1. To re-establish her entity (all her colonies) and her sovereignty
if she does nothing to aid the victory of the Totalitarians, and much
more, if she contributes to British victory.

2. In case the French Government handed over its air and naval
bases to the Totalitarians, Great Britain would no longer answer for
the future of France and her Empire.

(E) *Attenuation of the Blockade in Case France Would Help a British Victory Either Actively or Passively.*

1. The British Government will consider the transportation of
colonial food products from Dakar, from Casablanca, and the North
African ports to ports of Provence (Southern France) as belonging to
the coast trade; which does not come under the blockade.

2. The English Government will send an economic expert to Ma-

drid, who will come to an understanding with a French economic expert regarding the eventual exchanges with Morocco.

(F) *Accord Concerning the Status of the French Colonies That Have Remained Faithful to Vichy (Government).*

1. The English Government promises to try no longer to take by force or to undermine by propaganda the French colonies that have remained faithful to the Vichy Government.

2. All English aggression against the French colonies will be repulsed by arms, to avoid joint defense of said colonies by the Axis, which would be the same thing as yielding the African colonies and their bases to the Axis.

(G) *Radio Accord*

1. The British radio will abstain from all criticism addressed to the person of the French Head of State, Marshal Pétain.

(II) French View Point

(A) *Engagement Concerning the Colonies and the Bases.*

1. The French Government promises not to try to retake by force the colonies that have gone over to de Gaulle.

2. The French Government promises not to turn over to the Axis the ports of Provence (Southern France) nor the bases of North Africa, of Morocco and Occidental Africa.

3. The French Government will re-engage the Empire in the war the day that the English and their eventual Allies will have given proof of their strength, will be in a position to debark in number and to equip the colonial troops, who are at present without munitions, without heavy material, air defenses, anti-tank guns, and means of transportation.

(B) *Engagement Concerning the Fleet.*

The French Government, in conformity with the solemn assurances it has already given several times to the British Government, promises to scuttle the units of her fleet rather than to allow them to fall into the hands of the Germans and the Italians. Orders to this effect, annulling all previous orders, have already been given to all ship commanders.

The above drawn up in the office of Mr. Strang, at the Foreign Office, and submitted to the corrections and approval of the Prime Minister, Winston Churchill.

London, October 28th, 1940

3

Letter from President Roosevelt to the Appointed Ambassador to France, Admiral Leahy

Washington, December 20, 1940.

My dear Admiral Leahy:

As Ambassador of the United States near the French Government, you will be serving the United States at a very critical time in the relations between the United States and France. I impose entire confidence in your ability and judgment to meet all situations which may arise. Nevertheless, for your general guidance, I feel that I may properly outline some of the basic principles which at present govern the relations of the United States with France.

(1) Marshal Pétain occupies a unique position both in the hearts of the French people and in the Government. Under the existing Constitution his word is law and nothing can be done against his opposition unless it is accomplished without his knowledge. In his decrees he uses the royal "we" and I have gathered that he intends to rule.

Accordingly, I desire that you endeavor to cultivate as close relations with Marshal Pétain as may be possible. You should outline to him the position of the United States in the present conflict and you should stress our firm conviction that only by defeat of the powers now controlling the destiny of Germany and Italy can the world live in liberty, peace and prosperity; that civilization cannot progress with a return to totalitarianism.

I had reason to believe that Marshal Pétain was not cognizant of all of the acts of his Vice Premier and Minister for Foreign Affairs, Monsieur Laval, in his relations with the Germans. There can be no assurance that a similar situation will not exist with the new Foreign Minister. Accordingly, you should endeavor to bring to Marshal Pétain's attention such acts done or contemplated in the name of France which you deem to be inimical to the interests of the United States.

(2) I have made it abundantly clear that the policy of this administration is to support in every way practicable those countries which are defending themselves against aggression. In harmony with this principle this Government is affording and will continue to afford to the Government of Great Britain all possible assistance short of war. You may wish from time to time to bring to the attention of Marshal

Pétain and members of the Government concrete information regarding the American program to this end.

(3) I have been much perturbed by reports indicating that resources of France are being placed at the disposal of Germany in a measure beyond that positively required by the terms of the armistice agreement. I have reason to believe that aside from the selfish interests of individuals there is unrequired governmental coöperation with Germany motivated by a belief in the inevitableness of a German victory and ultimate benefit to France. I desire that you endeavor to inform yourself with relation to this question and report fully regarding it.

You should endeavor to persuade Marshal Pétain, the members of his Government, and high ranking officers in the military forces with whom you come into contact, of the conviction of this Government that a German victory would inevitably result in the dismemberment of the French Empire and the maintenance at most, of France as a vassal state.

(4) I believe that the maintenance of the French fleet free of German control is not only of prime importance to the defense of this hemisphere but is also vital to the preservation of the French Empire and the eventual restoration of French independence and autonomy.

Accordingly, from the moment we were confronted with the imminent collapse of French resistance it has been a cardinal principle of this administration to assure that the French fleet did not fall into German hands and was not used in the furtherance of German aims. I immediately informed the French Government, therefore, that should that Government permit the French fleet to be surrendered to Germany the French Government would permanently lose the friendship and good will of the Government of the United States.

Since that time I have received numerous assurances from those in control of the destiny of France that the French fleet would under no circumstances be surrendered.

On June 18, 1940, Monsieur Paul Baudoin, then Minister for Foreign Affairs, assured Ambassador Biddle "in the name of the French Government in the most solemn manner that the French fleet would never be surrendered to the enemy."

On July 1, 1940, President Lebrun informed Ambassador Bullitt that "France would under no conditions deliver the fleet to Germany." On the same day, Marshal Pétain assured Ambassador Bullitt that orders had been issued to every Captain of the French fleet to sink his ship rather than to permit it to fall into German hands, and Admiral

Darlan told Ambassador Bullitt that he had "given absolute orders to the officers of his fleet to sink immediately any ship that the Germans should attempt to seize."

When Marshal Pétain came into power as Chief of the French State I received renewed and most solemn assurances that the French fleet would not be surrendered to Germany. Vice Premier Laval reiterated these assurances to Mr. Matthews on November 14 when he said that "The French fleet will never fall into the hands of a hostile power."

On November 16, Marshal Pétain, when the subject was again raised, told Mr. Matthews: "I have given the most solemn assurances that the French fleet, including the *Jean Bart* and the *Richelieu*, should never fall into Germany's hands. I have given these assurances to your Government. I have given them to the British Government, and even to Churchill personally. I reiterate them now. They will be used to defend French territory and possessions. They will never be used against the British unless we are attacked by them." And most recently, Marshal Pétain, in a conversation with the present Chargé d'Affaires ad interim, Mr. Murphy, said on December 12: "I hope your President understands that I have kept and will continue to keep the solemn promise I made that the French fleet will be scuttled before it is allowed to fall into German hands."

I feel most strongly that if the French Government after these repeated solemn assurances were to permit the use of the French fleet in hostile operations against the British, such action would constitute a flagrant and deliberate breach of faith to the Government of the United States.

You will undoubtedly associate with high officers of the French Navy. I desire, therefore, that in your relations with such officers, as well as in your conversations with French officials, you endeavor to convince them that to permit the use of the French fleet or naval bases by Germany or to attain German aims, would most certainly forfeit the friendship and good will of the United States and result in the destruction of the French fleet to the irreparable injury of France.

(5) You will undoubtedly be approached from numerous quarters regarding food for the French people.

There is no people on earth who have done more than the American people in relieving the suffering of humanity. The hearts of the American people go out to the people of France in their distress. As you are aware we are continuing our efforts to arrange for the forwarding through the Red Cross of medical supplies and also tinned or powdered milk for children in the unoccupied regions of France. Nevertheless, the primary interest of the American people, and an interest which overshadows all else at the moment, is to see a British victory. The American people are therefore unwilling to take any measure which in the slightest degree will prejudice such a victory. Before the American people would be willing to have influence exerted upon the British Government to permit the shipment of food through the British blockade to France, it would be necessary that the American people be convinced beyond peradventure that such action would not in the slightest assist Germany.

(6) In your discussions regarding the French West Indies and French Guiana you should point out that our sole desire in that region is to maintain the status quo and to be assured that neither those possessions nor their resources will ever be used to the detriment of the United States or the American republics. To accomplish this we feel that it is essential that the naval vessels stationed in the ports of those islands or possessions be immobilized and that we have adequate guarantees that the gold which is at present stored in Martinique be not used in any manner which could conceivably benefit Germany in the present struggle.

(7) I have noticed with sympathetic interest the efforts of France to maintain its authority in its North African possessions and to improve their economic status. In your discussions you may say that your Government is prepared to assist in this regard in any appropriate way.

Very sincerely yours,

Franklin D. Roosevelt

4

De Gaulle from Brazzaville: Organic Declaration Completing the Manifesto of October 27, 1940

In the name of the people and of the French Empire

In view of the law of February 15, 1872, relative to the eventual role of the General Councils in case of exceptional circumstances;

In view of the constitutional laws of February 25, 1875, of July 16, 1875, of August 2, 1875, and of August 14, 1884;

In view of the state of war existing between France and Germany since September 3, 1939, and between France and Italy since June 10, 1940;

In view of our assumption of authority and the creation of a Council of Defence of the French Empire by Ordnances dates from October 27, 1940, in the free Territories of the French Empire;

Considering that this assumption of authority and its creation has as its goal and objective the liberation of all France; and that in consequence of this it is necessary to inform all Frenchmen, as well as foreign powers under what conditions of law and order we have taken and exercised this power.

We, General de Gaulle,

Chief of Free Frenchmen

Considering that all the territory of metropolitan France is under the direct or indirect control of the enemy; that in consequence, the so-called organism called the "Government of Vichy" which pretends to replace the Government of the Republic, does not enjoy a free liberty of action, indispensable to the integral exercise of its authority;

Considering that this organization tried in vain to justify its actions and existence under the semblance of a revision of the constitutional laws, which in reality are but repeated and flagrant violations of the French Constitution;

That, without denying that a revision of the Constitution could be useful in itself, the fact of having instigated and realized it at a moment of confusion and even panic in Parliament and public opinion, is sufficient reason in itself to take away from this revision that character of liberty, coherence and serenity without which such an act, essential to the State and the Nation, cannot have a real constitutional value;

That the President of the Republic has been deprived, without having handed in his resignation, of the rights and prerogatives of his functions;

That, under the formal terms of the Constitution of 1875, the Chamber and the Senate sitting separately, must each vote for such revision, that only after this the proposals for the revision are to be submitted to the National Assembly, which Assembly can only hold council in Versailles;

That these simple rules considered by the principal legislators of the Republic, in particular Gambetta, and Jules Ferry, as a necessary guarantee for the enlightened consentment of the Chambers, thus avoiding hasty or perfidious revisions of the Constitution, were respected in appearance only, or were violated;

That, in reality neither of the two Chambers or the National Assembly were able to deliberate freely, and that certain fundamental principles, treated disdainfully as "questions of procedure" by the representatives of the so-called Government, advancing this project, were manifestly misunderstood.

That in particular a certain number of members of the Assembly, were prevented from attending, the ship on which they were, having been kept at sea either by order of the Government or in accord with it; that during the course of these public debates, a pressure was exercised upon the members present by the intervention of other persons with no qualifications; that in violation of the rules no official report of the meetings was published;

That the so-called National Assembly was at Vichy, whereas in designating Versailles as the seat of the Assembly, the legislator had proved that he had not considered that one would ever take advantage of the distress of a Parliament obliged to flee and dispersed by armies on the march, to convoke suddenly in a local district with the object of compelling by intimidation the manipulation of the fundamental laws of the Republic;

Considering that, if such a project of revision had been decided upon normally, the Assembly of Vichy ought by right to have deliberated its contents article by article, and have voted on the final text, which would have then become, after its promulgation, one of the constitutional laws of the country; but that far from realizing the essential object of its function, the said Assembly, relinquishing a competence which belonged rightly to itself alone, was led to make the decision, as unconstitutional as it was senseless, to confer to a third party a veritable blank check, which had the effect of enabling this third party to develop and apply a new constitution;

Considering that the law of 1884 decrees that "the Republican form of Government cannot be the object of a proposition of revision";

That, nevertheless, in spite of this solemn promise made to the nation, the pseudo-Government of Vichy which styled itself "Government of the Republic" in view of obtaining full rights, pronounced the abolition article by article, in form as well as meaning, of the Republican Constitution;

That it prohibited by these pretended constitutional actions, even the word "Republic" attributing to the Chief of what it called "the French State," powers as vast as those given to an *absolute* monarch, permitting him to exercise this power for his lifetime or to transfer it to any other person chosen by him alone and even to become hereditary;

That, finally, it did not hesitate to annihilate the free rights of the people, a sacred and traditional right, by conferring on the Head of the State the permission, simply by his signature, to conclude and ratify all treaties, even treaties of peace, or cession of territory, a fact which harmed the integrity, the independence and the existence of France, of its colonies, and the countries under its protectorate or mandate;

That, frankly, the blank check that was delivered to this self-styled government, declares that the so-called new Constitution will be "ratified by the nation and applied by the Assemblies which it will form," but that this disposition is obviously without meaning, considering that the so-called "Chief of State" has the choice of deciding by himself the composition of the future assemblies, as well as the forms of the ratification;

That he can delay this ratification to any future date which pleases him, even indefinitely;

That in default of a free Parliament functioning regularly, France could have made known her desires by the voice of the General Councils; that the General Councils could have, by virtue of the law of February 15, 1872, and on account of the illegality of the Vichy organization, taken over the general administration of the country, but that the said organization, by the so-called decree of August 20, 1940, forbade their reunion, and that by the so-called law of October 12, 1940, replaced them altogether by commissions nominated by the central power;

Considering, in summing up, that, in spite of the aggressions committed at Vichy, the Constitution remains legally in force and vigour, that, under these circumstances all Frenchmen, and especially all Free Frenchmen, are freed from any loyalty in respect to the Vichy pseudo-government, the result of a parody of a National Assembly, which ignores the rights of man and of citizen and the free disposition of the people, a government above all, whose every act proves incontestably that it is under the control of the enemy;

Considering that the defence of territories overseas, as well as the liberation of the metropolis, demands that the French forces scattered over the world, should be placed without delay, under a central provisional authority;

And as it so happens that the establishment of this provisional central authority cannot at present, for unavoidable reasons, be established following the conditions of the law;

That the authors of the Constitution could not conceivably have foreseen that a day would come when Frenchmen would be obliged to proceed to the formation of a government outside of continental France, that one cannot either consider creating this power under the elective system, because the details of such a system in the midst of war, and the fact that it would be essential to organize it nationally, would create insurmountable difficulties and, in any case, long delays;

That it should suffice, at the present time, that the desires of Free Frenchmen should be freely expressed without restraint or uncertainty on this subject, with the formal reservation that the provisional authority thus constituted should, as all other authority, be responsible for its actions before the representatives of the Nation, as soon as these will have the possibility of freely and normally exercising their mandate.

In consequence,

We, General de Gaulle,
Chief of Free Frenchmen,
the Council of the Defence of the Empire included:

Realizing that, at all points of the globe, individually and collectively, millions of Frenchmen, or French subjects, and French territories have called Us to the task of directing them in the war;

Declare that the voice of these Frenchmen, the only ones which the enemy or the organization of Vichy which depends on it, has not been able to silence, is the voice of the Country and that We have, in consequence, the sacred duty to assume the charge that has been imposed upon Us.

We declare that We will accomplish this mission in the respect of the institutions of France, and that We will give an account of all our actions to the representatives of the French nation, as soon as these have the possibility of functioning freely and normally.

Ordered that the present organic declaration shall be promulgated or published everywhere that it is considered necessary.

Brazzaville, November 16, 1940.

C. de Gaulle.

5

The Question of the Treveneuc Law of February 15, 1872 and the Liberation of France

There exists a French law which deals with the protection of the constitution and provides for the restoration of the constitutional rights to the people should they be infringed upon by usurpation of power by any political faction or by enemy occupation of the country. It is the Treveneuc Law of February 15, 1872, framed by the National Assembly of 1871 after the military defeat and revolutionary uprisings of the preceding year.

Here is an accurate translation of the text of this law which appears to foresee the present total enemy occupation of France. This law offers the only legal procedure to be followed at the time of the invasion which will provide a provisional administration for the country, as it is liberated, based on the will of the people, and at the same time guarantees that the sovereignty of the state will be restored, in due course, to the French people.

LAW OF FEBRUARY 15, 1872, RELATING TO THE PART TO BE PLAYED BY THE GENERAL COUNCILS IN THE EVENT OF EXTRAORDINARY CIRCUMSTANCES.

Article 1. If the National Assembly, or those which may succeed it, should be illegally dissolved or prevented from meeting, the General Councils shall have the full right to assemble immediately at the capital town of each Department, without requiring special convocation. If their customary place of assembly does not appear to offer sufficient guaranties of security for free deliberation, they may meet anywhere else in the Department. The Councils are only validly constituted by the presence of the majority of the members.
Article 2. Until such time as the Assembly, to be mentioned in Article 3, shall have made known the fact that it is regularly and legally constituted, the General Council shall immediately provide for the maintenance of the public peace and legal order.
Article 3. An Assembly composed of two delegates elected in secret committee by each General Council shall meet at that place where the members of the legal government and such deputies as have been able to escape violence have reached.

The Assembly of Delegates shall not be validly constituted unless at least one half of the Departments are represented therein.

Article 4. This Assembly shall be charged with the responsibility of taking such urgent measures for the whole of France as may be required for the preservation of order, and especially those measures which are designed to restore to the National Assembly complete independence in the exercise of their rights.

It shall further be charged provisionally with the general administration of the country.

Article 5. The Assembly of Delegates shall be dissolved as soon as the National Assembly has been reconstituted by the assembly of the majority of its members at any point in the territory of the country.

If this reconstitution can not be accomplished within one month after the extraordinary events, the Assembly of Delegates shall decree an appeal to the nation for general elections.

The powers of the Assembly of Delegates shall cease on the day that the new National Assembly is constituted.

Article 6. The decisions of the Assembly of Delegates shall be executed under pain of forfeit, by all public officers, agents of authority, and commanders of the public force (military, naval, and police forces).

The validity of this Law has never been questioned, but on the contrary, has many times been affirmed. The most striking illustration of this is shown in the now famous joint letter of August 31, 1942 from Jeanneney, president of the Senate, and Herriot, president of the Chamber of Deputies, to Marshal Pétain. They say, "You have nullified the General Councils which gave expression to the wisdom of every part of France and have substituted your own choice for that of the people. . . . Your plan to abolish national representation . . . you have followed it since then. At present it is no longer enough for you to have forbidden any activity whatsoever to the legislative assemblies . . . deported their bureaus. . . . You are putting an end to their very existence.

"To make the pretense, as you do, that these bureaus should have been elected each year, is to fail to say that their reëlection has been prevented by you yourself in forbidding the assemblies to meet.

"If, in spite of engagements taken, you had the plan to take away from the nation its right of freely choosing for itself its final government . . . we would have, by this letter, protested ahead of time in the name of the sovereign rights of the people."

Since the German occupation the contingency foreseen by the Law of 1872 in which the National Assembly would be unable to meet is now a reality. Also the suppression of the Senate and The Chamber by the Vichy government is certainly an act of dissolution. Consequently both conditions of Article 1. of the Treveneuc Law exist, justifying,—in fact, demanding the application of this Law at the liberation of France.

It will be seen by Article 1. that as a Department of France is liberated the members of the General Council of the Department "shall have the full right to assemble immediately" and this meeting will be valid as soon as the majority of the members are present, at whatever place decided on in the Department. A further reading of the Law shows how the administration is to be enlarged as the country is liberated and finally handed over entirely to the decision of the people in the form of general elections. Consequently in applying this Law at the outset the administration of the mainland of France is left to the people whom we shall find in France, when we arrive.

Another great problem will have to be met in France, namely: the purging of administrative personnel and government officers, who after so many years of German occupation are today bound to be in varying degrees collaborators with the enemy.

The law of 1872 allows for the purging of any such officials by the people who have stayed in France and who are consequently better able to judge correctly an official's disloyalty to the State than could anyone coming from outside. It must always be borne in mind that the General Councils, as such, are the only political bodies in France who can never be accused of having collaborated with the enemy or with the Vichy government as they were dissolved at the time of the Armistice and have not met since.

If any individual councilor personally has been sympathetic to a policy of collaboration he can be expelled from the General Council by his colleagues, a prerogative essential for all political bodies in a democratic government.

It must be constantly borne in mind in thinking of France today that because of lack of communication, transportation, censorship, the entire country is broken up geographically into countless small local groups. This gives the General Councils an even greater importance as a natural and representative means for control and administration.

Four times General de Gaulle's and the de Gaullist movement's attitude toward the Law of 1872 has been affirmed. On November 16,

1940, General de Gaulle in his Brazzaville Proclamation, which is one of the basic declarations of the Free French movement, criticizes the Vichy government for having prohibited the meeting of the General Councils and concludes "that without a free parliament working regularly. France would be able to make known her will by the great voice of its General Councils in virtue of the Law of February 15, 1872, and in view of the illegality of the Vichy organism would even be able to provide for the general administration of the country."

Again in the December 1940 issue of *La France Libre* Professor Cassin, the official legal spokesman for the de Gaullist movement, discusses the Law of 1872 and the powers that it vests in the General Councils. He points out the illegality of the action of the Vichy government in suspending these General Councils.

In the spring of 1943 during the exchange of notes between General de Gaulle and General Giraud while the Committee at Algiers was being formed General de Gaulle reaffirmed that he considered the only way to ensure the protection of the rights of the French people and to guarantee order in France at the time of liberation was in applying the Law of 1872.

More recently in the last few months General de Gaulle stated that when he returned to France he would hand over the administration of the country according to the laws of the republic.

Nevertheless, the much discussed plan adopted by the Committee of Liberation, known as the Menthon plan, concerning "the constitution of the government of the Republic at the time of the liberation of metropolitan France," is in direct conflict with the Treveneuc Law of 1872.

Mr. de Menthon has based his plan on the premise of his statement, "we are not now in the situation provided by the Treveneuc Law which presupposed an illegal dissolution." This can only be construed as a deliberate misreading of the text of the law. He also says, "Their mandates (meaning that of the General Councils) will have expired." This assumption has no grounds by the texts of the law. But when Mr. de Menthon goes as far as to say, "The French Committee of National Liberation guarantees to exercise power immediately in liberated territory. This immediate seizure of power is in conformity with the necessity of maintaining public order," it is evident that the many declarations we have heard from Algiers of the Committee of Liberation's desire and intention to return to the laws of the republic are, indeed, cynical.

The Consultative Assembly at Algiers has not adopted the Menthon plan and are at this moment preparing a plan of their own; but, nevertheless, the de Gaullist press that is held under strict censorship by the Committee of Liberation has urged the Consultative Assembly to accept this Menthon plan without discussion, saying that in so doing the Assembly will be doing its war duty like the French soldiers in Italy.

But it is difficult to understand why any new plan need be discussed or decided upon when the application of the already existing Law of 1872 covers the problem and is the only legal procedure in existence.

If the de Gaullists and the Committee of Liberation at Algiers insist, as they do, that it is only in their name that the resistance groups of France will coöperate with us, the heroic action of the French North African army in Tunisia must not be forgotten. It was not in the name of anyone or of any committee but in the name of France that 70,000 soldiers took up what were originally inadequate arms and suffered 16,000 casualties (more than the British and the Americans together). There is every evidence that we shall find in France just such courage and patriotism on an even larger scale.

How could General de Gaulle who always most dramatically presents himself as the symbol of France hold any objection to our adopting the Law of 1872 as our guide? In fact, he, himself, should maintain that any other action would be a breaking of faith with the French people.

I was in North Africa since June 1941, attached to Mr. Murphy, and thus had a chance of studying at first hand the *technique de coup d'état* (agents, press, disdain shown for the premises upon which American and English recognition of the Committee of Liberation was based, the martyrdom, the xenophobia, etc.) used by the de Gaullists to transform ostensibly a civilian population that certainly was not 10% de Gaullist before the Allied landing to being almost wholly de Gaullist one year later.

In spite of the control of the press and the constant repetition on the part of the French Committee for National Liberation at Algiers that they have a mandate from the French people, there is absolutely no proof that this is true or that General de Gaulle and the Committee would ever be accepted for even a short time as a government by the people of France if this people knew in detail the history of de Gaullism. In fact, in judging the situation, the enormous difference between the point of view of 40,000,000 French within France and those outside must never be forgotten.

Therefore, in France should we, by any recognition, however defined or limited (do not forget North Africa), favor or aid, even slightly any political group to take over power in the country without the voice of the great mass of the occupied French people being heard through the legal processes of the Law of 1872, we not only risk, but assure internal dispute amongst Frenchmen, hindering the war effort, a further weakening of France in eventual unnecessary internal disorders, and a rupture of French-Anglo-Saxon relations for the future with the grave consequences that can ensue.

Certainly in following the procedure of the Treveneuc Law we shall be continuing our very honorable policy of never mixing ourselves up in the internal problems of other countries, above all, in those of our allies.

Kenneth Pendar
February, 1944.

6

To My Children

In captivity, at Koenigstein
January, 1941

I do not know how long I will stay here, perhaps months, perhaps years. It is possible that I may be buried beside my friend, Dame. No matter, I am ready for anything. To you I entrust the responsibility of taking my place in the sacred task of France's restoration. I forbid you to resign yourselves to defeat, and to accept a fate for France like that of Italy, Spain, Denmark, or Finland. The means are not so important. The goal alone is the essential thing, and everything must be subordinated to it. To it you must sacrifice your personal interests, your tastes, your theories, your faith.

In the beginning, there is no need of making a frontal attack on the enemy, who is entrenched on our soil and has totally disarmed us. Stresemann has demonstrated the method for us to use and we have only to copy it intelligently.

Of prime importance is the liberation of our territory inside the frontiers which have been given to us.

Then, physical, moral, and social reconstruction:

a. To bear children. To help those who have them.

b. To raise them as they should be raised—for France.

c. To assure each family its place in the sun.

In the third place, to be ready, at any moment, to take advantage of the opportunities which will be offered us, if there is still any confidence in us. By this means to re-establish a modern army instantaneously. This assumes that we shall adopt the right kind of program.

From this distance, I propose the following principle:

The spiritual requirements are fulfilled in France.

The training is carried out in the colonies.

The material is obtained from abroad.

In spite of all the surveillance, such a program is possible, providing it is camouflaged. Nothing resembles military experience so much as scouting experience. Nothing resembles a military airplane so much as a transport plane. A tractor on caterpillar treads only needs armor to become a tank, etc., etc.

But, above all, the spirits of our people must be equal to their task. They must wish to be French, completely.

Nobody should exile himself from the occupied or temporarily cut off territory in order to preserve French thought abroad.

On the other hand, nobody should hesitate to exile himself if the possibility is offered to him abroad to be useful to France.

All of you, Pierre, Henri, André, Bernard, and you, my dear daughters, remember that the storm passes but the mother country remains forever. A nation lives when it wishes to live. Tell this to everyone around you. Compel the others to think as you do, to work as you do. We are sure of success if we really want it.

Resolution—Patience—Decision

H. Giraud

7

September 9, 1942 Protest to Pétain and Laval from Jeanneney and Herriot

We learn in the Journal Official of your decrees that the bureaus of both houses of Parliament cease their functions August 31. That act is in contradiction to your engagements. In July, 1940, to obtain a vote of full powers by the National Assembly, you promised through Pierre Laval that the Chambers would not be suppressed. Your Constitution Act of July 11, 1940, stipulated that the Senate and Chamber should continue until new assemblies provided by a new constitution were ready. But by the same act you adjourned the Chambers and decreed that they could meet again only when you convoked them. (Here part of a sentence was missing from the dispatch.)

Now, not content to have forbidden any legislative activity, you have suppressed all the prerogatives of the members of Parliament. You have deported the Chambers from Vichy to Châtelguyon. (100 words censored here.)

You now want to terminate their existence. You pretend that the Chambers should have elected officers every year, but you omit to state that you have prevented their renewal by failing to convoke the Parliament. You recognize the legality of the parliamentary bureaus by decreeing their removal to Châtelguyon. Can you say that the bureaus lose their reason to be when the assemblies no longer sit?

Your own Keeper of the Seals, Barthelémy, replies to you implicitly on page 525 of his treatise on constitutional rights of 1933: "Bureaus do not disappear during the interval between sessions." There is no doubt that bureaus must exist as long as assemblies exist. Only those charged by the assemblies with mandates have the quality to act for them. But you have faced us with an accomplished fact. We can only accept. But you must realize that we republicans shall not stay silent against this new attack on republican institutions. (Some material censored here.)

You have put the brakes on the essential rules of our civil and penal rights. You have substituted unlimited dictatorship for guarantees that all civilized nations grant to accused persons. You have re-established *lettres de cachet*. The French are ready to accept any sacrifice to repair the national disaster. They will accept any necessary discipline, but they will keep their faith in the institutions of liberty. The National Assembly at Vichy gave you your full powers. The government of the Republic, under the authority and signature of Pétain, promulgated in one or more decrees a new constitution of the French State. Furthermore, it specified that the constitution be ratified by the nation and applied by the assemblies it created. Whether you like it or not, the National Assembly gave its mandate to the government of the Republic. The mandate is violated when you try to eliminate the essential institution of the Republic. The mandate is violated in that not only has the word "Republic" disappeared from the *Journal Officiel* and the front of public buildings, but everywhere you have abolished the principle of elective representation.

Such acts are more than misuse of power. No government can bear the mandate of a parliament if it ceases to be a government of a republic. We cannot clearly see your aims, but if, despite your solemn engagements, you intend to deprive the nation of the right to decide for itself freely its definite regime, or if without authorization of Parliament you try to draw France into war against our allies, which you yourselves declared "honor forbids," we, by this letter, protest in advance in the name of national sovereignty.

The great and imminent danger is that liberty cannot be reconquered without those convulsions which, in truth, it is your duty to avoid. All the time talking union, you have never ceased excluding Frenchmen from the French community. You have molested many. You have mutilated municipal assemblies that are the heirs of secular and communal traditions. You have wiped out General Councils that reflected the wisdom of our provinces and you have substituted men of your own choice.

You pretension now to deprive us of titles that do not depend on you but upon our suffrage cannot reflect our total devotion to France or our attachment to democracy, which we refuse to disavow.

(Signed) Herriot
Jeanneney

8

New York Herald Tribune, *June 6, 1942*

FRENCH TO ISSUE NEW DE GAULLIST PAPER IN BRITAIN

La Marseillaise to appear June 14 as 66th foreign war periodical in London.
by Eric Hawkins.

London, June 5th

Almost coinciding with the second anniversary of the fall of France, a new French newspaper, *La Marseillaise*, will begin publication in London June 14, it was announced today. It will be published weekly and will be the 66th foreign wartime publication appearing in the British capital.

La Marseillaise will reflect directly and officially the views, policies, and interests of the Free French movement, it was revealed, and will be edited from Carlton Gardens, General Charles de Gaulle's headquarters in London. Theoretically, it will be designed exclusively for the fighting forces of France and in this sense it will be a French counterpart of the *Stars and Stripes*, published for the American forces in Great Britain.

It will, however, be distributed without charge, part of the agreement with British authorities being that it will not be put on sale.

La Marseillaise will be the seventh French language publication edited in London. Of the sixty-six publications representing directly and indirectly the views of the United Nations and the free governments established here, Poland has twenty-one, Czecho-Slovakia fourteen, Belgium seven, Austria six, Russia, Denmark, Holland, Belgium and Norway two each and Greece one.

Many of the publications are assisted by funds from the British Ministry of Information or the British Council. Few are self-supporting, and lack of funds has caused some of the periodicals to cease publication after a good start. Shortage of paper has been another cause of their disappearance and also has compelled a number of original dailies to be converted into weeklies and weeklies into fortnightlies and monthlies.

Of the daily newspapers supporting the Allied cause, the most important is *France*, which, it was explained today in connection with the forthcoming appearance of *La Marseillaise*, in no way officially represents the de Gaullist government. Contrary to widely held belief, *France* is an independent paper giving strong support to General de Gaulle as a military leader and giving prominence to every Free French activity, but maintaining no political attachment.

9

La Marseillaise attack on Herriot and Jeanneney

London

"Laval has just suppressed not only the Chamber of Deputies themselves, but the offices of the Assemblies, which means that M. Jeanneney and M. Herriot are now nothing. To be frank, for the last two years they have not been very much.

"The President of the Senate, and the President of the Chamber of Deputies are therefore without jobs, 'on relief' so to speak. I must confess that their plight leaves me unmoved for two reasons. The first because neither one or the other showed, during the crucial and decisive hours when their authority could have helped the country, that force of character which commands respect. The second, because the republican strain which I inherited from peasant ancestry, and a postman father, is not upset by the slight fracas made by the collapse of one of the last remnants of a regime already rotten long before its final shameful end, and which M. Jeanneney and M. Herriot had themselves abandoned on the 10th of July 1940.

"For to speak truthfully, there was the National Assembly of Vichy. And it was therefore the Republic of these gentlemen which was in question and also the Republic of France. They knew the conditions of the armistice. They knew that Alsace-Lorraine had been immediately torn apart from us, and they kept silent.

"Brought up in the palace, and being great dignitaries they knew down to their finger tips, as did Pétain, Laval and Marquet and 'tutti quanti' all about the plot that unfolded before their eyes. They knew that the constitutional acts draughted by M. Alibert, whose co-helpers demanded the vote, overthrew the Republic and confiscated its liberties, and they remained silent.

"Neither one or the other took this occasion to unmask the traitors. Neither one or the other demanded a statement of accounts. Neither one or the other breathed a word to a fairly strong opposition, which in the final counting was able to muster 80 votes, and which perhaps at the call of one or the other might have been turned into a majority.

"Neither one of them, knowing they were defeated, pronounced words of vengeance which, while it does not remedy the crime, or prevent what follows, does not let the people be swept by the deluge and delivered without a word to its enemies. Neither one or the other uttered that cry to which a humiliated people could anchor its pride. A cry echoing from its own heart which could have saved its honor and its soul, and would have assured the continuance of its destiny.

"In all our history books they had put, these great republicans, an engraving representing Beaudin falling from the scaffold in '48. But they were not Beaudin, nor did they share his risk.

"And since then what have they done? I know very well that it is not possible for everyone to derail trains, or to throw bombs. But Ledru-Rollin and many others accepted exile. We who are nothing, and who, once the country is given back to itself, shall ask, after our sufferings, only for peace for those who are nothing. We who often were not of their clan, hoped for this exile, for a very simple reason it is true,—to fight. But during all this time, they, like Candide, 'cultivated their garden.'

"Because the obscure multitude from which we come, resists, it has created an optical illusion and a logomachy of the Resistance. From the moment an official personage does not do harm to France, or from the moment he goes under cover, it is said that he 'resists.' A strange pessimism this, that demands of its vested representatives only the immobility of any oyster glued to its shell.

"They also say that if Laval has enforced his decree, it is because he is afraid of an initiative such as the convocation of the Chambers on the day the Allies land in France. Well, it is possible that we may see them arrive before our own volunteers.—These important volunteers who, like trout, have been kept for so many months shivering with fear in the shade.

"It can even happen that this new France, which is finding herself through suffering, will go through the malady of youth, and in the exuberance of her new-found liberty may give a provisional confidence to some of those who have ill served her. But will this matter? The future, the great future, and stability are still far away.

"It is also said that among the majority of Frenchmen, quarreling has ceased; not only the divisions caused in regards to Germany and Vichy, but that men who opposed each other in former days, meet now with mutual aspirations. This is true. And these two statements are not contradictory.

"The prostration of the first months having been overcome, the sorcery of the old Marshal Pétain aired, French people regrouped themselves. Quite naturally, and as nothing else had been proposed to them, they frequently drifted back to their former affiliations. But what did every one of these sporadic penitents spread to the four corners of France, do? Well, they agitate the already existing feeling against party orthodoxy which begins to unravel, thread by thread.

"What does this mean? It means that a revolution is under way. Traditional etiquette indicates other ways of accomplishing this, and it is not certain that the same etiquette brings always the same results.

"To deduce consequences from this fact is impossible. Political predictions of the French problem have been for a long time uncertain, outside of a few fixed principles and indisputable premises, such as the establishment of a Republic, and the restoring of liberty. Only these facts of social and economic order are on solid ground, because they are known, and because the fact that we neglected them was the cause of our disaster, because also they are in the soul of everyone and correspond to pressing needs, and, lastly, because they are the original thoughts and dominant occupation of all revolutions.

"There is no problem more pressing than the one of reconciling

France with her workers, or one more urgent than to give French agriculture a position where it will no longer be a luxury of the State, or a despised means of livelihood for the worker.

"The work being done by the constituents is vast, and of permanent value. But the first shock that caused the spark was a social shock: the collision of the people with the nobles. And the first gesture was the abolition of feudal rights, on the night of August 4th. After this, all that was left of the monarchy was swept out like straw.

"This is why, when I hear of 'rejuvenated institutions' I am skeptical. To undertake the reconstruction of France on this political basis, and to which a form of conservatism still clings, would risk opening the doors to chaos.

"To remove the seat of M. Jeanneney from the Luxembourg, and put it in the Palais Bourbon in place of M. Herriot's armchair, or vice-versa, is not enough of an innovation to satisfy a new France. And this is why I fear that in this France of which I speak, M. Jeanneney and M. Herriot will continue to be without a job."

F. Quilici

10

For Release Monday Morning,
September 14, 1942.

Statement by the Five Members of the French Chamber of Deputies now in the United States

The five members of the French Chamber of Deputies now in the United States belonging to various political parties from the left and the right have issued the following statement in connection with the letter addressed by M. Jeanneney and Herriot to Marshal Pétain.

The five French deputies at present in the United States associate themselves whole-heartedly with the courageous declaration made against the Vichy government's abuse of power. Messrs. Jules Jeanneney and Edouard Herriot, President of the Senate and of the Chamber of Deputies.

Their forceful protest proves the illegitimate and arbitrary character of this government. The acts it performs do not bind France, which at present lacks a regular government.

The undersigned deputies—convinced that they are expressing the opinion of the great majority of their colleagues—are aware that

Messrs. Jeanneney and Herriot are interpreting an opinion that is almost unanimous among the French people. In allying themselves with the two Presidents, these deputies also express the feeling of the Frenchmen scattered throughout the world, and especially of those who are at present the guests of the generous American nation.

As this is their first opportunity to make a joint statement, they are eager to express to General de Gaulle their feelings of admiration and of gratitude for the task which he has undertaken in creating and inspiring the movement of Fighting France.

> Pierre Cot, Deputy for Savoie, Former Minister
> Edouard Jonas, Alpes Maritimes.
> Henri de Kerillis, Seine.
> Hervé de Lyrot, Ile et Vilaine.
> Pierre Mendés-France, Eure, Former Under-Secretary of State.

11

October 3, 1942

General de Gaulle in a statement made to a correspondent of the *News Chronicle* said: "The courageous attitude openly adopted by President Herriot has today been ennobled by his being placed in prison. I salute President Herriot. In my opinion the personal ordeal to which he is subjected is a great service rendered to France and to the Republic."

12

Extracts from a Report Made by the General Staff of the French Army in July 1943 and Communicated to the British and American Governments Dealing with the Desertions Instigated by de Gaullist Agents in the French Regular Army in North Africa

On June 7th the French Committee of National Liberation published the following decision:

"While waiting till it becomes possible to proceed to the fusion of the French forces whose totality should constitute a united national army, *it is obligatory for everyone to remain at his post.* In consequence it is forbidden for any man having irregularly left his regiment, or having received an order to which he has not as yet conformed, to incorporate himself in any other unit. All recruiting of a clandestine nature should immediately be suspended."

.   .   .   .

The report in question fixes the total desertions provoked by the de Gaullists in Algeria alone (not counting Tunis or Morocco) as of July 1st, 1943, at 2,750 officers, petty officers and soldiers, of which 2,000 were from the army, 500 from the aviation, and 250 from the navy.

Procedure and methods of propaganda employed

Every method and argument suitable for rallying men (or a staff forming the nucleus of a regiment, either European or native) to the Free French (de Gaullist) Forces has been used with psychological finesse, and, it must be added, with great cleverness, by the Free French Forces and their recruiting agents, both masculine and feminine:

a. Material arguments:
Important premium for enlistment (25,000 to 30,000 francs).
Higher military pay.
Higher rank given immediately on admission with promise of rapid advancement.

b. Moral arguments:
The prospect of serving in units equipped with modern armament and soon going into battle.
Promise made to Senegalese troops that they would be immediately repatriated. (An argument well calculated to appeal to natives from French West Africa)
Promises of no sanctions being taken for deserting.

c. Practical methods:
Distribution of false leave permits and false identity papers to enable deserters to escape arrest.

.   .   .   .

The conclusion of the report is as follows:

.   .   .   .

Conclusion

If the efforts of the de Gaullists were to be successful it would inevitably result in a fratricide war between the two armies. In fact, as soon as the number of effectives of one army was lowered to a point where they approached the number of the other, constantly increasing, two military forces of similar strength would find themselves face to face: The first army being the regular army, ardently patriotic, and imbued with strong anti-German feelings, but still composing a solid anti-de Gaullist front, and yet forced back into Pétainism from exasperation with the extremist spirit of the second army. This latter is composed of a nucleus of ultra de Gaullists, who have lured deserters out of the regular army and placed them under the orders of a chief determined to triumph at any costs.

13

1943.—D.—No. 465.

IN THE HIGH COURT OF JUSTICE.
     King's Bench Division.
Folios 23.

Writ issued the 6th day of August, 1943.

    Between—

          Maurice Henri Dufour—Plaintiff
                —and—
          General Charles de Gaulle
          Lieutenant-Colonel André Passy
          Captain Roger Wybot
          Captain François Girard
          Colonel Louis Renouard
          Major de Person (Male),
          Major Etienne Cauchois and
          Major Pierre Simon
                        Defendants

＊＊＊＊＊＊＊＊＊＊＊＊＊＊＊

STATEMENT OF CLAIM

1. The Plaintiff is a French national at present residing in England. The Defendant General de Gaulle is or was at all material times the Leader of the Free French Forces. The other Defendants are members of and officers in the Free French Forces employed therein by the Defendant General de Gaulle and serving him; and each of the acts hereinafter alleged as done by each of them were done in the course of such employment and service.

2. On 2nd September 1939, the Plaintiff was mobilised with the French Army, wherein he then held the rank of sergeant. On 1st May 1940, he was appointed an *aspirant* or cadet. Thereafter he fought in the Battle of France and for deeds of valour therein was awarded the *Croix de Guerre* and made a *Chevalier* of the Legion of Honour. On 23rd June 1940, he was severely wounded in the region of the kidneys and taken prisoner by the Germans. On 1st November 1940, six months having then elapsed since his appointment as *aspirant*, the Plaintiff, in accordance with French military regulations, automatically became a *sous-lieutenant*.

3. On 13th March 1941, the Plaintiff was released by the Germans on account of his wound and was sent to a hospital in France from which he was discharged on 7th June 1941. He was then employed by the Vichy Government at an internment camp in what was then un-occupied France. While so employed he came into contact with the British Secret Service, by which he was employed in certain activities, it became necessary for the Plaintiff to escape from France. He left France on 15th February 1942 and arrived in England on 28th March 1942.

4. In April 1942, the Plaintiff reported at the headquarters in London of the Free French Forces and was interviewed by the defendant General de Gaulle. On 11th May 1942, the Plaintiff signed a document described as an *acte d'engagement*, whereby he purported to engage himself to serve in the Free French Forces for the duration of the war. The said *acte d'engagement* is invalid under French law. The Plaintiff never in fact served in the Free French Forces.

5. On 18th May 1942, the Plaintiff was requested to proceed to 10 Duke Street, Manchester Square, W.1, which is the headquarters of the *Bureau Central Renseignements Affaires Militaires* of the Free French Forces. The Defendant Lt. Col. Passy is or was at all material times the officer in command of the said Bureau and the Defendants Capt. Wybot and Capt. Girard served under the Defendant Lt. Col. Passy in the said Bureau. On or after 18th May 1942, the said three Defendants wrongfully conspired together to procure from the Plaintiff information to which they were not entitled concerning his said activities with the British Secret Service, and for this purpose to assault, beat, imprison and otherwise maltreat and injure the Plaintiff. Each of the acts hereinafter alleged as being done by the Defendants Capt. Wybot and Capt. Girard was an overt act in the said conspiracy. The Defendant Lt. Col. Passy was at all material times well aware of the

commission of the said acts and caused and permitted the same to be done.

6. The Plaintiff arrived at the said Bureau at 2:45 p.m. on 18th May 1942. From 3:00 p.m. until 6:30 p.m. on the said day the Plaintiff was interrogated by the Defendant Capt. Wybot about his activities. Thereafter, after an interval of about 2 hours, during which he was kept in the custody of 2 French soldiers and given no food, he was again interrogated from 8:30 p.m. until about 10:30 p.m. by the Defendants Capt. Wybot and Capt. Girard and other officers in the Free French Forces, whose names the Plaintiff does not know; during this interrogation the Plaintiff was kept under a bright light. At about 10:30 p.m. the Plaintiff was directed to strip to the waist, which he did. The Defendants Capt. Wybot and Capt. Girard then struck the Plaintiff with their fists repeatedly in the face and beat him across the small of his back with a steel rod bound in leather, striking him particularly in the place where he had been wounded as aforesaid thus causing him a severe pain and suffering. They threatened to kill him and threatened also that a girl with whom he was friendly and who was then serving in the British F.A.N.Y. Service would be raped, saying "We have arrested Mlle. Borrel and we shall make her speak by whatever means are necessary even if we must rape her one after the other." They continued to treat the Plaintiff in this manner until about 3:00 a.m. on 19th May, when he was taken down to a cellar in the basement of the premises at 10 Duke Street aforesaid.

7. The Plaintiff was confined in the said cellar from 19th to 29th May 1942 inclusive. The said cellar was about three metres in length and two-and-a-half in width. It had no furniture, no light and little ventilation. It was so low that the Plaintiff could only just stand up at one end. During this period the Plaintiff was brought up nearly every night, and interrogated, beaten and maltreated by the Defendants Capt. Wybot and Capt. Girard in the manner hereinbefore described.

8. On 29th May 1942, the Plaintiff was removed in custody to an office of the Free French Forces at Dolphin Square. Before being taken there, he was told by the Defendant Capt. Wybot that he would be there required to sign a second *acte d'engagement* and that he was to do what he was told. The Plaintiff did in fact sign a second *acte d'engagement* whereby he purported to engage himself to serve in the Free French Forces for the duration of the war. The said *acte d'engagement* is invalid under French law. Further and alternatively, the same was in the premises signed by the Plaintiff under duress and is in any

event null and void.

9. The Plaintiff was then sent to the Free French Forces camp at Old Dean Park, Camberley, where, except for an interval from 17th July until 17th August 1942, during which he escaped and was at large, he was imprisoned from 23rd May until early in December 1942. His imprisonment as aforesaid was effected by the Defendant Major de Person, the officer in command of the said camp, pursuant (inter alia) to an order given by the Defendant, Col. Renouard, the officer in command of the Free French Land Forces in Britain, in or about the beginning of June 1942 and to a *mandat de dépôt* dated 10th July 1942 signed by the Defendant Major Cauchois and countersigned by the Defendant Major Simon. From and after 29th May 1942, the four Defendants named in this paragraph, conspired together to imprison the Plaintiff as aforesaid and each of the acts alleged in this paragraph was an overt act in the said conspiracy.

10. In the beginning of December 1942 the Plaintiff escaped for the second time from the said camp and is now residing in London.

11. By the Allied Forces Act of 1940 and orders made thereunder the Defendant General de Gaulle is invested with certain powers over members of the Free French Forces for securing discipline and internal administration. The Defendants or some of them claim that the Plaintiff is a member of the Free French Forces and have requested the British authorities to arrest the Plaintiff. Unless restrained by this Honourable Court, the Defendants will arrest the Plaintiff or cause him to be arrested, and will again imprison him.

AND THE PLAINTIFF CLAIMS:—

   1. Against all the Defendants:

      (a) A declaration that the Plaintiff is not and never has been a member of the Free French Forces within the meaning of the Allied Forces Act of 1940 or the Allied Powers (War Service) Act of 1942 or any others made under either of the said Acts or otherwise subject to the jurisdiction or authority of the first Defendant.

      (b) An injunction to restrain the Defendants and each of them, their servants or agents from arresting or detaining the Plaintiff or causing or permitting him to be arrested or detained.

   2. Against the Defendants General Charles de Gaulle, Lieutenant-Colonel André Passy, Captain Roger Wybot and Captain François Girard damages for assault and false imprison-

ment and for conspiring to assault and falsely to imprison the
Plaintiff.

3. Against the Defendants General Charles de Gaulle, Colonel
   Louis Renouard, Major de Person, Major Etienne Cauchois
   and Major Pierre Simon damages for false imprisonment
   and for conspiring falsely to imprison the Plaintiff.

PATRICK DEVLIN.

Delivered the 6th day of August 1943, by Thomas Cooper & Co. of 71,
St. Mary Axe, in the City of London, Solicitors for the Plaintiff.

1943.—D.—No. 465.

IN THE HIGH COURT OF JUSTICE
King's Bench Division.

D U F O U R
v.
DE GAULLE AND OTHERS.

STATEMENT OF CLAIM

Thomas Cooper & Co.,
71, St. Mary Axe,
London, E.C. 3.

14

A Proclamation by General de Gaulle

General de Gaulle's message to the organizations of the French resistance was given to the international press on the 24th of last June, 1942.
It was published in France by the underground newspapers of the two
zones, notably by *Combat, Liberation* and *Franc-Tireur.*

The text consecrates the union between the resistance of the interior
and the French Fighting Forces of the exterior. It resulted in the exchange of views between the National French Committee and the
representatives of the many clandestine organizations.

It was on Easter Monday that the accord took place between General de Gaulle and an authorized representative of the resistance organizations.

The importance of this accord becomes greater when one realizes that after the negotiations which took place in July and August 1941, an understanding was established between the organizations of resistance and the Syndicatist Cegetistes and Catholic organizations, which had been dissolved by the Vichy regime, but which had nevertheless continued to exist and to function.

"The last veils behind which the enemy has screened his acts of treachery against France have now been torn aside. The outcome of this war has become clear to all Frenchmen, it will be a choice between independence or slavery.

"The sacred duty of all must be to contribute to the liberation of the country by the total annihilation of the invader. There is no hope for the future except in victory. But this gigantic task has revealed to the nation that the danger which threatens its existence has not come only from without, and that a victory which does not bring in its wake a courageous and fundamental rebirth will not be a victory. A moral, social, political and economic regime which abdicates following defeat, after having emerged from a criminal capitulation, now exalts itself under a personal dictatorship.

"The French people condemns both, and while it unites for victory, it also gathers together for the revolution. In spite of the gags and chains which hold the nation in slavery, a thousand indications coming from its innermost depths testify to its hopes and desires.

"These we now proclaim in its name: We desire that all which belongs to the French nation should be returned to it. The end of the war means for us the restoration and the complete integrity of the territory belonging to the Empire, this, combined with the complete sovereignty of the nation itself, is our inheritance. Any usurpation, whether it comes from within or without should be destroyed and stamped out. In the same manner we desire that France alone should be the one and unique mistress of her territory. And that at the same time when Frenchmen shall be freed from the oppression of the enemy, individual liberty shall be given back to them. Once the enemy is banished from the territory all the men and women of our nation will elect a National Assembly which will decide the destiny of the country.

"We desire that everything which has or which does harm the rights and interests of our national honor shall be punished and abolished. This means first, that the enemy leaders who abuse the laws of war to the detriment of French persons or property, as well as the traitors who coöperate with them, must be punished. It means secondly, that the totalitarian system which raised the weapon which the enemy now uses against us, as well as the system of the coalition of special interests which was used against the national welfare, should be simultaneously and forever abolished.

"We desire that Frenchmen should live in security. Material guarantees must be given against perpetual tyranny and abuse of power which will assure to everyone liberty and dignity in his work and existence. National security and social security are for us essential goals and they are united in importance. We desire that mass organization of the people which was undertaken by the enemy—in defiance of religion and all moral and charitable laws—under the pretext of becoming strong enough to oppress others, should be definitely done away with. We desire at the same time, that in this strong renewing of the resources of the nation and the Empire under a well directed technique, the time honored slogan of "Liberty, Equality and Fraternity" shall from now on be put into practice in our country, so that everyone shall be free in his thoughts, his beliefs, and his actions, so that everyone shall have at the beginning of his social activities an equal chance with others, and that each one shall have the respect of all, and be entitled to any aid if necessary.

"We desire that this war, which affects in the same manner the destiny of all peoples, and which unites the democracies in a single and combined effort, should have as a consequence a world organization, to establish in a desirable and solid manner a mutual aid to all nations in all countries. And we expect that France will occupy, in this international system, the eminent place to which her value and her genius entitles her.

"France and the whole world struggles and suffers for liberty and justice, and the right for individuals to decide their own fate. This right of individuals to their own lives, this war for justice and liberty must be won in fact as well as in theory, for the good of each individual as well as for the good of each state. Such a victory is the only one that can compensate for the ordeals which France has suffered, the only one which can open for us the new road to grandeur. Such a victory is worth all possible effort and all possible sacrifice. We shall win it."

15

Ernest Lindley   For Monday, July 12, 1943.

British Views on de Gaulle

Copies of a statement of British policy toward General de Gaulle have been placed in the hands of British and American officials in Washington. The statement was originally prepared, it is understood, to acquaint British officials and the British press with the views of the Prime Minister.

To weigh in full its significance, it is necessary to bear in mind that after the fall of France, the British government devoted itself energetically to building up General de Gaulle. It invested millions of pounds sterling yearly in paying and supplying his armies and his administrative overhead. Except for small revenues from the colonies under Free French control, these were de Gaulle's only financial resources. Moreover, it was the British broadcasts to France which made his name the symbol of resistance among his conquered countrymen.

The British stuck with de Gaulle through thick and thin, condoning his faults and mistakes. Some months ago the British Government began to modify its policy toward de Gaulle. But this was interpreted in some quarters as a reluctant concession to the United States Government, which had assumed primary responsibility for the Allied venture in French North Africa.

The British statement now at hand, it is felt here, destroys that hypothesis as well as several others advanced by de Gaulle's American and British supporters. Among its high points are these:

1. De Gaulle can no longer be considered a reliable friend of Britain. In spite of all that he owes to British assistance and support, he has left a "trail of Anglophobia" wherever he has been.

2. From August 1941 on, he has tried to play Great Britain against the United States, and the United States against Britain.

3. He has striven to create friction between the British and French in Syria.

4. He clearly has "Fascist and dictatorial tendencies."

5. In spite of these grounds for complaint, the British Government has treated de Gaulle fairly and recognizes the value which his name has come to have in France—chiefly through British publicity. It still hopes that he will coöperate loyally as co-President of the new French

National Committee of Liberation. So far, however, he has struggled for complete mastery.

6. Peace and order and smooth communications in the French North African territory are essential to the great military operations now being prepared. (The statement was written before the invasion of Sicily.) Likewise it is highly important to avoid throwing into turmoil the French forces which the United States is now arming.

The statement alludes to President Roosevelt's strong views on the subject, and to the need for taking care that the differences among the French are not allowed to affect British-American relations. But the reasons given for dissatisfaction with de Gaulle were based on British experience and observation.

In the Syrian difficulties, referred to in the statement, the United States has played no part. The Free French, with British military support, wrested Syria from the Vichyites in August 1941, to forestall an Axis *coup*. The Free French assumed civilian and local military control. The British retained over-all military control. Syria is an important base of the Middle East Command. Its stability is essential to the conduct of the war. But there, as in North Africa and elsewhere, de Gaulle, according to this statement, has sought to set the French against the British.

It is not difficult to arouse popular support among one's own people by playing to their nationalist sentiments. This is de Gaulle's tactic, and it may be that it is winning some success. But it is not the way to wage coalition warfare. The restoration of France depends on American and British arms: even the new French Army in North Africa is being equipped with American arms.

The United States and Britain are not trying to foist a puppet on the French people. They have given their solemn pledge that the independence of France will be restored and that the French people will be given the opportunity to form a government of their own choosing. They do have a right to expect the full collaboration of patriotic Frenchmen in the vast military effort necessary to liberate France, if it is to be liberated.

But de Gaulle, it is felt in Washington and, as this statement shows, in London, is chiefly concerned with his own political power. He is behaving as an opponent of Britain and the United States, rather than as an ally.

> Washington *Post* and Des Moines *Register and Tribune* Syndicate

16

U. S. Critics of Gen. de Gaulle

LONDON *TIMES* JULY 16, 1943
CONFLICTING EVIDENCE   from our own correspondent.
Washington, July 15, 1943

In its editorial columns this morning the Washington *Post* returns to the question of the document on which Mr. Ernest Lindley and others before him have based their attacks on General de Gaulle.

"The statement," Mr. Lindley said, "was originally prepared, it is understood, to acquaint British officials and the British press with the views of the Prime Minister," and the *Post* finds it "highly significant that the British Embassy denies any knowledge of any such document." It further notes that the Prime Minister's words in the Commons on July 1st were "something very different from what Mr. Lindley says is contained in the privately circulated statement" of his views, and then remarks:—

"We are asked to believe, in short, that Mr. Churchill is capable of making one statement of his views to the Commons, the body to which he is constitutionally responsible, and another contrary statement for the benefit of British and American officials and certain favored and apparently carefully chosen newspaper men."

The newspaper speaks of "pipeline journalism" as a "sinister phenomenon" and says that in this case either the British or the American Government "should clear up the matter before the United Nations get bogged down in conspiracy." It reiterates that "the only way to depersonalize our relations with France is to recognize the French Committee."

17

Prime Minister and General de Gaulle in the House of Commons, July 21, 1943

LONDON *TIMES* JULY 22, 1943
A SECRET DOCUMENT.

Mr. Boothby (Aberdeen, E., U.) asked the Prime Minister if he had considered the document, a copy of which had been sent him, purporting to have been officially prepared to acquaint British officials and the

British press with the views of the Prime Minister on the subject of General de Gaulle, and what steps he was taking to put a stop to the dissemination of mis-statements liable to prejudice the relations of this country with the United Nations.

Mr. Churchill—"Contrary to the statement in my honorable friend's question, no document has been received from him, but only a cutting from a newspaper which refers to a document. I take full responsibility for this document, the text of which was drafted personally by me. It is a confidential document. I am not prepared to discuss it otherwise than in secret session, and then only if there were a general desire from the House to have a secret session."

Mr. Boothby—"May I ask whether a document purporting to be this document has not in fact been published in a Washington newspaper, and does he not think that these continued Press attacks on General de Gaulle are or may be harmful to the Allied cause, and will he use his great influence with the United States to try to get them to join us in an effort to increase and not decrease the prestige and unity of the French Committee of National Liberation?"

Mr. Churchill—"I said I was not prepared to discuss the matter otherwise than in a secret session, and I adhere to that."

18

Recognition of the French Committee of National Liberation
Statement by the President
(Released to the press by the White House August 26, 1943.)

The Government of the United States desires again to make clear its purpose of coöperating with all patriotic Frenchmen, looking to the liberation of the French people and French territories from the oppressions of the enemy.

The Government of the United States, accordingly, welcomes the establishment of the French Committee of National Liberation. It is our expectation that the Committee will function on the principle of collective responsibility of all its members for the active prosecution of the war.

In view of the paramount importance of the common war effort, the relationship with the French Committee of National Liberation must continue to be subject to the military requirements of the Allied commanders.

The Government of the United States takes note, with sympathy, of the desire of the Committee to be regarded as the body qualified to insure the administration and defense of French interests. The extent to which it may be possible to give effect to this desire must however be reserved for consideration in each case as it arises.

On these understandings the Government of the United States recognizes the French Committee of National Liberation as administering those French overseas territories which acknowledge its authority.

This statement does not constitute recognition of a government of France or of the French Empire by the Government of the United States.

It does constitute recognition of the French Committee of National Liberation as functioning within specific limitations during the war. Later on the people of France, in a free and untrammeled manner, will proceed in due course to select their own government and their own officials to administer it.

The Government of the United States welcomes the Committee's expressed determination to continue the common struggle in close co-operation with all the Allies until French soil is freed from its invaders and until victory is complete over all enemy powers.

May the restoration of France come with utmost speed.

19

Excerpt from the Daily Telegraph & Morning Post *of Tuesday,*
May 9, 1944

ALGIERS HAS ITS ROOT-AND-BRANCH
PLAN FOR LIBERATED FRANCE

Political and Press Control: Two Significant Ordinances
By E. B. Wareing,
formerly chief of the The Daily Telegraph Paris staff,
who has recently re-visited Algiers

The restoration of French nationhood through the revival of self-respect, the deepening of a sense of solidarity with the Allies, and, above all, the achievement of domestic unity are not matters that concern France alone. They are of basic importance to the post-war world and a vital necessity to Britain—four air-minutes removed, in either direction, from the French coast.

Weakened still, but convalescent, the spirit of France presents a problem of the utmost delicacy on the eve of operations which will bring Frenchmen into brusque contact with the Allied Forces, whose preliminary moves, of sad necessity, have taken the form of destructive bombing of French territory, costing innocent lives despite every care.

One calls to memory Gen. de Gaulle's proclamation of June, 1940, calling for resistance. It is as fine a piece of political prescience as ever existed. It is as true now as then.

"Nothing is lost, because this war is a world war. In the free universe immense forces have not yet swung into operation. Some day these forces will crush the enemy. On that day France must be present at the victory. She will then regain her liberty and her greatness. Such is my goal, my only goal!"

Gen. de Gaulle's Prestige

How far has Gen. de Gaulle justified himself since? How far has he proved himself capable of being the unquestioned leader of all Frenchmen? Does France need a leader with overruling personal powers? These were the questions which I set myself on my recent and third visit to Algiers.

The general impression which I received was that the prestige of Gen. de Gaulle personally had increased since my last visit in December, whilst that of the Committee of National Liberation as a whole had diminished. The tendency is to blame the Committee for what goes wrong and to praise de Gaulle for what goes right.

The European population of Algeria blames the Committee for the deplorable living conditions there. The ordinary citizen receives no milk, no butter and no cheese, very little coffee, no fresh vegetables, no tea and extremely little meat, the butcher's shops being often closed for weeks at a time. There is a rapacious black market, and Frenchmen who have escaped from France have told me that they can live better and more cheaply, except for the bad quality of the bread and the shortage of wine, in Paris than in Algiers.

Value of the Assembly

To whom the blame should, in equity, be attached seems an open question; the authority nominally responsible is the Governor-General of Algeria, but the presence of the Committee which claims the status of a Government naturally causes criticism to be shifted on to its shoulders.

The Consultative Assembly, composed mainly of resistance delegates selected by de Gaullist organs, is also felt to be very much divorced from the realities of life.

It falls between two stools: owing to the absence of fresh contacts with France, it is necessarily rather more of a debating society than of a Parliament. One of its members in a private conversation with me likened it to the *Conférences Môle* which are attended in Paris by young men intending to devote themselves to public service or to enter the Chamber of Deputies, and which held debates on the parliamentary model in much the same way as the Oxford Union.

Under the able chairmanship of M. Gouin, discussions are conducted in a businesslike way and reveal a high level of oratory and political thought, preponderantly of Left Wing tendency. They have, however, an academic flavour, and when the Committee of National Liberation has decisions of practical importance to take they are embodied in ordinances and decrees on which the Assembly is not publicly consulted.

It was chiefly busy during the last session with two pieces of legislation which cannot be applied until the liberation of France has been accomplished—namely, an ordinance regarding the civil and political administration of France, which was a compromise between the original projects put forward by members of the Assembly, and other ordinance regarding the control of the Press.

The former was adopted by the Committee and is ready to go into force, whilst no final decision has been taken regarding the Press ordinance.

Foreshadowing a Coup

It may now be stated publicly that behind this legislation was a lengthy scheme, elaborated last October by the Central Committee of Resistance Movements in France, which has hitherto been kept relatively secret. This was shown to me on the understanding that no reference should be made to its military clauses.

On its political side it is a rather startling document, of totalitarian trend, which provides for nothing less than what is called a "lightning insurrection." This is to take place "in the short space of time between the departure or decisive weakening of the Germans and the arrival of the Anglo-Saxons."

The body which drew up the scheme represents all but two sections of the action groups of the resistance movement co-ordinated under the National Council of Resistance. The Communists and the para-military groups, for different reasons, are opposed to the political character of the action outlined. The purposes of the "lightning insurrection" on its political side are:

1. To paralyse . . . the Vichy organisation, rendering impossible
any attempt by Pétain to change sides.

2. To guarantee the elimination within a few hours of all officials
and their replacement in order to confront the Allied authorities with
the *fait accompli* of an administrative machine working in a regular
way and representing the will of French resistance.

3. To guarantee within a few hours the revolutionary repression of
treason and, when this has been done as a matter of legitimate reprisal,
to ensure public order, to which the Allied military authorities naturally attach great value.

4. To give, by manifestations of force and mass, a popular and democratic basis to the Provisional Government and to bring about international recognition for the de facto Government of Gen. de Gaulle.

5. To call upon the Committee of National Liberation to let its
actions be inspired by the will of the nation and not by diplomatic
opportunism, and to impose upon the Provisional Government immediate revolutionary social and economic measures so that, as Gen.
de Gaulle has promised, "the French people shall have their say
again."

The insurrection is to be put into effect by Committees of Liberation, each having five to eight members. There is to be one for each
Department, with local sub-committees.

Since this scheme was first put forward the Central Committee of
Resistance Movements in France has been expressing considerable im-
patience and it has sent a number of sharp reminders to Algiers that
time might be short and that the bodies in France were finding their
work impeded by the slowness with which Algiers is acting. Since then,
however, the Committee of National Liberation has passed ordinances, some of them secret, which are understood to go far towards
satisfying the demands of the Central Committee.

The Communists still maintain reserve and have criticised the
Committee's action in passing secret legislation, pointing out its dangerous implications.

The ordinance on the Press can also best be described as totalitarian,
and, if applied in full, it would bring the French Press and news
agency organisation even closer to the Italian Fascist model than they
are at present.

Treatment of the Press

Last month a hitherto unknown body described as "The National

Federation of the Clandestine Press in France," and said to represent 13 underground papers of all shades of opinion, called for even more drastic action than the ordinance provides. It asks that this should include the expropriation "from the first day of liberation" of all Press concerns without exception, but with compensation for proprietors of proved patriotism.

All seized property would then be handed over to the resistance organisations and other political bodies.

How far this "Federation" effectively exists or, in present circumstances, can consult affiliated newspapers scattered throughout France is an open question. In any case its proposals bear a striking resemblance to those before the Committee of National Liberation, whose hands will be strengthened against criticism of the draft ordinance. "These radical measures," it will be said, "are willed by the people of France: here is the proof."

One newspaper, and one alone, the *Echo d'Alger*, is being allowed to criticise the treatment of the Press and to demand that liberty be restored. On March 15, for example, it wrote: "The censorship ought to be lifted except for military secrets. We protest against the steel brakes and the golden curb which it is thought fit to apply to us."

Even the strongly de Gaullist organ, *Alger Républicain*, on March 29, published a mysteriously worded complaint about "the friend whom we meet every day" who brings items of news "at the end of a piece of elastic which returns them to his hands at the moment when they are about to be used."

According to the writer, this "friend"—and the reference is obviously to an official of the Information Service who pays a nightly visit to all the newspaper offices—gives advice in the following terms:

"You can publish this but with discretion. Do not give it too large a headline but bury it among other items. In fact, publish it without appearing to have noticed it."

Effects of "Discretion"

"Discretion" is the keynote of the handling of the Press. Thus, the written directives which are sent out in Fascist countries are replaced in North Africa by telephone calls or private visits, but the effect is very much the same. Editors have told me that they are, in fact, as much subject to control as they were under the Vichy regime. Certainly the resemblance of the Algiers newspapers to one another the morning after the nightly visit is more than surprising.

On the day of Pucheu's execution the fact was announced with precisely the same headlines and text by the de Gaullist and the non-de Gaullist newspapers.

Comment on matters regarded as of international interest is for the most part permitted only in the form of quotations from political or diplomatic correspondents of the *France-Afrique* News Agency. This, it will be remembered, lost its independence as the result of action taken a few days after the receipt by Gen. de Gaulle of a letter from three Communist leaders complaining that Pucheu's defence had been circulated by the agency to the newspapers.

20

Letter from Henri de Kerillis to Félix Gouin

My dear President and friend:

In Washington on Thursday, October 14, 1943, I was informed of a telegram from M. Philip, Commissioner of the Interior, summoning members of parliament resident in America to Algiers on November 3rd for the purpose of electing deputies and senators destined to become members of the Consultative Assembly provided for in the de Gaullist Constitution.

This summons left me only 26 days in which to get ready, whereas medical formalities and government regulations normally require four weeks, barring exceptional cases, and the journey alone takes two or three, save under extraordinarily favorable circumstances.

I saw in this action, with respect to the members of Parliament, not only a lack of consideration, but above all a cold determination to prevent them from carrying out the mission for which they were supposedly being convened.

You will therefore permit me to make this formal protest.

I have every reason to fear furthermore that the measures taken to prevent French members of Parliament in exile in America from going to Algiers is part of a systematic campaign to bar from French politics any influence favorable to America. As you can see for yourself, most of the Algiers Committee have, in many a case, begun again on the anti-Anglo-Saxon propaganda of the Vichy government, more subtly but just as efficaciously.

This said, my dear colleague, I also wish to protest against the purpose of the summons that has been sent to us.

I do not recognize the right of anyone, unless it be the French people, to destroy the Constitution of the Republic to which they have given themselves of their own free will and which they themselves will certainly wish to amend in order to adapt it to the new era.

Now, the creation of a Consultative Assembly is tantamount to destroying the legislative power, just as the creation of the Committee of Liberation amounts to destroying the executive power as the constitution of the Third Republic intended them to be.

The Assembly to which the deputies are summoned, in the humiliating proportion of 20 members to 80, has only to advise. The executive authority will have the right to veto. We are reverting to the darkest ages of Absolute Monarchy, when the King assembled the States-General reserving the right to disregard their advice and invoking his famous: "Such is our good pleasure." Moreover, the King represented a power recognized as legitimate in those days. Again, the deputies of the States-General were elected by the three Orders, whereas 52 members out of 80 on the Consultative Assembly will be practically chosen by the executive power.

Let us have the courage to acknowledge and broadcast the fact that the new Algiers Constitution is the most dictatorial France has ever seen. And how could I, for my part, approve of it when one of the main objects of this war is to save Democracy and crush individual power? I share the opinion expressed by President Roosevelt on September 17, 1943, before the American Congress, when he declared that the war would not be won unless the forms of Fascism, not only the evil forms of Fascism, were eradicated.

Let me add that I consider the regulations set forth in M. Philip's letter against the deputies who voted on July 10, 1940, in favor of Marshal Pétain, unacceptable. Those deputies are all declared outcasts. And they are invited to seek absolution in order to be admitted to their colleagues' transactions. You know how opposed I am to Marshal Pétain (who, by the way, has taken my French nationality from me) because of the part the Marshal played before the armistice, then in concluding the armistice, and later in collaborating with M. Laval and the Germans. But the deputies who voted for Marshal Pétain on July 10, 1940, were merely interpreting the will of the French people who, helpless, overwhelmed by the disaster, fell into the arms of the man in whom they saw the "Hero of Verdun." Besides their vote was formally submitted to the consent of the people when it could be freely expressed after the war. Save for a few exceptions those deputies are guilty only of having participated in a mistake common to all

Frenchmen. Many of them, since then, have suffered cruelly at the hands of the Germans. Some of them are in prison or hunted. Some are resisting heroically and are sacrificing themselves for the nation. Certain members of the Committee of Liberation who have not known the enemy yoke, who have been fortunate enough to shield their families from the hardships of invasion, have no right to declare those deputies outcasts. The National Committee of London and afterwards the Algiers Committee of Liberation have brought notorious "Pétainist" officials into the administration. On the other hand, "Pétainist" officers and soldiers have died in great numbers on the battlefields of Tunisia. Would one dare to brand them as infamous? And if not, why bear down on those particular deputies, precisely when it is the sacred duty of all Frenchmen to stand shoulder to shoulder united against the Germans?

The ulterior motive seems clear to me. In the Washington and London governments there are friends of France, staunch democrats, who want the liberating countries to restore France, after victory, to the same political condition she was in when Germany defeated her. They do not intend to prevent her from changing a constitution which has proved to be lamentably deficient. But they want her to have time to recover her prisoners and her children scattered in exile, to rid herself of the deadly poisons German propaganda has injected into hearts and minds, and finally to know what is going on outside in a world which for years has been hidden from them behind their prison walls. They want all this to save France from civil war and disastrous adventures. And to stop France's good friends who advocate that solution from being heard the de Gaullists are trying to discredit Parliament, the only legitimate trustee of the will of the French people. And that is the spirit in which the Committee of Liberation wrote the letter summoning the deputies in terms equivalent to an affront.

If therefore I had been able to answer the call, it would have been to raise formal protest in Algiers and to vote both against the establishment of the Consultative Assembly and against the manner in which the representatives of the French people have been treated.

The French people, moreover, gave us an absolute and inviolable mission—that of defending our Country and the Republic. We have no right to abdicate. The nation has entrusted us with control over the executive power and the authority to enact laws. The nation expected us to be judges and we have no right to turn defendants. We shall be responsible to the French people and to History, until such time as the nation may be called upon, in perfect freedom, to elect our successors. If the French people crushed by the enemy's armies must suffer new trials in the future through the fault of masters who, under cover of the defeat, seized political power, we would be guilty in their eyes, and this time cast out forever by the people themselves.

Let me remind you that when the Vichy government, under pressure from the Germans, browbeat, humiliated and dissolved the Parliament, the Presidents of the Chamber and of the Senate in their forceful protests expressed the shout of condemnation that rose from the French consciousness.

Today the Algiers government copies the Vichy government, in its turn represses parliamentary assemblies, replaces them by a servile assembly, outrages and humiliates the nation's representation and would certainly draw down on its head the same indignant protest if those two great Frenchmen were not prevented by the enemy from doing so.

It is our duty, in absence of those two men, to interpret their thought which is the thought of the people.

I shall ask you to be so kind as to read this letter to my colleagues that it may appear in the *Journal Officiel*. If they try to prevent you by force from doing so, I would ask you to convey it to each one of them. I am greatly distressed that I cannot be with you all in these dramatic moments. At least I have the consolation of thinking that now, just as on the day when Marshal Pétain seized power, one can do more for France from the outside, as a free man, than inside, as a prisoner, under the sombre shadow of a military dictatorship.

Rest assured, my dear President and friend, that I have unfailing faith in the future of France and that I shall work to the very end with all the strength of my being for her deliverance and for her greatness. That was the spirit in which on June 17, 1940, in London, I rallied enthusiastically to General de Gaulle's cause, when that cause stood for a refusal to accept the armistice, loyalty to the British alliance, a fight to the finish. In those days I believed that General de Gaulle was going to lead the heroes who came at his call to join him from all the corners of the globe, from battle to battle; and that with his own hands he would unfurl our flag on the battlefields of liberation: In the same spirit I cannot approve either the conditions under which the Algiers government was formed, or the measures it takes, measures contrary to our democratic ideal, nor certain general lines of policy which it assumes the right to map out and which can involve the

future of France for years to come against her will and even without
her knowledge.

I send you my protest from an anguished heart. In the night of exile
and grief for our martyrs, I hope soon to be able to fling across the
Atlantic a cry of faith and enthusiasm on the announcement that
France has found again the bright road of her destiny.

With affectionate greetings to you and to my dear colleagues,

Henri de Kerillis